Social Studies for the Preschool/Primary Child

SEVENTH EDITION

Carol Seefeldt

UNIVERSITY OF MARYLAND, COLLEGE PARK

PEARSON

Merrill
Prentice Hall

Upper Saddle River, New Jersey
Columbus, Ohio

Library of Congress Cataloging in Publication Data

Seefeldt, Carol.
   Social studies for the preschool/primary child / Carol Seefeldt.—7th ed.
      p. cm.
   Includes bibliographical references and index.
   ISBN 0-13-140812-7 (pbk.)
      1. Social sciences—Study and teaching (Primary)—United States. 2. Social
   sciences—Study and teaching (Preschool)—United States. I. Title.

LB1530.S37 2005
372.83—dc22   2003064997

Vice President and Executive Publisher: Jeffery W. Johnston
Publisher: Kevin M. Davis
Editor: Julie Peters
Editorial Assistant: Amanda King
Production Editor: Sheryl Glicker Langner
Design Coordinator: Diane C. Lorenzo
Photo Coordinator: Sandy Schaefer
Cover Design: Linda Sorrells-Smith
Cover Image: Corbis
Production Manager: Laura Messerly
Director of Marketing: Ann Castel Davis
Marketing Manager: Autumn Purdy
Marketing Coordinator: Tyra Poole

This book was set in Berling Roman by Carlisle Communications, Ltd. It was printed and bound by R. R. Donnelley & Sons Company. The cover was printed by Phoenix Color Corp.

Photo Credits: Pearson Learning, pp. 1, 9, 29; Laima Druskis/PH College, pp. 5, 123, 171; Anne Vega/Merrill, pp. 6, 40, 67, 94, 149, 212, 300, 302; Todd Yarrington/Merrill, p. 12; PH College, p. 31; Kenneth P. Davis/PH College, p. 35; Barbara Schwartz/Merrill, pp. 55, 157, 174; Scott Cunningham/Merrill, pp. 63, 131, 141, 166; Dan Floss/Merrill, p. 70; Silver Burdett Ginn, pp. 72, 151, 221; Anthony Magnacca/Merrill, pp. 77, 88, 105, 110, 116, 185, 255, 298; Shirley Zeiberg/PH College, p. 89; Karen Mancinelli/Pearson Learning, p. 128; courtesy of Carol Seefeldt, pp. 135, 206, 224, 235, 246, 278; Ken Karp/PH College, p. 194; Jo Hall/Merrill, p. 197; Merrill Education, p. 201; Tracey Wheeler/Silver Burdett Ginn Needham, p. 228; Eugene Gordon/PH College, p. 260; John Paul Endress/Silver Burdett Ginn, p. 269; KS Studios/Merrill, p. 284; L. Morris Nantz/PH College, p. 291.

Pearson Education Ltd.
Pearson Education Singapore Pte. Ltd.
Pearson Education Canada, Ltd.
Pearson Education–Japan
Pearson Education Australia Pty. Limited
Pearson Education North Asia Ltd.
Pearson Educación de Mexico, S.A. de C.V.
Pearson Education Malaysia Pte. Ltd.

10 9 8 7 6
ISBN: 0-13-140812-7

To the loving memory of Reba Henessee who taught me how to live.

Preface

Social Studies for the Preschool/Primary Child was designed as a textbook for early childhood preservice teachers and a resource for inservice teachers, and preparing the seventh edition has been a stimulating and rewarding experience. Since the first edition was published in 1977, much in the field of early childhood education has remained the same, but even more has changed. This edition retains the continuity while addressing contemporary changes in early childhood education and the social studies.

CHILD GROWTH, DEVELOPMENT, AND LEARNING

The seventh edition continues to be based on knowledge of children. Although the world has changed, children have not. Today's children grow, develop, and learn in much the same ways as they always have. This new edition of *Social Studies for the Preschool/Primary Child* is based on a solid theoretical and research foundation of child growth, development, and learning. One chapter focuses on child development. In addition, each chapter incorporates current research and theory on child growth, development, and learning into all areas of the social studies.

DIVERSITY AND INCLUSION

This edition features diversity and inclusion. A separate chapter on celebrating diversity offers preservice and inservice teachers a solid foundation of curriculum methods and practices based on the latest theory on and research into teaching young children to value themselves and each other. Each chapter also includes ideas and practices designed to celebrate diversity and provide full inclusion into the social studies curriculum for all children, regardless of special needs or individual differences.

LEARNING THROUGH ACTIVITY

This text assumes that all young children will be educated in enriching, stimulating educational environments that foster and promote play as well as mental, physical, and social activities that are known to lead to learning. Research clearly documents that humans learn best when they are active—when they can play with things, objects, others, and ideas. Because play is so critical to learning, it serves as the integrator of the social studies curriculum and is viewed as the basic mode for children's learning. Play and activity are featured in each chapter; however, a separate chapter on resources for children's learning gives teachers ideas for arranging the environment to enable children to learn through their own activity.

AN INTEGRATED APPROACH

The wholeness of the child is honored in this text through the advocacy of an integrated social studies curriculum. The wholeness of learning, the intimate relationship between children's cognitive growth and their social, physical, and emotional growth, is recognized and respected.

Social studies are approached as an integrated experience, one that involves the school, parents, and community. The social studies are also presented as a continual experience, one that builds as children move from a child-care setting or a preschool to kindergarten and the primary grades.

Even though the text presents separate chapters for teaching social studies content, it is based on the theory that learning is a continuous, integrated activity. Thus, teaching social studies involves all curriculum content areas. Integrated throughout this seventh edition of *Social Studies for the Preschool/Primary Child* are suggestions for incorporating content from the visual arts, music, movement, science, health, and the language arts.

CHANGES IN THE FIELD AND TO THIS EDITION

While children and the way they learn have not changed since the first edition of *Social Studies for the Preschool/Primary Child*, the world has changed—dramatically so. Wars have come and gone, and the velvet revolutions in Eastern Europe have literally changed the face of the world.

The expansion of technology has also affected worldwide changes. E-mail brings us closer to each other regardless of how far apart we are. Technology brings us closer to information and knowledge as well. Thus, this seventh edition offers teachers ideas for using current technologies in today's classrooms, from using digital cameras in the classroom to obtaining resources from the Internet.

Changes in the field of early childhood education itself form another underpinning for this text. As the field of early childhood education enters the future, it does so with a new sense of professionalism and newly established standards. The National Association for the Education of Young Children has set new standards for quality in programs serving children from birth through age 8, standards for appropriate curricula, and standards for the professional preparation of early childhood teachers. The assumption that all children will be taught by professional, highly intelligent, and qualified early childhood teachers continues in this edition. Teachers are needed who take their cues from children, who understand children, and who know how to follow their lead. This text offers a multitude of practical ideas, suggestions, and guides for teaching social studies; but the most important component of any social studies program is a reflective, thoughtful, highly educated teacher who will plan, implement, and assess the social studies concepts, skills, attitudes, and learning experiences found herein.

STANDARDS AND POSITION PAPERS

Recognizing the need to prepare children to become effective, fully functioning citizens in a rapidly changing world, authorities have called for reforms in social studies education. Developed by the Office of Research and Improvement of the U.S. Department of Education, position papers and national standards in history, geography, economics, and civics education suggest new directions for social studies curriculum.

These position papers and standards lead to the conclusion that social studies has been a long-neglected topic in schools for young children. *Social Studies for the Preschool/Primary Child* can remedy this neglect. Structured around the concepts considered key to the social science disciplines—the attitudes, values, and skills believed essential for citizens of a democratic society—this text presents a multitude of ideas for introducing children to social studies content. These suggestions will give young children an opportunity to build a foundation of knowledge in history, geography, economics, and other social science disciplines as well as skills and attitudes that will enable them to become fully functioning members of a democratic society in the future.

SPECIAL FEATURES

In this teacher-friendly text, each chapter does the following:

- Begins with questions that serve as advanced organizers and objectives
- Concludes with a summary that organizes the information presented

- Offers suggestions for expanding and extending student knowledge, attitudes, and skills
- Provides extensive information about resources for teachers
- Integrates children's literature into each chapter by identifying appropriate books and poems
- Provides examples and ideas for inclusion and valuing diversity
- Is replete with examples and ideas of how to translate social studies theory and research into practice

STRUCTURE OF THE SEVENTH EDITION

Social Studies for the Preschool/Primary Child is organized into three parts. Part 1 introduces the social studies with chapters defining the social studies, celebrating diversity, planning to teach, and resources for learning.

Part 2 provides information about social skills, thinking and concept formation, and attitudes and values. The chapters discuss development of these processes and how teachers foster them through experiences with the social studies.

Part 3 is devoted to content from the social studies disciplines of history, geography, and economics. Current position papers and standards from these fields are reflected throughout these chapters.

ACKNOWLEDGMENTS

I acknowledge the support and encouragement of my friends and colleagues. My colleague, Dr. Alice Galper, who redefines the definition of friend; Dr. Irene Schmalz, who motivates me; and to Dr. Barbara Wasik, whose trust supports me, are constant guides and mentors.

Many others have my thanks as well. The dedicated work of Sheryl Langner, production editor, and Dawn Potter, copyeditor, is deeply appreciated.

Special thanks are given to Dr. Fran Favretto, director of the University of Maryland at College Park's Center for Young Children, and the center's faculty for always permitting me to visit and learn. The innovative, child-centered curriculum and practices of the Center for Young Children are reflected in this text.

The thoughtful insights and comments of these reviewers are greatly appreciated: Margaret S. Carter, James Madison University; JoAnne Buggey, University of Minnesota; Barbara Hatcher, Southwest Texas; and Huey-Ling Lin, Alabama State University.

Brief Contents

Contents

Chapter 7 / **Thinking and Concept Formation**   193

Chapter 10 / Production, Distribution, and Consumption: Economics   **289**

Index   **309**

Note: Every effort has been made to provide accurate and current
Internet information in this book. However, the Internet and information
posted on it are constantly changing, and it is inevitable that some
of the Internet addresses listed in this textbook will change.

Educator Learning Center:
An Invaluable Online Resource

Merrill Education and the Association for Supervision and Curriculum Development (ASCD) invite you to take advantage of a new online resource, one that provides access to the top research and proven strategies associated with ASCD and Merrill—the Educator Learning Center. At www.EducatorLearningCenter.com you will find resources that will enhance your students' understanding of course topics and of current educational issues, in addition to being invaluable for further research.

HOW THE EDUCATOR LEARNING CENTER WILL HELP YOUR STUDENTS BECOME BETTER TEACHERS

With the combined resources of Merrill Education and ASCD, you and your students will find a wealth of tools and materials to better prepare them for the classroom.

Research

- More than 600 articles from the ASCD journal *Educational Leadership* discuss everyday issues faced by practicing teachers.
- A direct link on the site to Research Navigator™ gives students access to many of the leading education journals, as well as extensive content detailing the research process.
- Excerpts from Merrill Education texts give your students insights on important topics of instructional methods, diverse populations, assessment, classroom management, technology, and refining classroom practice.

Classroom Practice

- Hundreds of lesson plans and teaching strategies are categorized by content area and age range.
- Case studies and classroom video footage provide virtual field experience for student reflection.
- Computer simulations and other electronic tools keep your students abreast of today's classrooms and current technologies.

LOOK INTO THE VALUE OF EDUCATOR LEARNING CENTER YOURSELF

A 4-month subscription to the Educator Learning Center is $25 but is **FREE** when used in conjunction with this text. To obtain free passcodes for your students, contact your Merrill/Prentice Hall sales representative, and your representative will give you a special ISBN to give your bookstore when ordering your textbooks. To preview the value of this website to you and your students, please go to www.EducatorLearningCenter.com and click on "Demo".

Discover the Companion Website Accompanying This Book

THE PRENTICE HALL COMPANION WEBSITE: A VIRTUAL LEARNING ENVIRONMENT

Technology is a constantly growing and changing aspect of our field that is creating a need for content and resources. To address this emerging need, Prentice Hall has developed an online learning environment for students and professors alike—Companion Websites—to support our textbooks.

In creating a Companion Website, our goal is to build on and enhance what the textbook already offers. For this reason, the content for each user-friendly website is organized by topic and provides the professor and student with a variety of meaningful resources. Common features of a Companion Website include:

FOR THE PROFESSOR—

Every Companion Website integrates **Syllabus Manager™,** an online syllabus creation and management utility.

- **Syllabus Manager™** provides you, the instructor, with an easy, step-by-step process to create and revise syllabi, with direct links into Companion Website and other online content without having to learn HTML.
- Students may logon to your syllabus during any study session. All they need to know is the web address for the Companion Website and the password you've assigned to your syllabus.
- After you have created a syllabus using **Syllabus Manager™,** students may enter the syllabus for their course section from any point in the Companion Website.
- Clicking on a date, the student is shown the list of activities for the assignment. The activities for each assignment are linked directly to actual content, saving time for students.
- Adding assignments consists of clicking on the desired due date, then filling in the details of the assignment—name of the assignment, instructions, and whether or not it is a one-time or repeating assignment.

- In addition, links to other activities can be created easily. If the activity is online, a URL can be entered in the space provided, and it will be linked automatically in the final syllabus.
- Your completed syllabus is hosted on our servers, allowing convenient updates from any computer on the Internet. Changes you make to your syllabus are immediately available to your students at their next logon.

For the Student

- **Introduction**—General information about the topic and how it will be covered in the website.
- **Web Links**—A variety of websites related to topic areas.
- **Timely Articles**—Links to online articles that enable you to become more aware of important issues in early childhood.
- **Learn by Doing**—Put concepts into action, participate in activities, examine strategies, and more.
- **Visit a School**—Visit a school's website to see concepts, theories, and strategies in action.
- **For Teachers/Practitioners**—Access information you will need to know as an educator, including information on materials, activities, and lessons.
- **Current Policies and Standards**—Find out the latest early childhood policies from the government and various organizations, and view state, federal, and curriculum standards.
- **Resources and Organizations**—Discover tools to help you plan your classroom or center and organizations to provide current information and standards for each topic.
- **Electronic Bluebook**—Paperless method of completing homework or essays assigned by a professor. Finished work can be sent to the professor via email.
- **Message Board**—Virtual bulletin board to post and respond to questions and comments from a national audience.

To take advantage of these and other resources, please visit the *Social Studies for the Preschool/Primary Child*, Seventh Edition, Companion Website at

www.prenhall.com/seefeldt

PART ONE

PLANNING FOR THE SOCIAL STUDIES

CHAPTER 1

These Are the Social Studies

The purpose of the social studies is to help young people develop the ability to make informed and reasoned decisions as citizens of a culturally diverse, democratic society in an interdependent world.

National Council for the Social Studies, 2003

After you read this chapter, you should be prepared to respond to the following questions:

- What is the definition of the social studies?
- How were social studies taught in the past?
- Which theories have most influenced social studies today?
- What characterizes social studies today?

After the Fourth of July fireworks and parades, my grandfather would take a key from his pocket and open a metal box containing his important papers. From the box he would take a small package wrapped in a soft chamois cloth. Carefully he would unwrap the package. We knew what was inside—a small leather folder holding his citizenship paper. Opening the folder, he would unfold the paper declaring him a citizen of the United States. Then he would tell the story of how he came to America, his trip across the ocean, and the sorrow he experienced when he said goodbye to parents, brother, and sisters, knowing he would never see them again. He would finish the story by saying, "You do not have to leave your home to be a citizen of the United States. All you need to do is go to school, and there you will learn how to be a citizen of this wonderful country."

Grandfather was right. By participating in the small democracies of their classrooms, young children will gain the knowledge, skills, and attitudes required to assume the office of citizen. Although all of children's early educational experiences are designed to prepare children for the role of citizen in a democratic society, the integrated study of the social sciences—the social studies—is uniquely suited to do so. Through the social studies, children have the opportunity to learn they are deeply respected as individuals and at the same time learn to give up some of their individuality for the good of the group.

As defined by the National Council for the Social Studies (NCSS), social studies are

> the integrated study of the social sciences and humanities to promote civic competence. . . . social studies [provide] coordinated, systematic study drawing upon such disciplines as anthropology, archaeology, economics, geography, history, philosophy, political science, psychology, religion and sociology, as well as appropriate content from the humanities, mathematics, and natural sciences. (NCSS, 1998, p. 1)

The two main purposes of the social studies—those of preparing children to assume "the office of citizen" and to integrate knowledge, skills, and attitudes within and across disciplines—distinguish the social studies from other subjects.

It seems overwhelming. The field of social studies is enormous, and children are so young. Preschool and primary children are too new to this earth to be expected to learn all about economics, history, and geography, much less the attitudes and skills necessary to participate in a democratic society. Yet it is because children are so young that the subject of social studies is critical during early childhood. In these early years the foundation for later and increasingly mature understanding is constructed (NRC, 2000, 2001).

Realizing that children have a long time in which to grow and learn, however, makes teaching social studies in the preschool-primary classroom less overwhelming. During their early years, children need only to develop anticipatory, intuitive ideas and interests that will serve as a foundation for the elaboration of the more complex understandings, attitudes, and skills of adults (NCSS, 1988; NRC, 2001).

Then, too, social studies learning takes place naturally as children participate in an early childhood classroom, which is itself a small democratic society. Within an early childhood program, the rights of the individual are constantly balanced with those of the group; children naturally learn and use the knowledge, skills, processes, dispositions, and attitudes that will serve as a foundation for later social studies learning (Mitchell, 2000; Pohan, 2003).

Looking to the past helps today's educators understand how social studies and young children can be brought together in meaningful, appropriate ways. Over the years, a number of approaches to social studies education for young children have been developed and implemented.

Social studies take place naturally in good schools for young children.

As you read about historic approaches to the social studies curriculum, think about how each of these approaches continues to influence today's social studies. You might recall your own experiences with social studies education or observe how social studies are being taught in today's schools.

As you do, relate the following to what is being taught in today's schools:

1. Lucy Sprague Mitchell's here-and-now expanding communities approach
2. the social-living curriculum
3. the holiday approach
4. more recent approaches stemmig from social forces and research and theory

PAST APPROACHES TO THE SOCIAL STUDIES

Here-and-Now Curriculum

Before the 1930s, social studies were concerned with an unchanging body of facts—facts to be memorized. Appalled by this dry memorization of things children knew

Children's world expands to the study of the community.

nothing about and had no experience with, Lucy Sprague Mitchell (1934) developed a practical and detailed account of the ways in which teachers could enlarge and enrich children's understanding of the world around them and their place in it. Encouraged and influenced by the child development theory and progressive education movement of John Dewey (1944), Mitchell created a curriculum that was a direct attack on the elementary school's concentration on facts totally unrelated to children's lives.

Mitchell's basic educational concept was that children need to experience things for themselves. She believed that the social studies curriculum should be based on children's experiences and their discovery of the things and culture of the world around them—on the "here and now."

Mitchell believed it was dangerous to teach anything to children before they had an opportunity to experience it for themselves. The teacher should not pour in information but provide experiences that will enable the child to absorb information through firsthand manipulation and encounter.

Even today, the dominant organizational pattern for social studies teaching is based on Mitchell's work (Wade, 2003). For example, the typical social studies curriculum begins with the child in the neighborhood and then expands so that the child is introduced gradually to societies farther away in time and space. This is known as the spiral curriculum.

Grade	Emphasis
K	Home and neighborhood
1	Community and community helpers
2	United States
3	People in other lands

Unfortunately, many misinterpreted Mitchell's theories and ideas. Although convinced that social studies for young children should be solidly based on the here-and-now of children's lives, teachers ignored the complexities of children's here-and-now world. Instead of focusing on the relationships of things in the environment, or the web of interdependency within it, social studies instruction revolved around the trite. Kindergarten children learned that they live in a family, first graders that firefighters help them, and third graders that they live in a neighborhood. In the end, Mitchell's strong concern for relationship thinking and intellectual development was ignored (Wade, 2003).

Mitchell (1934), however, saw the children's world—"whatever and where ever it may be"—as complex and full of opportunities to enhance their knowledge and foster thinking (p. 16). She wrote that, at first glance, her suggestion that geography learning begin with children's explorations of their immediate environment seems preposterous because the environment is too complex. "Modern children are born into an appallingly complicated world. The complications of their surrounding culture, however, instead of making this attack impossible, make it imperative" (p. 8). By enlarging and enriching children's understanding of their immediate environment, their world, and their place in it, Mitchell aimed to develop children's intellectual capabilities in terms of "relationship thinking, generalization from experience, and the re-creation of concrete experience through symbolic, dramatic play" (p. 11).

Mitchell's insights into the intellectual processes of young children—in terms of relationship thinking, generalizing from experience, and re-creating concrete experience through symbolic or dramatic play—are consistent with the theories of Piaget (Piaget & Inhelder, 1969) and Vygotsky (1986). Further, the philosophy articulated in *Developmentally Appropriate Practice* (Bredekamp & Copple, 1997) is congruent with Mitchell's ideas. Current research and theory (Piaget & Inhelder, 1969; NRC, 2000, 2001; Vygotsky, 1986) support the principles she first advocated:

- The younger the child, the greater the need for firsthand sensory experiences.
- One experience, fact, or idea needs to be connected in some way to another; two facts and a relation joining them are and should be an invitation to generalize, extrapolate, and make a tentative intuitive leap—even to build a theory.
- What children learn must be useful to them in some way and related to daily life.
- Play and active learning are necessary.

Certainly, nothing can be more potent for fostering intellectual development than real experiences, and the here-and-now of children's lives can provide a foundation for social studies experiences—that is, if the total of children's here-and-now lives is considered.

Today, children's here-and-now world has expanded; it is increasingly diverse, multicultural, and global. "Will my school get bombed?" asked 6-year-old Kala after the bombing of Baghdad. This doesn't mean that 6-year-olds should study maps to locate Iraq, but it does mean that today's teachers should recognize the complexities and totality of children's here-and-now environment. Building on children's interests and fostering their understandings of both their immediate world and what is far away in space and time are part of teaching social studies to young children.

Social-Living Curriculum

As Mitchell (1934) was formulating her theories, Patty Smith Hill (1923), in an attempt to apply the principles of democracy to school organization, initiated a curriculum with the goal of habit and social skill development. Training children in the skills and habits necessary to function in a democratic society would prepare them to participate in a democracy. Her book, *A Conduct Curriculum for the Kindergarten and First-Grade*, specified all the social skills and habits that children should learn, stated in measurable form. It primarily focused on the realm of moral and social conduct.

Hill's social-living curriculum grew from child development and psychoanalytic theories coupled with the growing 1930s concern about education for citizenship. The social-living approach maintained that young children were developmentally ready to learn skills required for them to live with a group. Having learned in infancy and early childhood who they were and how they fit into their family unit, children were then ready to develop the social skills necessary for nursery school and kindergarten.

Psychoanalytic theory, with its strong emphasis on the psychosocial segment of life, lent support to the social-living curriculum. The concepts that children should learn to express feelings and to find emotional and social support in the school situation were readily translated into the social-living curriculum.

Curricula in many nursery schools established in the 1930s and 1940s were based on the social-living curriculum. A number of these schools were established by faculty wives at universities to provide socializing experiences for their young children; others were established for children of immigrants or poverty-stricken families. They shared the goal of supporting and fostering the social and emotional growth of young children by leading children to do the following:

- Learn to share materials and ideas
- Develop healthy relationships with others
- Become self-reliant
- Feel responsibility for their own behavior
- Develop interest and attention span
- Cooperate with others in a friendly, willing spirit
- Appreciate the worth and contribution of others
- Develop self-concept and self-respect

Implementation of these goals led to social studies programs that included large blocks of time for free play, interaction with others, discussions of feelings, emphasis on sharing and cooperating behaviors, and rule learning. Rather than becoming a strong, interdisciplinary, interrelated curriculum based on an individual's relationship with others and the environment or focusing on complex social studies concepts such as interaction, cooperation, and interdependency, the social studies curriculum called social living became a curriculum of benign neglect. Children were given a rich environment of toys and materials and left alone to learn to live with themselves and others. Even worse, in

To express ideas and to work with others are both social and cognitive skills.

some programs elaborate plans and procedures were developed and implemented to teach children how to share, hang up their coats, take care of materials, blow their noses, tie shoes, and cooperate, with little concern for their intellectual development.

Through the 1930s the social studies curriculum continued to revolve around the promotion of social skills (Freeman & Hatch, 1989). Only today has the social skills curriculum been pushed to the background. With the passage of the No Child Left Behind Act and increasing pressure for academic accountability, the social-living approach to the curriculum has all but disappeared. Now the focus is on specific language and mathematic skill development, to the exclusion of social skills.

Perhaps the real failure of the social-living approach in social studies was proponents' inability to view the child holistically. Many teachers failed to understand that learning to relate to others, see another's point of view, and understand the complex social rule system are cognitive as well as social tasks. Relating to others demands communication—a facility with language. The ability to express ideas, share thoughts with others, listen, and speak are cognitive skills. Nevertheless, fostering children's language development, enhancing their cognitive growth, and even developing concepts of rules, moral values, and understandings—which should have been an integral part of the curriculum designed to foster social living—were neglected or ignored.

Holiday Curriculum

Another common approach to social studies in early childhood education—a total embarrassment to those teachers who do guide children through valuable learning episodes—is the holiday curriculum. Celebrating holidays is an enjoyable diversion from the regular school routine. Unfortunately, in too many cases these celebrations have become the basis for teaching social studies. Year after year, the same celebrations are repeated without much concern for the knowledge, skills, attitudes, or values gained from them (Myers & Myers, 2002).

Commercial companies have fostered the holiday approach with unit plans, posters, and entire curriculum packages, all centering around the celebration of holidays. Children follow a pattern to make Pilgrim hats, cut out a pumpkin at Halloween, sing songs, and listen to contrived stories that are more myth and legend than fact. Given this curriculum, children's social studies learning is superficial, an unrealistic perpetuation of myths—untrue at best, stereotyping groups of people at its worst.

This does not mean, however, that there is no place for the recognition of holidays in the social studies curriculum. Celebration of holidays can promote identification with family, community, and nation (Vygotsky, 1986). Further, acquaintance with the holiday customs of many lands, when appropriately introduced, fosters an appreciation of other cultures. The use of stories, video, role playing, music, bulletin boards, and discussions to clarify the meaning of virtues such as honesty, bravery, and kindness can help children develop historical understandings (National Center for History in the Schools, 1994; NCSS, 1998).

Figure 1.1 summarizes the strengths and weaknesses of historical approaches to the social studies.

Social Forces and Theories Affecting the Curriculum

In the recent past, two major social forces influenced the social studies curriculum: the Soviet Union's launching of Sputnik and the civil rights movement of the 1960s. Theories, especially those of Piaget (Piaget & Inhelder, 1969) and Vygotsky (1978), also influenced the curriculum.

Sputnik's Challenge

Following the launch of Sputnik, the first satellite to circle the earth, U. S. educators began reevaluating their theories and practices. In 1959 the famous Woods Hole Conference was held, where scientists and educators met to determine the content of various disciplines and how to present that content to children. After this conference Jerome Bruner (1960) stated that the "curriculum of a subject should be determined by the most fundamental understanding that can be achieved of the underlying principles that give structure to that subject" (p. 31).

This idea, that curriculum content should emphasize the structure of a discipline, caught the imagination of curriculum planners and educators and has guided curriculum development since that time. Concepts and theories key to a discipline became the core of the curriculum, and inductive thinking became the method of teaching. A number of mathematics, science, and social studies curricula were developed based on this theory.

In 1965 Robison and Spodek published *New Directions in the Kindergarten*, a description of a program for 5-year-old kindergarten children that focused on the struc-

Date	Approach	Concept	Weakness	Strength
1920s–1930s	Social skills	Social skills are necessary for living in a democracy.	Translated into habit training and formation. Ignored the complexities of social learning.	Social skills are required to function in a democracy. The ability to cooperate, share, negotiate, and give up some of oneself to consider the rights of others is necessary.
1934	Here-and-now	Children's learning is firsthand, based on experiences in their immediate environment.	Misunderstood and translated into meaningless simplistic units of "my family," "community helpers," etc.	When complexities of the immediate here-and-now world are considered and used to support thinking, this approach is current and supported by both theory and research.
1930s+	Holiday curriculum	None	Stereotypic and sterile in content, ideas; limits thinking, problem solving.	None.

Figure 1.1   Historical foundations of social studies in early childhood education.

ture of subject matter and included curriculum content from science, mathematics, language, and social studies. Robison and Spodek concluded that young children could successfully learn concepts that once were believed to be beyond their grasp.

The ideas of the past are reinforced with current knowledge of how children learn (NRC, 2001):

- Children develop ideas and concepts about their world when they are very young.
- The embryonic concepts or preconcepts children bring to school are the foundation for new and more conventional knowledge of their social world.
- Children's learning is continual. They deal with ideas over long periods of time.
- Children think. They pose questions, and gather information in many ways. They use the tools of the social scientist.
- Children transfer their understandings when approaching new situations.

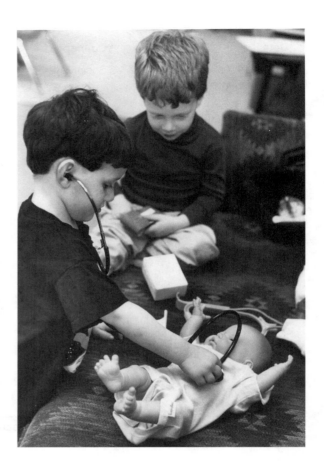

Piaget helped us realize that children construct knowledge through social, physical, and mental activity.

Civil Rights

As this reexamination of curriculum and educational practices was taking place, Americans were becoming aware of the inequality of educational opportunities for many people in our society. The recognition that large groups of people had for many years been systematically discriminated against led to organized efforts to gain full civil rights and educational opportunity for all citizens, regardless of ethnic background or race. This drive for civil rights was manifest in the Johnson administration's War on Poverty.

The War on Poverty included the Elementary-Secondary Education Act of 1965 and the Head Start Program. Using the theories of J. McV. Hunt (1961) and Benjamin Bloom (1963), who believed that intelligence was malleable and could be influenced by early, enriching educational experiences, the government looked to early childhood education as a means of increasing children's intelligence and an instrument to break the poverty cycle. Preschool programs that were enriching and stimulating and involved the child's total family were thought to increase young children's intelligence as well as change their attitudes and the attitudes of their families toward school. Thus, early childhood education was designed to increase children's motivation to learn and achieve while improving basic cognitive skills; all of this would, in turn, lead to success in later school experiences and in a chosen career.

Of all the programs within the War on Poverty, the Head Start Program has had, and continues to have, the most influence. The program is not only popular with families, educators, and members of the community but has demonstrated long-lasting positive effects (NRC, 2001). Twenty years after participating in a model early-intervention program, children had repeated fewer grades, were less likely to be placed in special education programs or to be involved in delinquency, and had been more productive when compared with those of comparable backgrounds who had not participated in such a program (Washington & Bailey, 1995).

Because social studies emphasize the development of self-concepts, skills in relating with others, and multicultural understanding as well as knowledge, the discipline proved to be an excellent vehicle for fostering the goals of Head Start. Many social studies experiences—taking field trips, exploring the environment, observing adults at work, talking to classroom visitors—help Head Start children better understand themselves and their place in the world.

Piaget

Linked with renewed concern for providing equality of educational opportunity for all children was an emerging acceptance of the work of Jean Piaget (Piaget & Inhelder, 1969), a Swiss psychologist who had been exploring children's thought processes since the early 1900s. During the 1960s, his research and theories began receiving attention from psychologists and educators in the United States. Piaget's work may have become well known at this time because his writings were then being translated into English. On the other hand, the interest may have arisen because his theories offered psychologists a different way of looking at children's learning.

According to Piaget, children, like humans of any age, construct their own knowledge through maturation and interaction with the total environment. He suggested that, as children mature, they pass through four stages of cognitive development: (1) the sensorimotor period, from birth through age 2; (2) the preoperational period, ages 2 through 7 or 8; (3) the concrete operational period, ages 8 to adolescence; and (4) formal thought, after adolescence. To progress through these stages requires mental activity and interaction with the social and physical environment.

The social studies curriculum was heavily influenced by knowledge of Piaget's stages of intellectual growth. His descriptions of young children's abilities and their conceptions of the world, time, and space offered insights for social studies curriculum planners and teachers. Further, the Piagetian interview—the probing technique used to uncover children's concepts—can be used as a model for evaluating the outcomes of lessons, units, and other teaching sequences.

Vygotsky

The current focus on the social and cultural influences of all aspects of children's development has promoted the ideas of another theorist, Lev Semenovich Vygotsky

(Glassman, 2001). A student of literature, philosophy, and aesthetics, Vygotsky was born in the late 1800s into a middle-class Jewish family in Belorussia. He graduated from the University of Moscow in 1917 and entered the field of psychology in the 1920s. During the 1920s and 1930s, his written research was banned by the Soviet Union. Vygotsky died in 1934, before the ban was lifted. His works were translated into English in the 1960s and 1970s and gradually became popular. They are now used to support curriculum development (Glassman, 2001), especially social studies curricula.

Vygotsky believed the following:

- A person's social and psychological world are connected.
- Child-adult interaction is important for cognitive development.
- The capacity to use language to regulate thought and action is distinctly human and the source of conscious mental life.
- Social experience is extremely important for cognitive growth.
- Education leads development.
- Teaching must be geared to the zone of proximal development; that is, it must match what is to be taught to what the child already knows and can accomplish independently as well as with adult help.

Vygotsky's ideas are similar in a number of ways to Piaget's. Both believed that learning is the result of firsthand experiences that stem from the child's environment. Both regarded play as a major educative activity; and both believed that social interaction with others, whether peers or adults, is critical for learning to take place.

SOCIAL STUDIES TODAY

Today's social studies are based firmly on the past. The theories of both Piaget and Vygotsky continue to influence the field. Mitchell's work in the 1930s (e.g., Mitchell, 1934), because of its similarity to Piagetian and Vygotskian thought, continues to provide the foundation for approaches to social studies (see Figure 1.2).

Today's social studies is integrated, meaningful, and of high interest. Whatever is introduced to children is

❏ *Integrated* into and with children's cultural background, personal knowledge, family, and community and embedded into the total curriculum

❏ Filled with *meaning* because it is appropriate for their development, matching their cognitive, emotional, social, and physical maturity

❏ *Of high interest* to children when based on their firsthand experiences, self-choice, and social interaction

---

Figure 1.2   Social studies today.

Social studies in today's schools, however, are based on more than just the past. Current learning theory and research are reflected in today's social studies curriculum.

Active Children

In order to learn, children from birth through the primary grades and even beyond must be physically, mentally, and socially active. Every type of play, whether alone or with others—sociodramatic play, play with materials, or physical play—provides children with physical, mental, and social activity (Colker, 2002).

Both the theories of Vygotsky (1986) and Piaget and Inhelder (1969) support the premise that children's play is necessary for concept formation. Play, according to the theorists, permits children to do the following:

- *Develop more hierarchical and long-term goals.*   Play may be the first context in which children are able to delay gratification, to keep on working at something until they achieve their goal.
- *Take the perspective of others, which is necessary to learning.*   When children play with others they are forced to consider the ideas of others. If children did not consider each other's ideas, they could not play as if they were mothers, fathers, doctors, beauticians, and so on. This initial ability to coordinate, to think about multiple ideas, will develop into reflective thinking and metacognition (Bodrova & Leong, 2003).
- *Use mental representations.*   Children may use objects as substitutions for other objects. For example, a child may use a block to represent a scissors as they play barbershop. To be able to use symbolic substitutes for real objects is essential to the development of abstract thought.

Because play is so critical to children's cogntiive development, large blocks of time in child-care, preschool, and kindergarten settings will be arranged for children's play. Throughout the primary grades, children need opportunities to continue to play with others, with materials, and with board and other games in order to solidify their learning.

Integrated

Social studies are not isolated bits of information or knowledge that children memorize but, as Vygotsky indicated, are deeply rooted in children's cultural background and personal experience. The more situated in context and the more rooted in cultural background and personal knowledge an event is, the more readily it is understood, learned, and remembered (Popkewitz, 1999). Thus, today's social studies are embedded within the context of children's family, school, and neighborhood (Garcia, 2003).

No one social science discipline can be separated or segregated from another or from the development of skills, attitudes, and values. Just as social studies are an integrated subject, so is the entire early childhood curriculum. The social studies cannot be separated from any other subject matter of the school. Try to find a key concept or a suggested activity in any of the chapters of this text that does not involve children when they are studying other subjects in school. Most social studies concepts and activities involve children in using language through listening, speaking, reading, or writing; in applying mathematics or science concepts; or in expressing their ideas through art, music, or movement. Many social science concepts overlap those of science and mathematics (Jantz & Seefeldt, 1999).

Meaningful

To be meaningful, social studies content must match children's intellectual growth. Meaningful teaching requires matching the richness of the learning environment to the intellectual growth of the child. The richness of an environment for intellectual growth is a function of the appropriateness of this match between inner organizations and external circumstances in a child's succession of encounters with his or her environment. Vygotsky (1978) explained the importance of matching what is to be learned with the nature of children's cognitive maturity: "It is a well known and empirically established fact that learning should be matched in some manner with the child's developmental level" (p. 85). Sue Bredekamp (1998) calls matching what one wants to teach children to their existing knowledge "teaching on the edge of children's knowledge."

Today, early childhood educators have increased their understanding of the problem of this match. The National Association for the Education of Young Children has published *Developmentally Appropriate Practice in Early Childhood Programs Serving Children from Birth through Age 8* (Bredekamp & Copple, 1997) as well as *Reaching Potentials* in two volumes: *Appropriate Curriculum and Assessment for Young Children* (Bredekamp & Rosegrant, 1992) and *Transforming Early Childhood and Assessment* (Bredekamp & Rosegrant, 1995).

Recognizing that curriculum must match children's maturation as well as the context in which they live, the National Council for the Social Studies does not specify scope, content, or sequence in its standards. These decisions, the council believes, are in the hands of those who teach social studies, the people who know the children and the world in which they live.

The search for matching content to a child's intellectual development continues. By organizing the social science disciplines—skills, attitudes, and values—around key concepts or principles and then describing what we do know about how children grow in understanding these principles, teachers have an opportunity to plan ways of presenting social studies material and content that will have meaning because it will match children's developmental level.

A measure of meaningfulness is guaranteed when teachers realize that children are very young and do have a long time to grow. Then social studies are conceptualized as an initial foundation of social and physical knowledge on which later logical knowledge will be built. The social sciences are meaningful when young children are not pushed to attain concepts beyond their intellectual reach. Learning is a much more complex and drawn out process than is generally acknowledged. The type of complex, meaningful learning that occurs in school and throughout the life span takes place over weeks, months, and years; and there is good reason to believe that the nature of the learning process changes as the tasks of mastering a complex body of knowledge unfold.

Of High Interest

Interested children learn. Interest leads to "meaningful learning, promotes long-term storage of knowledge, and provides motivation for further learning" (Hidi, 1990, p. 549). Whether studying history, geography, economics, current events, or cultures, children must find the material of high interest. It is their interest that motivates them to satisfy their curiosity about themselves and the world in which they live, promoting a sense of competence (Wigfield, 2002). At least three other factors stimulate children's interest in social studies: firsthand learning, self-choice, and social interaction. All the social studies in this text begin with children's firsthand interactions with their world. All of social studies teaching is grounded in children's firsthand experiences, play, and spontaneous activity.

Child choice is encouraged. Through centers of interest, children can select their own learning experiences and activities. Children who are given choices—who initiate their own learning experiences and activities, choose the centers in which they will work, and then make choices within the centers—are more likely to succeed because the problem of match is at least partially solved (Seefeldt & Galper, 2000).

As social beings, children want to be with others and learn to relate ever-more effectively with them. Relating with others, children are exposed to different ways of thinking, knowing, and valuing—all of which lead to expanding cognitive powers (Pattnaik, 2003). Feeling competent socially and cognitively, children are fully motivated to want to continue to learn more about themselves, others, and the world in which they live (Stone, 2003).

Skills, Attitudes, and Knowledge

Using the recommendations of the NCSS (1998) and national history, geography, and civics standards, today's social studies revolve around introducing children to the skills, attitudes, and knowledge required of citizens of a democracy.

Focus on Skills

Within the small democracy of the preschool or primary classroom, children begin to develop the social and participatory skills required of citizens in a democracy. They will be taught and gain the skills necessary to cooperate and share and begin to assume responsibility for themselves as the total group. The *National Standards for Civics and Government* (Center for Civic Education, 1994) state that students in school should learn to do the following:

- Respect the rights of others.
- Respect the privacy of others.
- Promote the common good, clean up the environment, and care for the school.
- Participate in voting and in developing class rules and constitutions.

Civics and government standards suggest that these skills are best developed by "providing students [with] opportunities to practice these skills and to observe and interact with those in their community who are adept in exercising them" (Center for Civic Education, 1994, p. xiii). Good citizenship is not just a matter of the observance of outward forms, transmitted from the old to the young, but also a matter of reasoned conviction, the end result of people's thinking for themselves (Center for Civic Education, 1994).

Citizens of a democracy need to have the skills of thinking and inquiry. Those skills are promoted throughout the social studies curriculum. "Intellectual skills and civics are inseparable" (Center for Civic Education, 1994, p. xii), and being a citizen of a democracy means being "able to think critically" (p. xii). Wade (2003) suggests a civics curriculum focused on civic projects and aimed at developing concepts of a common good. In this way, young children are most likely able to develop the concepts key to citizenship in a democracy.

Involving children in study of their here-and-now world gives them the platform for posing questions and finding answers. As children study their world, they collect data, observe, survey, weigh, measure, compare, and contrast things in their here-and-now world. After considering the information collected, children reach conclusions. Through inquiry, they use an array of tools appropriate for study of their world. Teachers scaffold children's use of tools and provide time and opportunity for children to reflect on and reconsider the results of their activity. Only as children make sense of their own world, whatever or wherever that world is, will they develop the thinking skills and knowledge of content necesssary for productive citizenship.

Focus on Attitudes and Values

Children need to develop attitudes and values congruent with the democratic way of life if democracy is to continue. The attitudes and values of respect for each individual, freedom of speech, setting and following rules, learning to make choices, and participating in the democracy of the classroom are fostered through the social studies.

The NCSS (1998, p. 3) maintains that the focus of education is on how values are formed and how they influence human behavior rather than on building commitment to specific values. The values and attitudes of the fundamental rights to life, liberty, dignity, equality, and speech are best taught by helping students to weigh priorities in situations in which conflicts arise.

Focus on Standards and Knowledge

More than ever, children need knowledge and a basic understanding of the world in which they live. Without knowledge of history, geography, economics, current events, and global interrelationships, children will be ill-prepared to assume responsible citizenship in the future.

In the past, social studies content was limited in scope, trivial, and lacking in connection to major social education goals (Brophy & Alleman, 2002). Today, however, there is an awareness of the richness of concepts key to the social studies and how these concepts can be meaningfully introduced to very young children (Levstik, 2002).

National associations have identified social studies content that children are to learn during the primary grades. Geographers, historians, economists, civic educators, and social studies authorities have all identified what children should know and be able to do from kindergarten through grade four. Pre-kindergarten standards developed by CTB/McGraw-Hill (2002) and reviewed by the Carnegie Corporation of New York articulate what children 3 to 5 years of age should know and be able to do in the field of the social studies. Additionally, the NCSS identifies themes around which social studies teaching can be organized. Eight of those themes are reflected throughout this book:

- *Culture.*   The study of culture—the art, language, history, and geography of different cultures—takes place across the total curriculum. To become a global citizen, children must recognize the universals of human cultures everywhere. Chapter 3, "Celebrating Diversity," guides teachers on ways to develop children's ideas about the things that unite all humans everywhere.

- *Time, continuity, and change.*   In the context of their lives, children come to understand themselves in terms of the passage of time and develop the skills of the historian. This theme is reflected in Chapter 8, "Children's Study of Time, Continuity, and Change: History."

- *People, places, and environments.*   Children learn to locate themselves in space, become familiar with landforms in their environment, and develop beginning understanding of the human-environment interaction. Chapter 9, "People, Places, and Environments: Geography," presents these themes.

- *Individual development and identity.*   Personal identity is shaped by one's culture, by groups, and by institutional influences. How people learn, what they believe, and how people meet their basic needs in the context of culture are themes within this topic. Chapter 5, "Self, Others, and the Community: Social Skills," begins with a focus on developing children's sense of self.

- *Individuals, groups, and institutions.*   Institutions such as schools, families, government agencies, and the courts play a role in people's lives. Children can develop beginning concepts of the role of institutions in their lives. Chapter 5, "Self, Others, and the Community: Social Skills," introduces children to the fact that within a democracy, individual rights are balanced with those of the group.

- *Power, authority, and governance.*   Understanding how individual rights can be protected within the context of majority rule can be introduced to young children in the context of their classroom. The idea of power and rights is developed in Chapter 5, "Self, Others, and the Community: Social Skills."

- *Production, distribution, and consumption.*   Because people have wants that often exceed the resources available to them, a variety of ways have evolved to answer questions such as "What is to be produced?" and "How is production to be organized?" Chapter 10, "Production, Distribution, and Consumption: Economics," is designed to enable young children to develop embryonic ideas of these concepts.

- *Science, technology, and society.*   This theme deals with questions such as "How can we cope with change?" and "How can we manage technology so that all benefit from it?" The theme draws on the natural and physical sciences, social sciences, and the humanities, which are discussed in Chapters 8, 9, and 10.

SUMMARY

Knowledge of the content, skills, and attitudes that make up the social studies is necessary if children are to be prepared to take their place as fully productive members of a democratic society. Only when social studies are integrated, meaningful, and of interest to children, however, will the discipline fulfill its purpose.

Today's social studies are also grounded in current thinking about social studies education. Using current theories of learning as well as the recommendations of the NCSS and the standards stemming from each of the social studies disciplines, teachers have a basis for fulfilling the primary goals of the social studies, which involve preparing children to fulfill their role as citizens and integrating the total curriculum.

Extend Your Knowledge

1. Observe a group of young children at play. As you observe, make a list of all the topics the children discuss or even mention. Then write a description of the nature of the child's here-and-now world. What were the most frequently mentioned topics? Where did children become acquainted with these topics?

2. Obtain copies of social studies standards such as *Curriculum for Social Studies: Expectations of Excellence* from the National Council for the Social Studies, 8555 Sixteenth Street, Silver Spring, MD 20910; *National Standards for Civics and Government,* Center for Civic Education, *www.civiced.org; National Standards for United States History: Exploring the American Experience, K–4,* National Center for History in the Schools, *www.ssnet.ucla.net;* and *Geography for Life: National Geography Standards,* National Geographic Association, *www. nationalgeographic.com.* Read and discuss them with other students. Which of the ideas presented in these reports will affect how you teach social studies to young children?

3. Interview a teacher of young children. Ask him or her to define the social studies. What is included in this definition? How does the teacher decide what to include in the social studies curriculum? You may be able to interview a number of teachers, asking the same or similar questions. The goal is to determine how teachers define the social studies and make decisions about what to teach.

4. Describe your own experiences with the social studies. What was your first experience with them? Which memories are based on your feelings, which on knowledge?

Interview a group of your peers, and ask the same questions. What conclusions do you reach about your own experiences with social studies education as a child?

Resources

Successful teachers identify and use available resources. A number of organizations are concerned with social studies education and the education of young children. These associations offer publications, educational materials, services, and other resources for teachers. Why not write and request information about these services?

Associations

Associations have many resources for teachers. Contact the following associations and ask for their free or inexpensive resources for teachers of young children:

Association for Childhood Education International
17904 Georgia Avenue, Suite 215
Olney, MD 20832
Phone: (800) 423-3563
E-mail: ACEIED@aol.com
Website: *http://www.udel.edu/bateman/acei*

Government Printing Office
Washington, DC 20402
Website: *http://www.governmentprintingoffice.org*

National Association for the Education of Young Children
1509 16th Street, NW
Washington, DC 20036-1426
Phone: (800) 424-2460
E-mail: membership@naeyc.org
Website: *http://www.naeyc.org*

National Council for the Social Studies
8555 16th Street, Suite 500
Silver Spring, MD 20910
Website: *http://www.ncss.org*

Your local school system, state department of education, and local affiliates of national associations also have excellent resources to use in teaching the social studies.

Publications

Bredekamp, S., & Copple, C. (1997). *Developmentally appropriate practice in early childhood programs* (Rev. ed.). Washington, DC: National Association for the Education of Young Children.

Bredekamp, S., & Rosegrant, T. (Eds.). (1995). *Reaching potentials: Vol. 2. Transforming early childhood curriculum and assessment*. Washington, DC: National Association for the Education of Young Children.

National Council for the Social Studies (NCSS). (1988). *Social studies for early child-hood and elementary school children: Preparing for the 21st century.* Washington, DC: Author.

References

Bloom, B. (1963). *Stability and change in human characteristics.* New York: Wiley.

Bodrova, E., & Leong, D. J. (2003). Chopsticks and counting chips: Do play and foundational skills need to compete for teacher's attention in an early childhood program? *Young Children, 58* (3), 10–17.

Bredekamp, S. (1998). *Tools for teaching developmentally appropriate practice: The leading edge in early childhood education.* Cincinnati: Resources for Instruction and Staff Excellence.

Bredekamp, S., & Copple, C. (1997). *Developmentally appropriate practice in early childhood programs serving children from birth through age 8.* Washington, DC: National Association for the Education of Young Children.

Bredekamp, S., & Rosegrant, T. (1992). *Reaching potentials: Vol. 1. Appropriate curriculum and assessment for young children.* Washington, DC: National Association for the Education of Young Children.

Bredekamp, S., & Rosegrant, T. (1995). *Reaching potentials: Vol. 2. Transforming early childhood and assessment.* Washington, DC: National Association for the Education of Young Children.

Brophy, J., & Alleman, J. (2002). Learning and teaching about cultural universals in primary grade social studies. *Elementary School Journal, 103,* 99–114.

Bruner, J. (1960). *The process of education.* Cambridge, MA: Harvard University Press.

Center for Civic Education. (1994). *National standards for civics and government.* Calabasa, CA: Author.

Colker, L. (2002). Introduction. *Young Children, 57* (5), 10–12.

CTB/McGraw-Hill. (2002). *Pre-K standards.* New York: McGraw-Hill.

Dewey, J. (1944). *Democracy and education.* New York: Free Press.

Freeman, E. B., & Hatch, J. A. (1989). What schools expect young children to know and do: An analysis of kindergarten report cards. *Elementary School Journal, 89,* 595–607.

Garcia, E. (2003). Respecting children's home language and culture. In C. Copple (Ed.), *A world of difference* (p. 3). Washington, DC: National Association for the Education of Young Children.

Glassman, M. (2001). Dewey and Vygotsky: Society, experience, and inquiry in educational practice. *Educational Researcher, 30,* 3–15.

Hidi, S. (1990). Interest and its contribution as a mental resource for learning. *Review of Educational Research, 80* (4), 549–573.

Hill, P. S. (1923). *A conduct curriculum for the kindergarten and first grade* (pp. x–xix). New York: Scribner.

Hunt, J. McV. (1961). *Intelligence and experience.* New York: Ronald.

Jantz, R. K., & Seefeldt, C. (1999). Social studies for young children. In C. Seefeldt (Ed.), *The early childhood curriculum* (3rd ed., pp. 159–200). New York: Teachers College Press.

Kozulin, A. (1986). Introduction: Vygotsky in context. In L. Vygotsky, *Thought and language*. Cambridge, MA: MIT Press.

Levstik, L. S. (2002). Introduction: Social studies. *Elementary School Journal, 103*, 93–98.

Mitchell, L. S. (1934). *Young geographers*. New York: Bank Street College.

Mitchell, L. S. (2000). Social studies for future teachers. In N. Nager & E. K. Shapior (Eds.), *Revisiting a progressive pedagogy* (pp. 125–138). Albany: State University of New York Press.

Myers, M. E., & Myers, B. K. (2002). Holidays in the public school kindergarten: An avenue for emerging religious and spiritual literacy. *Childhood Education, 78*, 79–84.

National Center for History in the Schools. (1994). *National standards for history, grades K–4*. Los Angeles: Author.

National Council for the Social Studies (NCSS). (1998). *Standards for social studies: Expectations of excellence*. Washington, DC: Author.

National Council for the Social Studies (NCSS). (2003). *Social studies for early childhood and elementary school children: Preparing for the 21st Century* [On-line]. Available: *www.socialstudies.org/positions/elementary.shtml*.

National Research Council (NRC). (2000). *From neurons to neighborhoods: The science of early childhood development*. Washington, DC: National Academy Press.

National Research Council (NRC). (2001). *Eager to learn: Educating our preschoolers*. Washington, DC: National Academy Press.

Pattnaik, J. (2003). "Learning about the 'other': Building a case for intercultural understanding among minority children." *Childhood Education, 78*, 204–210.

Piaget, J., & Inhelder, B. (1969). *The psychology of the child*. New York: Basic Books.

Pohan, C. A. (2003). Creating caring and democratic communities in our classrooms and schools. *Childhood Education, 79*, 369–373.

Popkewitz, T. S. (1999). Dewey, Vygotsky, and the social administration of the individual. *American Education Research Journal, 35*, 535–570.

Robison, H., & Spodek, B. (1965). *New directions in the kindergarten*. New York: Teachers College Press.

Seefeldt, C., & Galper, A. (2000). *Active experiences for active children: Social studies*. Upper Saddle River, NJ: Merrill/Prentice Hall.

Stone, J. (2003). Communicating respect. In C. Copple (Ed.), *A world of difference* (p. 9). Washington, DC: National Association for the Education of Young Children.

Vygotsky, L. (1978). *Thought and language*. Cambridge, MA: MIT Press.

Vygotsky, L. (1986). *Thought and language* (Rev. ed.). Cambridge, MA: MIT Press.

Washington, V., & Bailey, V. J. (1995). *Project Head Start*. New York: Garland.

Wade, R. (2003). Beyond expanding horizons: New curriculum directions for elementary social studies. *Elementary School Journal, 103*, 115–131.

Weber, E. (1969). *The kindergarten: Its encounter with educational thought in America*. New York: Teachers College Press.

Wigfield, A. (Ed.). (2002). *The development of achievement motivation*. San Diego: Academic Press.

CHAPTER 2

Planning to Teach

Each school will make its own curriculum for small children.

L. S. Mitchell, 1934, p. 12

After you read this chapter, you should be prepared to respond to the follow-ing questions:

- Why is knowledge of children's growth, development, and learning neces-sary for planning the social studies?
- How does the nature of the community in which children live affect plan-ning? How does social studies content affect planning?
- What short-term plans will you set for social studies learning? What long-range plans?
- What are the benefits of planning to teach through themes, units, or projects?
- How will you know if children have learned what you have planned to teach them?

"But what do I teach?" asked one student after a discussion of the scope of the social studies. "I know social studies is a large, complex field, and I've read some of the stan-dards, but isn't there a workbook or something we can use that tells what to teach?"

If social studies are to be meaningful and totally integrated into children's culture, background of experiences, and social interactions, the teacher must, based on her knowledge of the children, knowledge of the community in which they live, and knowledge of the social studies, "make [her] own curriculum for small children" (Mitchell, 1934, p. 12).

Throughout the years, reflective teachers have understood this need. They understand that, to bring children and the social studies together, curriculum must hold meaning and interest for each child and be based on children's firsthand interactions with their immediate environment.

Today, as in the past, the teacher is the decision maker. The decisions teachers will make include the following:

- What short- and long-term goals and objectives will guide the curriculum?
- How will these goals and objectives be achieved?
- How can children's interactions with their environment and community be used to achieve these goals?
- What place will mandated curriculum plans hold in the curriculum? How can the goals and objectives of mandated plans be achieved in meaningful ways?
- How will the curriculum be evaluated?

As in the past, these decisions cannot be made without (1) knowledge of children, (2) knowledge of the community in which the children live, and (3) knowledge of social studies content.

KNOWLEDGE OF CHILDREN

"I am advising you to retain Judy in kindergarten for another year," the teacher said to 6-year-old Judy's parents. "She doesn't know which day comes before or after another, nor can she tell you the name of the month or the months that came before or after. She just won't make it in first grade until she can do so."

This is the problem of the match that Vygotsky (1986) discussed and Bredekamp and Copple (1997) described in *Developmentally Appropriate Practices*. If Judy's teacher had based her social studies instruction on knowledge of child growth and development, she would have known that isolated facts, such as the names of the days of the week or the months, have no meaning to children. Further, she would have known that children will learn these names automatically as they progress through the primary grades.

Without knowledge of children, teachers are unable to match the curriculum or its goals and expectations for children's learning to the developmental capabilities of children. Without this match, social studies are meaningless and uninteresting to children. As a result, children will fail. And once they have experienced failure, research shows they continue to think of themselves as failures.

Basing curriculum on the universal characteristics of children (i.e., those characteristics that make all children alike) and on the unique characteristics of each child (i.e., those things that make each an individual) is one way to ensure that children will live fully each day and be prepared to take their places in a democratic society.

Children Are Alike

Regardless of where children live, their ethnic background, or the structure of their family, they all have the same needs and share similar characteristics.

Children Have Similar Needs

Young children share certain characteristics. For instance, all young children need the following:

- Love, security, and the attention of a friendly, interested, sympathetic adult they can trust (NRC, 2001)
- Shelter, food, warmth, and clothing
- To feel good about themselves and learn to relate to others, make friends, and be a friend.

Children Are Active Learners

If children's basic needs for security and love have been met, they are curious, interested in their environment, and filled with the desire to learn more about themselves and their world. Their active minds and bodies demand that they move about physically and interact with one another. Children need to talk, question, and take things apart in their attempts to find out about and make sense of their world (Bredekamp & Copple, 1997; Piaget & Inhelder, 1969).

Children Pass Through the Same Stages of Thought

Between the ages of 2 and 7 or 8, children's thinking is preoperational. They are beginning to think abstractly and use symbols, to represent their actions mentally, to anticipate consequences before an action actually occurs, and to develop some idea of causes; but they don't yet think about abstract ideas or perform operations on them.

A child in the stage of preoperational thought relies heavily on the way things look. Perception dominates thought; the way things look is the way they are. Thus, a child under age 7 or 8 says there is more juice in a tall, skinny glass because it looks bigger than a short, squat one does or that there are more candies in a long, spread-out row than there are in a bunched group.

At around age 7 or 8, children's thinking changes; they begin to think operationally. They can tell you that the amount of juice poured into two containers of different shapes stays the same because no juice has been added or taken away. But even though children after age 7 or 8 can reason this way, their thinking is still tied to the concrete. They cannot think about the hypothetical or go from the real to the merely possible or from the possible to the real. Their thought is bound to the real, concrete world—hence the term *concrete operations*. Not until age 11 or 12 do children enter the last stage of thought, in which they can think formally and have the ability to manipulate abstract ideas.

Because children cannot think abstractly until nearly age 11 or 12, most of the goals and objectives planned for early social studies learning are based on the concrete here-and-now world and are introductory. During the preschool and primary grades, children need only to develop an interest in learning and a base of firsthand experiences from which to learn later abstract concepts.

So Alike, So Different

As individuals, however, young children are very different. Each child is unique. Understanding the general characteristics of all children, teachers recognize that each one brings to school a different background of experiences, interests, and motivations. Successful social studies are based on teachers' understanding of the experiences children have had before coming to school, the interests of each child, individual abilities, special needs, and the culture in which children live (Derman-Sparks, 2003; McCormick, Wong, & Yogi, 2003).

Experiences

For the most part, children entering school have a full, rich background of experience. Many have had opportunities to explore their immediate neighborhoods, become familiar with traffic systems and community helpers, discuss their experiences with adults, and recognize the relationships among their experiences. Teachers can determine children's background of experience in the following ways:

- Visiting their homes and talking with their parents about the things the children have done
- Walking around the children's neighborhoods to see what the community offers experientially
- Interviewing the children, asking them to tell about the things they do, places they have been, and things they would like to do

Whatever the children's backgrounds, they are important indicators of objectives and goals for the social studies program. Teachers plan objectives to support past experiences of children; introduce new experiences that can be incorporated into the children's previous experiences; and extend, clarify, and expand all experiences.

Interests

As anyone who has contact with young children knows, they are interested in learning about everything. They enter preschool interested in learning about ants, worms,

Children—so alike, yet so different.

cars, boats, water, air, space, foreign countries, letters, machines, trees, colors, families, seeds, rocks, love, hate, birth, death, friendship, war, peace, cosmic forces, good, and evil. To plan a social studies curriculum, some understanding of what the group, and each individual child within the group, is interested in will be necessary. To begin, you could do these things:

- Talk with children informally; ask them what they would like to know more about, what they would like to do, or what they know a lot about
- Observe children at play; note the things they play with, how they use materials, what they play, and which books they select
- Discuss children's interests with their parents, and ask what the children like to do at home

Abilities

Children not only bring a wide range of experiences and interests to the classroom; they also bring great differences in social, emotional, physical, and intellectual abilities. These differences in abilities form the basis of other goals and objectives of the social studies for the group and for individual children.

To determine the abilities of children, you might take these steps:

- Review past records of health and physical growth
- Observe children at play to note social skills and how they interact with others
- Structure some task for them to complete, observing how successful each child is
- Review results of standardized measures

Special Needs

All children are special, and each has individual needs, strengths, and weaknesses. Some, however, have needs and characteristics that require special planning and care. Public laws have been passed to ensure that the special needs of these children will be met. P.L. 94-142, the Education of All Handicapped Children Act of 1975, protects children with special needs by requiring that every child, regardless of handicapping condition, have access to free and appropriate educational experiences in the least restrictive environment.

P.L. 99-457, the Federal Preschool Program and Early Intervention Program Act of 1986, extends rights and services to handicapped infants, toddlers, and preschoolers. Until 1986, children between ages 3 and 5 received services only at each state's discretion. P.L. 99-457 requires appropriate public education for those children. From birth through age 2, the law requires that services be available for children who show signs of developmental delay, have identifiable physical or mental conditions, or are at risk because of medical or environmental problems (Diamond & Stacey, 2003).

Even without laws, teachers wishing to foster the principles of democracy in their classrooms would find ways to include all children and their families (see Figure 2.1). Democracy reflects the belief that young children, whatever their abilities or disabilities, can grow in self-confidence and increase their skills and abilities to interact socially with others when included in programs. As Diamond and Stacey (2003) assert, all children have the right to a life that is as normal as possible.

Teaching children with special needs is not a new aspect of early childhood education. The needs of exceptional children in the regular preschool or primary classroom have been recognized for decades, long before implementation of these laws. So what was new about P.L. 94-142 and P.L. 99-457? They protect children with special needs by requiring educational experiences in the least restrictive environment. The preschool or primary classroom is often determined to be the least restrictive environment, for it gives children with special needs the opportunity to

---

When talking with families of children with special needs, try to do the following:

- *Reduce education or professional terms.*   Instead of talking about methodologies or strategies, say, "This is what we will do," and "Here is how we will do it."

- *Use words instead of initials.*   Rather than saying, "P.L. 94-142," say, "the law providing for equality of educational opportunity." Say, "individual education plan" instead of "IEP."

- *Accept parents' feelings.*   Say, "Understandably, you are very worried," to parents who are expressing anxiety about their child. To angry parents, say, "Understandably, you are angry."

- *Use active listening.*   To clarify what parents have said, you might say, "I heard you say. . . . Did I understand you correctly?"

Figure 2.1   Talking with Families

Teachers find ways to include all children.

enter the mainstream of living and learning with other children their age (McDermott, 2003).

As a teacher of special children you need to (1) familiarize yourself with the complete text of P.L. 94-142; (2) ask your director, principal, or supervisor for your child-care center's or school system's guidelines for implementation of the law; (3) obtain resources and special assistance when mainstreaming children with special needs; and (4) perhaps request a classroom aide—a teacher of a specific skill such as sign language—or assistance in helping yourself acquire specialized skills.

Children with special needs who benefit from being in the mainstream preschool or primary classroom are those who have visual or hearing impairments, physical disabilities, mental retardation, emotional problems, or speech or language impairments, as well as those who are gifted. While labeling of individual children is discouraged, it does help to know something about the specific conditions children may bring to the classroom.

Visual Impairments

Children with visual impairments frequently can work and learn effectively in the regular classroom. They can participate in many activities without special assistance.

Teachers working with children who have visual impairments just have to remember the obvious: these children cannot see. This means remembering that children with visual impairments do not learn by looking or by imitating others. They will need systematic and deliberate introduction to the physical environment of the room, school, and playground as well as the activities of the school. You will need to maintain consistency in the physical environment, provide tactile guides in the room, and communicate by touching as well as speaking.

Hearing Impairments

Children with hearing impairments also find the mainstream preschool and primary classroom suited to their needs. You will want to learn how to communicate with the child who has a hearing impairment using the method the child uses and learn the care of hearing aids and how to assist the child with the aid.

Children with hearing impairments can participate in nearly all school activities. You need to communicate with these children in special ways. They learn by seeing, and they respond to touch. Marschark, Lang, and Albertin (2001) describe how a child with a hearing impairment was successfully included in a first-grade classroom through collaboration with children, the family, and others in the school.

Physical Disabilities

You may need to adapt the physical environment for children with physical disabilities and for those who use orthopedic aids. Ask specialists for assistance in adapting the physical plant to the needs of the child, both indoors and outdoors. Special chairs, tables, and play equipment can be purchased or made for children with physical disabilities, enabling them to participate in school activities.

You will want to learn all you can about the condition of a child with physical disabilities. You will need to know the child's limitations and potentials as well as how to care for orthopedic equipment and assist the child with the equipment.

Mental Disabilities

Children who differ markedly from average or normal intelligence or who have learning disabilities are also frequently mainstreamed in the preschool and primary classroom. The open schedule, free activity times, and emphasis on concrete learning as well as social, emotional, and language development are well suited for children who have mental impairments (Molenarr-Klumper, 2002).

You will need to analyze each task so that you can present it to the child in small steps. Specific experiences and instruction in listening and speaking, social skills, and self-help skills will enable children who have mental impairments to succeed.

Emotional Problems

Nearly everyone has lost control, felt afraid, or had difficulty interacting with others. At one time or another, all children experience difficulty handling strong emotions.

Children who have more difficulty than most in handling their emotions find a preschool experience very beneficial. Here they can learn techniques for channeling emotions appropriately and strengthening their ability to control behavior.

Probably all preschool activities will benefit children who need to learn to handle emotions, and the primary classroom environment can be modified to permit more activities designed for this purpose. When you have a child who is totally out of control—hitting, kicking, hurting self and others—it will be helpful to assign an aide or a volunteer to stay with the child for a while, offering the child support and guidance in learning to gain control over strong emotions (Greene, 2001).

Speech and Language Impairments

For children who have language impairments, you can arrange assessment for specific diagnoses and planned activities in listening and speaking. Speech and hearing specialists can assist you as you plan for these children, and volunteers or aides may help you implement specific lessons.

Remember that all of the language activities of the preschool-primary classroom will benefit children with speech and language impairments. The stories, poems, creative dramatics, and dramatic play will be of great benefit.

Gifted Children

Children who demonstrate intelligence higher than the norm or who have specific gifts and talents deserve to have their special needs met (Walker, Hafenstein, & Crow-Enslow, 1999). Typically, the needs of children who are gifted have been met by acceleration, enrichment, placement in special schools, or advancement to a higher grade. The social studies offer these children the opportunity to explore special interests and develop talents.

A Program of Inclusion

While public laws protect all children's rights to appropriate education, teaching children who have special needs requires much more than just being together in a classroom. Children with special needs require acceptance for who they are and an environment that fosters their autonomy and the development of alternative modes of interaction with the world (Diamond & Stacey, 2003).

Research suggests that early childhood programs should strive for the following goals:

- Develop an inclusive educational environment in which all children can succeed
- Enable children with disabilities to develop autonomy, independence, competency, confidence, and pride
- Provide all children with accurate, developmentally appropriate information about their own and others' disabilities, and foster understanding that a person with a disability differs from others in one respect but is similar in many others

- Enable all children to develop the ability to interact knowledgeably, comfortably, and fairly with people who have various disabilities
- Teach children with disabilities how to handle and challenge name calling, stereotypic attitudes, and physical barriers
- Teach nondisabled children how to resist and challenge stereotyping, name calling, and physical barriers directed against people with disabilities
- Encourage children to ask about their own and others' physical characteristics
- Provide children with accurate, developmentally appropriate information
- Enable children to feel pride, but not superiority, about their racial identity
- Enable children to develop ease with and respect for physical differences
- Help children become aware of our shared physical characteristics—what makes us all human beings

KNOWLEDGE OF THE COMMUNITY

"I found four signs with words and seven without," exclaimed an excited first grader returning from a walk around the block. The teacher explained to a parent volunteer, "There's so much available for children to learn in the environment that I rarely use a social studies book."

As Mitchell (2000) suggested, teachers must become aware of the nature of the here-and-now world in which children live. Then they must develop knowledge of the culture and values of the community. Just as teachers cannot plan a social studies curriculum without knowledge of child growth and development, they cannot successfully implement it without knowledge of the community.

The Child's Physical World

"The practical tasks for each school are to study the relations in the environment into which their children are born and to watch the children's behavior in their environment, to note when they first discover relations and what they are" (Mitchell, 1934, p. 12). To do this, you might drive or walk through children's neighborhoods. One teacher asked a parent to guide her through the school's neighborhood. As they walked and talked together, they noted the following:

- The physical nature of the area
- Places children enjoyed going
- The history of the neighborhood
- Neighbors who had special skills or resources
- Places of business
- Other resources for learning

Teachers locate community resources for children's learning.

Another day the teacher walked through the neighborhood again. This time she noted where children played, the pathways they took on their way home from school, and, most important, the way they interacted with peers, adults, and their parents. She also noted how people functioned in the neighborhood. The insights into the children's community and here-and-now world led to the teacher's decisions about the overall goals and objectives for the social studies curriculum.

Cultural Knowledge and Values

Less concrete than knowledge of the physical environment, but perhaps even more important, is knowledge of the culture and values of the community. Early in the school year, teachers try to become acquainted with each child's ethnic and subcultural backgrounds as well as the culture and values of the community as a whole (Garcia, 2003). This can be done in various ways:

- *Informal conversations.* Early in the school year, teachers can talk informally with parents and children. Teachers can ask them what the family does on weekends, in the evenings, before school starts, or on vacations. Teachers can note the traditions, customs, language, special foods, items of dress, and types of celebrations mentioned by the children or their parents during these conversations.
- *Resource persons.* A resource person might be able to inform teachers about the traditions, history, and meaning of a group's practices.
- *Formal inservice activities.* Teachers and administrators can initiate a variety of activities and programs designed to acquaint them with different cultures and

values. One school enrolled a large number of children from Cambodia. A resource person knowledgeable about Cambodian culture and its demands on children and their families was invited to talk with the teachers. In a short period of time, she was able to build a base of knowledge useful for understanding and teaching these children (Newman, 1995).

Other meetings might be sponsored by community organizations or local businesses and involve parents and other community residents. Slides, videos, and photographs of the community are helpful in illustrating the culture of a community.

KNOWLEDGE OF THE SOCIAL STUDIES

"I have to take two more courses from the social sciences if I want to teach young children? What in the world does my taking geography, history, and economics have to do with young children?" an undergraduate student complained to her advisor. Well, just about everything. Without complete, in-depth knowledge of the social sciences and the skills and values considered to be a part of social studies, teachers cannot be effective.

To make this vast, even overwhelming, amount of information accessible to children, teachers must have a basic grasp of the concepts key to each social science discipline. Selected concepts must be complete and accurate as well as match what children already know and are capable of understanding (Brophy & Alleman, 2002). Thus, knowledge of both child development and content is required. If a concept key to politics is setting and keeping rules, then 4-year-olds might decide on rules for using the woodworking bench, 5-year-olds could dictate a list of rules they will follow in their group for the coming year, and 6- and 7-year-olds might draw up rules for their class. Children in the middle grades might study the rules of their school; and those in junior high school and high school could study the lawmaking bodies of the community, state, and nation.

National standards also guide teachers in planning and selecting social studies content. National professional organizations in the fields that form the social studies have identified concepts key to history, geography, economics, civic education, and other fields. These standards are typically given for children from kindergarten through grade 4. The outcomes—what children are to do and learn—are generally suggested for children leaving fourth grade. The standards, therefore, are a useful framework to guide teachers' planning. But teachers will still need to adjust the standards to accomplish the following:

- Provide for the needs of individual children and the unique group of children they are working with
- Match the standards with the resources in the community so children can learn from their here-and-now world
- Offer developmentally appropriate learning experiences for children below grade 4

Teachers also need to be knowledgeable about social studies skills, attitudes, and values. Teaching skills is part of both the social studies and other areas of the curriculum. Some skills, however, are best fostered within the context of the social studies, such as map reading. Other skills, such as thinking and social skills, are present in the social studies but are developed throughout the curriculum. Skill development begins at birth and continues throughout life. In gaining proficiency, children will have the opportunity to practice thinking and social skills throughout their preschool and primary experiences.

Attitudes and values constitute the third major area of the social studies. Those included in the social studies are necessary for the perpetuation and continuation of our society. Teachers select goals and objectives for children's learning of content and skills congruent with the values of a democracy. The entire early childhood program is arranged around goals and objectives that will foster the following:

- Each child's own worth and dignity
- Respect for self and others
- Participation in and responsibility for the group
- The disposition of learning to learn

SHORT- AND LONG-TERM PLANNING

With an understanding of the children, their culture, and the social studies, you have a base from which to answer this question: "What am I trying to help the children learn, understand, and experience?" Before you begin to answer the question, consider some other factors:

- How can I involve the children in planning?
- How can I plan for spontaneous learning?
- How can I plan short-term lessons?
- How can I plan thematic, unit, or project lessons?

Involving the Children

Everyone benefits when children and teachers plan together. Teachers benefit because children who have been involved in planning their own learning are more highly motivated to learn and less likely to disrupt the group. Children benefit because they know they belong. They feel in control.

Teacher-child planning implies cooperation between teacher and child. It doesn't mean that children take over. Young children would feel insecure if that were the case; they do want and need an adult to make decisions and to protect and guide them. On the other hand, teacher-child planning doesn't mean that a teacher decides ahead of time and then fishes for answers until the children give the responses she had in mind. Here's an example of such fishing. "What should we make today?" asked a teacher.

"I'm going to build a garage," answered one child, and another said, "I'll make a painting."

The teacher continued questioning until a child asked, "Are we going to make valentines?"

"Yes, that's it. Today we're making valentines," said the teacher. Later, when asked why she proceeded this way, the teacher explained, "It's very important to involve the children in making plans."

Much teacher-child planning is informal and takes place when 3- and 4-year-olds are asked to plan what they will do next or during the morning. Five-year-olds may be able to make plans for a party next week or at the end of the month, and primary-age children can develop even more extended plans.

All children should be asked to take part in making plans. Those who may be too shy to speak in front of a group or not quick enough to take their turn may need other opportunities besides group discussions to contribute their ideas. Some planning can be done by talking with individuals or small groups of children as they play and work.

Children can plan many things:

- What they will begin to work and play with
- With whom they will play and work
- The materials they need to complete a project
- What things they would like to learn more about
- How they will celebrate a birthday or holiday
- Places they would like to visit to learn more about a specific topic

More formal ways of planning with children have been developed. Many teachers ask children to tell them what they *know* about a specific topic, what they *want* to learn, and (after the lesson) what they have *learned* (K-W-L) (Ogle, 1986) as a means of involving children in planning (see Figure 2.2).

A teacher from the University of Maryland's Center for Young Children sent a letter to each kindergarten child before school started. She asked each to return the enclosed self-addressed postcard to her, listing the things the child wanted to learn in the coming year.

After the children had settled into the kindergarten routine, the teacher organized their postcards into a graph. The children discussed the graph, counting the cards in a given area. Most of the children responded that they wanted to learn to read and do math, but they also included many other topics that the teacher incorporated into her plans.

K	*What do we **K**now about fire fighters?*
	They put out fires.
	Only men can be fire fighters, girls can't.
	Firemen are big.
W	*What do we **W**ant to learn about fire fighters?*
	Where do they sleep?
	How do they slide down the pole?
	What do they eat?
	Do they like to ride on the truck?
L	*What have we **L**earned about fire fighters?*
	Men and women can be fire fighters.
	They sleep and eat at the fire station, but they have a home too.
	A computer tells them where there is a fire.
	Fire fighters put on boots, fireproof clothing, and helmets.
	They carry air with them.
	The truck has another computer, hoses, and equipment.
	Fire fighters go to school and learn everything.
	They know how to stop, drop, and roll.
	Fire fighters are daddies and mommies too. They have children.
	Fire fighter Bob's little boy is named Daniel, and his girl is Catlain.
	They're nice.

Figure 2.2   A K-W-L Chart

Planning for the Spontaneous

Teaching young children is never predictable. Their curiosity, interests, and creativity can jump from one exciting event to an equally thrilling moment, none of which may have been planned by a teacher or a curriculum guide. Being able to respond to children's spontaneous interests and to incidental events—whether it be a bird that flies against the window, a dead fish in the aquarium, snow, or the need for a repair person—is part of being an effective teacher. When teachers ignore the changing interests, immediate needs, or incidental experiences of children, they miss too many opportunities for teaching; and children miss opportunities to follow their curiosity and have their needs for knowledge met.

Although you cannot ignore the opportunities for social studies teaching and learning that arise spontaneously, planning is still critical. You can keep in mind the broad goals and objectives of social studies, as well as specific objectives for individual children, and then use the spontaneous and incidental as a means of fostering the achievement of these objectives. With goals in mind, any number of spontaneous happenings become a lesson.

Being able to respond spontaneously to incidental events is part of the planning process.

You can also keep complete lesson plans or even unit plans handy. A lot of things seem to happen spontaneously or incidentally, yet they are really very predictable. For instance, the apple tree outside the window will bloom one day, it will rain or be windy on another day, and children will fight and argue over a toy. Aware of the many things that happen throughout the year, some teachers keep concept boxes on hand. These boxes contain props and equipment—perhaps a complete lesson plan with poems and books—on a variety of topics. They may focus on the weather, interpersonal disputes, recognition and safe release of feelings, the functions of school personnel, or mainstreaming children with special needs.

One day when an unpredicted wind came up, a teacher went to the storeroom and picked out a box labeled "wind." Using the small parachutes, kites, scarves, and poems about wind in the box, she led the children through a series of lessons that, although they seemed spontaneous, were in reality very carefully and thoughtfully planned to meet children's interests as well as specific goals and objectives of the social studies curriculum.

Lesson Plans

Teachers make plans for day-to-day experiences and activities as well as long-range plans. *Lesson plans* are created for short-term, day-to-day learning experiences, while units or *projects* are planned for learning experiences that extend over time.

Daily lesson plans are one useful tool for short-term planning. They enable a teacher to plan meaningful activities for the present—for today and perhaps tomorrow or even next week. Once you get into the habit of making lesson plans, planning becomes second nature, like driving a car does. Once they internalize the process of planning lessons, teachers can focus on the broader aspects of teaching, meet individual differences, relax, and take advantage of the spontaneous.

Lesson plans can revolve around an individual child, a small group, or the total group. They include elements such as the following:

- Arranging the room to provide different opportunities for children's play
- Presenting new materials or demonstrating possibilities with materials familiar to the children
- Providing opportunities for open-ended outcomes and creativity
- Giving teacher guidance in the form of feedback, listening to children, talking with them, and asking questions
- Planing for inclusion of children with special needs

Teachers use many types of lesson plans and formats. The format is not important, but every lesson plan includes the following:

- Preparation
- A statement of goals and objectives
- Procedures to obtain the stated goals and objectives
- Some way to evaluate the lesson

Preparation

"Is Jefferson City north or south of where we live?" a teacher asked a group of 6-year-olds. When no one answered, the teacher said, "I told you yesterday. Now listen: Jefferson City is north of us; north is always up," pointing to a globe she was holding.

If this teacher had been prepared, she would have known that concepts of north and south are meaningless to children until they are nearly 11 or 12 years old. She also would not have given children inaccurate information—that north is always up.

Before planning, you must be fully certain that you understand the concept, attitude, or skill you want to present. You can obtain references from the library or discuss the topic with an authority on the subject. If you are planning experiences in geography, you might attend a lecture at the local library, community center, or university. Teachers need to understand content for two important reasons: (1) translating subject matter into experiences for children demands knowledge of the scope and structure of the discipline; and (2) facts (e.g., the names of countries or the number of chemical elements) change so rapidly in today's world that continually updating knowledge is required to ensure accuracy.

It is also useful to observe children as they work and play and to interview them to find out what they already know about a topic and would like to know. Some teachers simply ask children to "tell me everything you know about _____."

The answers to this type of question provide valuable insights into children's ideas on any given topic. Other teachers ask children to make books about a topic. For example, they may have children make a booklet about dogs to discover their level of knowledge about the subject (Bredekamp & Rosegrant, 1997).

Your final preparation for planning involves locating resources for children's use, obtaining materials, arranging the room, or contacting experts who might visit the class. Outstanding resources in the community may lead you to select a goal you had not thought about; limited resources may cause you to eliminate an experience you were considering.

Objectives

The song "Happy Talk" from the musical *South Pacific* expresses the idea that you must first have a dream before you can make it come true. This same idea can be applied to teaching. How do you know when you have achieved your goals if you have never established any? Thus, the first and perhaps the most essential part of planning is determining your objectives.

State the lesson's major purpose, either specifically or generally. One or two carefully thought-out objectives stated in specific behavioral terms are more effective and realistic for a lesson plan than many less specific goals are. Teachers decide on objectives based on their knowledge of the children, the content of social studies, and their knowledge of the environment.

Today, nearly every educator is familiar with behavioral objectives. Although writing objectives behaviorally is somewhat tedious, stating them behaviorally is not at all mysterious or difficult. A behavioral objective, unlike the more general objective just mentioned, is a precise statement of behavior that will be accepted as evidence of the child's having achieved what was set out to be accomplished. A behavioral objective answers the following questions:

1. What will we teach?
2. How will we know when we've taught it?
3. What materials and procedures will work best to teach what we wish to teach?

In writing behavioral objectives, you will want to pay particular attention to your use of language. Since behavioral objectives are specific, your language must also be specific. Look at the following words and decide just how well each one communicates what will be taught and learned:

General	Specific
To know	To name
Understand	Identify
Appreciate	Construct
Enjoy	Compare
Believe	Solve

1. Identify the terminal behavior you desire by name. ("Name four ways to travel on land.")
2. Try to define the desired behavior further by describing the conditions under which you expect the behavior to occur. ("When given a set of pictures of vehicles, the children will be able to identify and name those that travel on land.")
3. Specify the criteria of acceptable performance by describing how well the learner must perform. ("The child will select three of the five vehicles that travel on land.")

Goals stated in these terms—specific student behaviors related to lesson content—facilitate the teaching-learning process as well as its evaluation. Once you determine the lesson's behavioral objectives, you need only to teach those behaviors identified in the objective and, after the teaching, check each child's performance only in regard to the specified behavior.

Behavioral objectives have been in use for a number of years. But while they enable teachers to plan more precisely, they are not without problems. Because they always specify the outcome, they can limit children's learning by leading teachers to ignore children's behaviors or outcomes not prespecified by an objective. Assuming only one correct response leaves little room for divergent thinking, choice, or selection of materials. In addition, behavioral objectives are very specific, breaking learning into isolated steps without considering the entire experience. A child can learn the 22 steps in shoe tying yet never be able to put them together to actually tie a shoelace.

Procedures

It is not necessary to excite or stimulate young children; however, every lesson plan includes some means to initially involve children and hold their interest. Some teachers find that an interesting picture, a photograph, a book, an object, or even a finger play engages children's interest in a lesson.

Learning activities are then specified. These describe what the teacher and children will do to achieve the stated goals and objectives.

Evaluation

The beauty of stating objectives behaviorally is that, once stated, evaluation is nearly complete. The teacher has only to check the children's behavior against the statement, and the lesson is evaluated.

On the other hand, most teachers now use more authentic forms of evaluation. Teachers familiar with authentic evaluation techniques know how to evaluate the success of a lesson by (1) observing the children as they play; (2) interviewing children informally to see if misconceptions have been corrected and concepts gained; and (3) structuring some informal task for children to complete—for example, asking each child to follow a map of the room to find a hidden treasure, to describe the things happening in a picture, to tell the story of something, or to select the pictures showing the objective taught.

Units, Projects, and Thematic Learning

Units, projects, and thematic learning share a number of similarities. Each is grounded solidly on theories of constructionism. In the early 1900s, Dewey's (1944) assertion that meaningful curriculum is not just the memorization of isolated facts but a unified whole led to the development of unit planning. Over the years, Piagetian and Vygotskian ideas of children's construction of knowledge through social, physical, and mental activity supported project and thematic learning (Piaget & Inhelder, 1969; Vygotsky, 1986).

All three approaches revolve around a theme that unites activities and learning into a congruent, consistent whole. The learning experiences in a unit of study allow children the opportunity to learn concepts as parts of an integrated whole rather than isolated bits and pieces of information under a particular content area (see Figure 2.3).

Units, which are organized around a theme and include project work, differ subtly from project and thematic learning. A unit is developed and planned in advance by the teacher to last for a specific amount of time, perhaps several days, a week, or even a month (Helm & Katz, 2001). Although a unit plan allows room for children to initiate, and teachers follow children's interests and cues as the unit is implemented, the teacher is the primary initiator. Thematic learning tends to be more teacher-directed than project learning does, while the word *theme* implies a more planned or crafted progression.

As opposed to a preplanned unit, project and thematic work stem from children's interests and follow children's questions and needs. Children actively investigate, bring in resources, and represent their ideas. Projects may last for several days, weeks, months or even the entire year. This does not mean that every day or week is taken up with the project but that the theme is studied throughout the year. An example of a year-long project is the web-based learning site Journey North (*http://www.JourneyNorth*). Journey North is a free online educational service supported by the Annenberg/CPB. The project uses media and communications to improve math, science, and social studies education for the nation's 44 million school children. Journey North tracks migratory species each spring. Children share their own field observations with classrooms across the hemisphere. In addition, students are linked with scientists who provide expertise directly to the classroom. You can choose the species you want to follow. Migration is tracked by satellite telemetry, providing live coverage of individual animals as they migrate. As spring sweeps across the hemisphere, students note changes in daylight, temperatures, and all living things as the food chain comes back to life.

Regardless, both project and thematic learning, although well planned and thought out by the teacher, leave more room for children to initiate than do some unit plans. The teacher takes more cues from the children; as a result, no prespecified time limits are projected.

Geography Standard

Understand the world in spatial terms.

Children will understand the characteristics and uses of maps, globes, and other geographic tools and technologies.

Goals

Children will create a map of their playground.

Objectives

Children will do the following:

- Learn the names of play equipment and their function
- Locate spaces and play equipment when asked to do so
- As a group, construct a map of the playground
- Follow a map of their playground to locate a hidden object

Beginning

- Before they go out to play, ask children to sing the North Carolina version of the song "On Our Holiday": "What will we do when we all go out, we all go out, we all go out to play? What will we do, what will we do, when we all go out to play?" List children's responses on a chart.
- As children play, take candid photos of them in different areas using different equipment. Make sure each child is included in a picture and that you have a photo of each area of the playground and each piece of equipment.

Continuing

- After you print the photos, place them on a table for children to look at and discuss. After they've had time to handle and talk about the photos, ask them to find the following:
  - Themselves at play
  - The picture of their favorite piece of equipment
  - Their favorite spot on the playground

  Then ask children to group the pictures by their function, grouping equipment in terms of climbing, sand, riding, swinging, or other types of equipment.

  Sing "What Will We Do?" again. This time change the tense, singing "What DID We Do?" List children's responses on the chart, comparing what they did to what they said they would do when they went out to play.
- On a large piece of brown mural paper draw an outline of the playground. Draw one landmark on the paper, perhaps the outline of the building with the entrance to the yard. Have children draw or build with small unit cubes the playground equipment on the paper. They can use the photos of themselves as guides. Take a picture of the created map.
- The next day, take the map outside and ask children to check it for accuracy. Are there any changes they need to make? If so, make them.

Evaluation

- Refine and duplicate the created map. Hide 5 objects on the playground. Mark one object with an X on each of the five maps.
- Organize children in groups of 3. Each group is given a map of the playground with the object they are to find marked with an X. The directions are to find the hidden objects.

Figure 2.3 Mini Lesson Plan: Mapping the Playground (5- and 6-year-olds)

- They equip students with knowledge, skills, and attitudes they will find useful both in and outside of school.
- They are based on goals selected to develop students' expertise, conceptual knowledge, and self-regulated application of skills.
- They balance breadth with depth by addressing limited content but develop this content sufficiently to foster conceptual understanding.
- They allow children to actively make sense and construct meaning.
- They build on children's prior knowledge.
- They foster children's higher-order thinking skills by relating what they are learning to their lives outside of school, thinking critically and creatively about it, or using it to solve problems and make decisions.
- They take place within a classroom designed as a learning community.

Figure 2.4   Why Use Projects, Units, or Themes?

Source: Adapted from J. Brophy and J. Alleman, *Learning and Teaching about Cultural Universals in Primary-Grade Social Studies.*

Units, projects, and thematic learning accomplish a number of goals (see Figure 2.4):

1. They offer opportunities for a group of children to build a sense of community by working together around a common interest, theme, or project. Working together on a project facilitates fruitful conflicts and investigations, permitting children to clarify and rethink their initial ideas (Helm & Beneke, 2003; New, 1999).

2. When children work together on a common theme or project, they have the chance to relate to one another. They check one another, spontaneously offering criticism and information as they exchange ideas and prior knowledge in a cooperative effort. Vygotsky (1986) saw this type of social activity as the generator of thought. He believed that individual consciousness is built from outside through relations with others. "The mechanism of social behavior and of consciousness is the same" (p. ii).

3. They give relevance to the curriculum. When content is a part of an organized whole, children see it as useful and relevant to their daily lives. Conceptual organizers such as themes, units, or projects, give children something meaningful and substantive on which to engage their minds. It is difficult for children to make sense of abstract concepts such as colors, mathematical symbols, or letter sounds when they are presented at random or devoid of any meaningful context.

4. They provide for flexibility of teaching and learning, following children's interests and building on their experiences. Because units and projects are flexible, they are planned for varying lengths of time. Some seem to end as quickly as they begin if children satisfy their interests immediately. Others extend for several weeks or even a semester as children expand their interests and seek other information (Bredekamp & Copple, 1997).

In one kindergarten, a police officer permitted children to sit in a police car. Following the visit, the children began building a police car in the classroom out of large blocks. A posted sign let others know what the block structure represented and that it was not to be disturbed. The teacher added a steering wheel, a piece that looked like an instrument panel, and some boards. The block structure expanded and became a more permanent car with seats, a dashboard, a horn, and a gearshift.

The children did research as they strove to make the car more and more realistic. Finally, the teacher added wires, bulbs, and batteries. With the help of a volunteer who guided and directed them in their discovery, the children made the right connections and were able to turn the lights in their car on and off. They consulted books, compared different types of cars and trucks, and held discussions. Videos of police cars in action were shared when the police officer visited the class again. The entire unit lasted for more than 6 weeks.

5. Units, projects, and thematic learning can meet individual children's needs through the variety of learning experiences and opportunities offered over time. Children can pace themselves, staying with a specific activity for a long period of time to satisfy their interests or needs, or select tasks that permit them to practice skills or gain mastery over new skills.

Planning Units, Projects, or Thematic Learning

Planning involves selecting a topic, specifying goals and objectives, and identifying content for the entire group. The plans, however, include specific ideas and experiences for individual children (Helm & Beneke, 2003).

Teachers need to make additional plans for children with disabilities so they can participate freely and fully. For example, a teacher who wanted his class to experience a field trip to a fast-food restaurant made special arrangements so that a child in a wheelchair could take part.

Plans are also made for children who are uninterested in the topic. In one second-grade class, a unit on fruits and where they come from bored two of the children. Observing them, the teacher noted their curiosity about an apple that was beginning to rot. She directed their attention to the molds growing on the apple. The two children completed an entire unit on that subject, concluding by presenting their findings to the class, while the others studied fruit.

Selecting Themes or Topics.   The theme for a unit, a project, or thematic learning can stem from a number of sources. Some topics may be suggested by the school system, state department of education, or national standards. In the child-care programs in Reggio Emilia (a city in northern Italy), the selection of a project topic is a complicated process, and the genesis may take a number of forms:

1. The teacher may observe something of interest and importance to the children and introduce it as a topic or theme.
2. A topic may stem from the teacher's interest or professional curiosity.

3. The topic or theme might stem from some serendipity that redirects the attention of the children and teacher to another focus. The topic may be concrete or abstract in nature, local or distant, present-day or historical, small or large scale; but whatever the topic, it should allow children to draw on their own prior understandings and should involve them in firsthand, relevant, and interactive experience (Helm & Beneke, 2003).

Objectives   Objectives direct teaching and learning. They tell what the unit, project, or thematic learning is to accomplish; describe how the children will change following the experience; and lead to evaluation. Here again, your careful selection of a few well-thought-out objectives will be more effective than listing numerous general objectives will be. Focusing objectives on each area of the social studies—knowledge, skills, attitudes, and values—helps balance children's learning experiences.

But objectives are flexible. At all times, teachers remain alert to children's interests, continually looking for new objectives and ways to extend rather than dampen children's enthusiasm and curiosity about the theme or topic.

Content   The content lists the major points to be covered. You will want to organize and specify the facts, information, and knowledge that will be presented. You should include a list of available materials and possible field trips. Flexibility is the key. Guided by the overall goals and objectives of the program, teachers select content that meets children's developmental and learning needs.

Procedures   The introduction is followed by learning experiences—the core of the unit or project—and a culminating activity.

Introduction   Almost anything that motivates and stimulates the children's interest can be used to introduce a unit, a project, or a theme. The purpose of the introduction is to arouse children's curiosity by stimulating their interest in the topic. This could be done in any of the following ways:

- *A teacher-initiated discussion.*   You might ask the children some questions to stimulate their thinking or interest, or you could say directly, "We all have to ride the school bus, so today we're going to begin learning the safety rules for riding the bus." This could begin a unit on safety.
- *An incidental experience.*   Sometimes a unit arises from an unplanned experience. A child's illness in school could begin a unit on health. Some event in the local community—fire prevention week, elections, construction—might initiate a unit. A kitten wandering into the classroom could stimulate interest in a unit on animals.
- *An audiovisual resource.*   A television show, a record, or slides could stimulate interest. You can make use of other media as well, such as newspapers or magazines.

- *Ongoing activities.*   Units, projects, and themes can lead to other units and projects. The study of the grocery store might lead to the study of food, purchasers, consumers, or transportation. A unit or project on seashells can lead directly to a study of life in the sea and then to life on land.

- *An arranged environment.*   You might display objects from some other country, place, or time; exhibit a poster or an open book; or prepare a bulletin board. Any of these steps would call children's attention to a topic and stimulate questions and interest. One teacher from a western state left a branding iron on the library table with a few books opened to pictures of cowhands at branding time. In this way he introduced a theme built around the history of the region.

Learning Experiences.   Learning experiences are the heart of the unit or project. These experiences are not isolated activities but are planned to foster the goals and objectives of the unit. You can plan some activities for individual children, others for small groups, and still others for the total group.

Since the purpose is to build a strong relationship between learning experiences and content, you will want to design the learning experiences to work together as a whole. You can plan a sequential presentation of learning experiences around the objectives of the unit. Analysis of each objective will suggest activities that will foster children's attainment of the objective. You might ask yourself, "What experience will foster this goal?" "Which experiences should come first and provide a base for further experiences?" "What will extend and clarify children's understanding?"

Learning experiences may come from any of the following:

- *Language experiences.*   Oral discussion; listening to records; recording ideas in writing; dictating to a teacher or a tape recorder; reporting to a group; and dictating or writing letters, booklets, or stories are all examples of language experiences you could plan to foster children's attainment of unit goals.

- *Community resources.*   Field trips in the school neighborhood or the community can be part of any unit or project plan. You could ask individuals from the community to visit and share information with the class.

- *Audiovisual experiences.*   Films, slides, CD-ROMs, models, graphs, murals, and digital photos are classified as audiovisual experiences. Children could make their own graphs or murals or illustrate some topic by taking their own photographs.

- *Arts and crafts.*   Painting, constructing, drawing, modeling with clay, paper weaving, and many other art activities can be coordinated with other learning experiences.

- *Music and physical activities.*   Songs, games, making and playing musical instruments, creative rhythms, and dance foster children's active involvement with stated objectives.

- *Mathematics activities.*   Opportunities to use mathematics include counting, ordering and sorting, and judging groups of more or fewer objects. One class, stimulated by the discovery of parsley caterpillars in their garden, recorded how many days the caterpillars spent eating, the caterpillars' length, how many days it took for each chrysalis to form, and the number of days it took for the butterflies to emerge. Because they were engaged in meaningful activities, the children gained not only counting skills but calendar skills as well.

- *Social skills.* Social skills are an integral part of the unit as children participate together in planning or work together on some activity. Children's interests might dictate that they work together to investigate some subtopic; later, they could report to the group. Young children can also improve their social skills by working together on a mural, a painting, a scrapbook, or a construction project.

Regardless of the number and type of learning experiences selected, continuity between experiences is planned. One experience builds on another. A thread of meaning runs through several experiences. Experiences and activities are juxtaposed to enable children to see the connections between past and present, among and between people, and between objects in their world (see Figure 2.5).

Culminating Activity. The culminating activity is time spent for review and summing up the unit; it provides closure for teacher and children. A concluding activity gives the teacher a chance to observe the children and learn what concepts they have formed about the topic or theme. It gives the children an opportunity to tie the pieces together. Units and projects could end simply with the children singing songs, acting out stories they have learned, or listening to the poetry they have enjoyed. Dictating experience charts or thank-you letters, compiling a booklet, or sharing experiences are other summary activities.

Anne Daniels, a teacher of 5-year-olds at the Center for Young Children at the University of Maryland, concludes a unit on Winnie the Pooh with a trip to the university apiary to collect honey for a snack. This activity, in turn, leads to a new theme—studying and identifying different types of insects, where and how they live, and what they contribute to our lives.

Evaluating Units, Projects, or Thematic Learning

You will want to be able to describe what children have learned and the skills and attitudes they've gained. The behavioral objectives offer a built-in evaluation; other types of evaluation might include asking the children to evaluate the unit themselves: "What did you like best about the topic? What did you learn? What can you do now that you couldn't do before? What would you like to do again? What could you do differently next time?" Children could dictate or write booklets reporting the "Things I've Learned." You can evaluate the success of the unit informally as you observe children at play or work. Or you can structure the evaluations by asking each child to tell about a topic, demonstrate a task, or respond to some questions. Informal checklists, developed around the goals of the unit and the specified content, might be used.

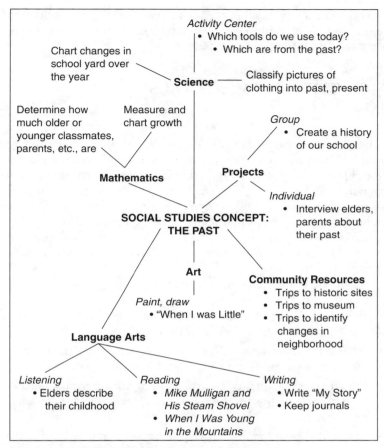

Figure 2.5 Social Studies: An Integrated Web

In addition to evaluating the children, teachers will want to evaluate their planning and teaching. A well-planned project or unit should include the following:

- Clear, realistic, obtainable goals and objectives
- Material of high interest to the children
- Activities that take into consideration children's different abilities, interests, and backgrounds
- Involvement of the children in planning the goals and activities of the unit
- Active experiences that fully involve the children
- Opportunities for children to work and play together

Following a unit, teachers can ask themselves if it did include those factors, how it could have been improved, what parts were highly successful and why, and what they would do differently next time.

EVALUATION OF THE SOCIAL STUDIES CURRICULUM

Evaluation is necessary and important. We all want and need good information about how and what children are learning. Teachers and parents want to know how their children are doing, school administrators want to know how effective their program is, and policy makers want to judge the worth of policies (National Education Goals Panel, 1998). When evaluation is authentic, it benefits children, teachers, and parents. Authentic evaluation takes place as a part of the curriculum. The tasks used to evaluate children's learning in the social studies are real, and they connect to children's daily experiences rather than detract from them (Helm & Beneke, 2003).

Authentic evaluation does the following:

- Provides evidence for teachers that can improve the quality of instruction for individual children as well as groups
- Clarifies goals and objectives that may help determine the extent to which the children are learning, growing, and developing in desired ways
- Functions as a quality-control system that permits teachers to determine which parts of the teaching-learning process have been effective and which have not
- Stimulates ideas for alternative procedures that may be effective in enabling the teacher to achieve a set of educational goals
- Gives feedback to parents; communicates something about children's growth and learning, the program, and the quality of the teaching

A broad and complex process, evaluation is not to be confused with tests and measurements. Authentic evaluation is ongoing, comprehensive, and an integral part of social studies instruction. Evaluation procedures can include these elements:

- Observation
- Portfolios
- Informal interviews
- Performance interviews
- Checklists
- Standardized tests

Observation

When they observe children's behavior systematically, teachers see indications of their achievement of social studies goals. Teachers look for behaviors that demonstrate children's skills, attitudes, values, or knowledge. Behavior observation is a valid way to evaluate social studies goals relating to social skills, problem solving, decision making, and acceptance of the values of others.

Observing means only noting the behavior that is occurring without making inferences. Teachers observe and record children's behavior in the following situations:

1. At free play
2. On the playground
3. During the routines of dressing, eating, resting
4. During group activity time
5. At discussion time

When you record repeated behaviors of children, you compile a record of their progress. You could structure your observations around the specific and general goals of the social studies program. You could observe and record children's behavior in applying knowledge, solving a problem, taking responsibility, or working with others. Or you might structure your observations around more specific goals. Children's use of maps during block building and their drawing of maps for use with wheel toys give real indications of their mapping concepts. Shopping at the play store, children reveal economic concepts through their behavior. As children play, you might note when they (1) use new vocabulary correctly; (2) demonstrate their understanding of making change, purchasing, or producing; and (3) follow social rules and procedures.

Digital and other photographs can help you observe and evaluate children's behaviors, knowledge, and progress. The photos let you reflect on what was happening and what children were doing when they were observed (Hoisington, 2002). Then the photos can be e-mailed to families or included in a child's portfolio for parents to see. Discussing what the child in the photo was doing, why, and when can be a fruitful form of evalaution.

Portfolios

Collecting samples of children's work in portfolios illustrates children's progress over time. Each child has an individual portfolio; whatever work or records are placed in the portfolio are dated, and often something about when, how, and under what conditions the work was completed is included. Growth charts, photos of children completing skills, and tape recordings of their speech can also be collected (see Figure 2.6).

Several times a year, teachers go over the portfolios and note the changing form of children's concepts, new vocabulary, expansion of ideas, and children's increasing ability to express their ideas. This analysis offers a base on which to evaluate both children's learning in the social studies and your teaching.

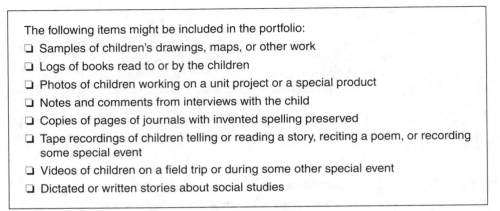

The following items might be included in the portfolio:

❑ Samples of children's drawings, maps, or other work

❑ Logs of books read to or by the children

❑ Photos of children working on a unit project or a special product

❑ Notes and comments from interviews with the child

❑ Copies of pages of journals with invented spelling preserved

❑ Tape recordings of children telling or reading a story, reciting a poem, or recording some special event

❑ Videos of children on a field trip or during some other special event

❑ Dictated or written stories about social studies

Figure 2.6   The Portfolio

The child, as well as teachers and parents, should have the opportunity to select work samples to place in the portfolio. Teachers can guide children when asking them to contribute work samples. Teachers might ask children to select something that was difficult to do, that illustrates a special accomplishment, or has special meaning and merit (Gronlund, 1998).

When the work in the portfolio is an accurate representation of a child's growth and achievement, teachers can use it to evaluate progress. The work is not to be compared with the work of other children; rather, each child's work should be analyzed and evaluated for progress toward a standard of performance consistent with the child's development and growth.

Informal Interviews

Another, more specific form of evaluation of children's progress in social studies is the informal interview method. You could conduct interviews during free play or anytime you and individual children can get together. You should look for the following as you interview children:

1. *Consistency.*   Does the child have a stable set of responses? Does the child reply in the same way to the same type of question?

2. *Accuracy.*   Are the answers correct? The child may not include all of the possibilities, but is the response somewhat accurate?

3. *Clarity.*   Is the response clear and acceptable?

4. *Fullness.*   How complete was the response? How many aspects of the concept were covered by the response?

5. *Extensiveness.*   How many illustrations of the concept were given?

Informal interviews with children yield information on children's thinking.

As they conduct interviews to discover children's thinking about a social studies topic, teachers sometimes use pictures or objects for the children to manipulate to demonstrate or illustrate the concepts. Not all concepts can be expressed by children verbally; you could ask them to act out a concept, show it, draw all the things they know about it, or find an example of the concept in the pictures.

The work of Piaget (1969) provides other guidelines for interviewing young children. The questions Piaget asks and the way in which he builds his questions on the child's responses to the first question exemplify the type of interview technique that reveals children's thinking. Here is another example of an interview directed by a teacher, which revolves around seeds. This teacher wanted to find out what children knew about seeds and plants. He asked children to tell him what grows from a seed, where one looks for seeds, and how one gets seeds to grow.

In administering Piagetian interviews, you must establish an atmosphere of security and trust by communicating to the child that she is in a safe, nonthreatening position. When a child responds to your question, accept the answer without judgment. You might use a small tape recorder to record the answer. Children's responses are often short, however, so they are not difficult to record by hand.

When the child responds, continue questioning by asking for justification. Do not assume that if a child gives a correct answer, he has done the proper thinking. Several questions may be necessary to understand his perceptions and thinking processes. You might ask the child, "Could you show me?" "Would you tell me more?" or, "What if . . . ?" You could ask the child to act out the answer, or you could challenge his answer by saying, "Well, another person said . . . " In this way, you will be able to uncover more of the child's thinking and ideas.

You will need to give the child plenty of time to answer. In many testing situations, time is limited. When conducting an individual interview, you will want to allow the child all the time necessary to think and answer.

Performance Interviews

Structuring tasks for children to demonstrate concepts and skills is another kind of informal evaluation. You might ask children to draw a map of the room, show on a graph which bus has the most riders, complete a puzzle, or sort pictures into categories. One teacher used a set of pictures to assess children's awareness of selected concepts in physical geography by asking them to select the four pictures that represented the concept and the four that did not.

Checklists

Some teachers find that checklists of behaviors or skills are a convenient way to evaluate children's progress. You can construct a checklist for yourself designed around the specific concepts, goals, and objectives of the social studies unit or lesson plan. Other checklists are often provided by the school or by the county or state department of education and might be based on the general goals of social studies. Publishers of textbooks and instructional kits sometimes prepare checklists. Table 2.1 shows a checklist developed by a teacher for use with a group of 5-year-old children.

Standardized Tests

Standardized tests are based on goals and objectives decided by someone other than the classroom teacher and meet the criteria for serving as a tool of summative evaluation. Thus, the content of standardized tests may have little to do with the goals of the classroom teacher or the experiences or activities of the children. Nor do standardized tests reflect the multiple forms of intelligence (Anderson, 1998; Seefeldt, 1998). Gardner's (1991) multiple types of intelligences, such as interpersonal, intrapersonal, linguistic, and logical mathematics intelligences, are not readily tapped by typical standardized tests.

Table 2.1 Example of a Checklist

NAME		DATE	
Behavior	*Always*	*Sometimes*	*Never*
Completes a task Works with others Assumes responsibility Cooperates in group work Listens to others			

Recognizing that all children are special and unique, most early childhood teachers want to consider a combination of evaluation techniques. In this way, they are better able to pinpoint children's strengths and needs. Using a variety of evaluation techniques is useful for other reasons. Keeping records of the children's work, systematically observing their behavior, or using informal interviews might be helpful in reporting progress to parents; in giving insights on how to improve your teaching methods; or in indicating which experiences, activities, goals, and objectives are appropriate to introduce at a given time. This type of evaluation, conducted by teachers for the purpose of evaluating the teaching and the attainment of specific goals, is often called formative. It is the type of evaluation that enables you to formulate your program; set goals; and know when the goals have been reached, what new goals should be set, and what goal modification should be made (Shepard, Kagan, & Wurtz, 1998).

SUMMARY

Planning is essential for successful teaching and learning. Having a clear idea of what children are like, the goals of society and education, and content knowledge of the social studies, you are prepared to plan. In planning, you must consider the reality of your situation, provide balance throughout the program, involve the children, and allow for spontaneity.

Long-term planning of social studies units and short-term planning of the daily lessons involve designing appropriate learning objectives. In setting specific goals for your teaching and children's learning, evaluation follows naturally as you assess the degree to which the goals have been reached.

Extend Your Knowledge

1. When you are shopping, walking in a park, or attending a community gathering, observe children under the age of 8. List the ways in which these children are alike, regardless of their age and individual characteristics. Then observe again, and make another list of the ways in which the children differ from one another as individuals.

2. Take a fresh look at the community your school is part of. What physical properties do you note that affect children's learning? For example, what kinds of stores are present? Are there gardens? Talk with some of the community members and others in the community. Ask what they expect children to learn in school, how they think children should be taught, and what they would do to change education. From these responses, can you determine some of the cultural values of the community? List these values and compare and discuss them in class.

3. Curriculum libraries at colleges, universities, or school systems contain guides from school systems throughout your state and nation. With a partner or in a

small group, compare the goals and objectives of unit and project plans suggested in two or more of these guides.

4. Design both a lesson and a unit, project, or thematic learning plan. When you have completed the plans, ask the class to critique them.

Resources

Often, curriculum guides are developed by local school systems or state departments of education. Inquire in your school system or at the state department of education about curriculum guides. The guides offer suggestions for objectives for many subject areas, including the social studies. They also contain abundant information and ideas for lesson planning and things to do with children.

The ERIC Clearinghouse on Early Childhood Education offers on-line library searchers and sample lesson plans. You can contact the clearinghouse at the following addresses:

Bank Street College
Website: *www.BankStreetCorner.com*

Early Childhood Social Studies
Website: *http://patricia_f.tripod.com*

ERIC Clearinghouse on Elementary and Early Childhood Education
Website: *http://ericeece.org*
E-mail: ericeece@uiuc.edu

Social Studies Development Center
2805 E. Tenth Street #120
Bloomington, Indiana 47405
Website: *www.socialstudiesdevelopmentcenter.com*

References

Anderson, S. R. (1998). The trouble with testing. *Young Children, 53*(4), 25–30.

Bredekamp, S., & Copple, C. (1997). *Developmentally appropriate practice in early childhood programs* (Rev. ed.). Washington, DC: National Association for the Education of Young Children.

Bredekamp, S., & Rosegrant, T. (Eds.). (1997). *Reaching potentials: Vol. 2. Transforming early childhood curriculum and assessment.* Washington, DC: National Association for the Education of Young Children.

Brophy, S., & Alleman, J. (2002). Learning and teaching about cultural universals in primary-grade social studies. *Elementary School Journal, 103*(2), 99–114.

Derman-Sparks, L. (2003). Developing antibias, multicultural curriculum. In C. Copple (Ed.), *A world of difference* (pp. 171–173). Washington, DC: National Association for the Education of Young Children.

Dewey, J. (1944). *Democracy and education.* New York: Free Press.

Diamond, K. E., & Stacey, S. (2003). The other children at preschool: Experiences of typically developing children. In C. Copple (Ed.), *A world of difference* (pp. 135–139). Washington, DC: National Association for the Education of Young Children.

Garcia, E. E. (2003). Respecting children's home language and culture. In C. Copple (Ed.), *A world of difference* (p. 16). Washington, DC : National Association for the Education of Young Children.

Gardner, H. (1991). *To open children's minds.* New York: Basic Books.

Greene, R. W. (2001). *The explosive child.* New York: HarperCollins.

Gronlund, G. (1998). Portfolios as an assessment tool: Is collection of work enough? *Young Children, 53*(3), 4–11.

Helm, J. H., & Beneke, S. (2003). *The power of projects.* New York: Teachers College Press.

Helm, J. H., & Katz, L. (2001). *Young investigators.* New York: Teachers College Press.

Hoisington, C. (2002). Using photographs to support children's science inquiry. *Young Children, 57*, 26–30.

Marschark, M., Lang, H. G., & Albertin, J. A. (2001). *Educating deaf students: From research to practice.* Oxford, England: Oxford University Press.

McCormick, L., Wong, M., & Yogi, L. (2003). Individualization in the inclusive preschool: A planning process. *Childhood Education,79*, 212–217.

Mc Dermott, J. (2003). A letter to teachers of young children. In C. Copple (Ed.), *A world of difference* (pp. 140–142). Washington, DC: National Association for the Education of Young Children.

Mitchell, L. S. (1934). *Young geographers.* New York: Bank Street College.

Mitchell, L. S. (2000). Social studies for future teachers. In N. Nager & E. Shapiro (Eds.), *Revisiting a progressive pedagogy* (pp. 117–124). Albany: State University of New York Press.

Molenarr-Klumper, M. (2002). *Nonverbal learning disabilities.* New York: Jessica Kingsley Publisher.

National Association for the Education of Young Children. (1991). Position statement: Guidelines for appropriate curriculum content and assessment in programs serving children ages 3–8. *Young Children, 46*(3), 21–40.

National Education Goals Panel. (1998). *Principles and recommendations for early childhood assessments.* Washington, DC: Author.

National Research Council. (2001). *Eager to learn: Educating our preschoolers.* Committe on Early Childhood Pedagogy. Commission on Behavioral and Social Sciences and Education. Washington, DC: National Academy Press.

New, R. (1999). An integrated curriculum: Moving from the what and the how to the why. In C. Seefeldt (Ed.), *The early childhood curriculum: Current findings in theory and research* (pp. 265–288). New York: Teachers College Press.

Newman, R. (1995). For parents particularly: The home-school connection. *Childhood Education, 71*, 296–298.

Ogle, D. M. (1986). K-W-L: A teaching model that develops active reading of expository text. *Reading Teacher, 39*, 564–570.

Piaget, J. (1969). *Science of education and the psychology of the child.* New York: Viking.

Piaget, J., & Inhelder, B. (1969). *The psychology of the child.* New York: Basic Books.

Seefeldt, C. (1998). Assessing young children. In C. Seefeldt (Ed.), *Continuing issues in early childhood education* (pp. 314–347). Upper Saddle River, NJ: Merrill/Prentice Hall.

Shepard, L. A., Kagan, S. L., & Wurtz, E. (1998). *Goal 1: Early childhood assessments resource group recommendations.* Washington, DC: Government Printing Office.

Vygotsky, L. (1986). *Thought and language* (Rev. ed.). Cambridge, MA: Harvard University Press.

Walker, B., Hafenstein, N. L., & Crow-Enslow, L. (1999). Meeting the needs of gifted learners in the early childhood classroom. *Young Children, 54*(1), 32–37.

Webster, T. (1990). Projects as curriculum: Under what conditions? *Childhood Education, 1,* 2–4.

CHAPTER 3

Celebrating Diversity

Schools reflect the diversity of society so that children are "living diversity" rather than "doing diversity."

Jyotsna Pattnaik, 2003, p. 204

After you read this chapter, you should be prepared to respond to the following questions:

- Why is it important for teachers to know themselves and to examine their own attitudes and values about diversity?
- What attitudes, values, and ideas about others do children bring to the classroom?
- How do children learn about others?
- What concepts are key to teaching children to celebrate diversity?
- How can teachers resolve conflicts that occur between children in the classroom?

"I celebrate diversity every day," said a first-grade teacher. "Among the 23 children in my class, there are children from several Central American countries, two are Hmongs, one is from China, two are from Iran, and two are from Eastern Europe. It's a very different classroom from the first one I taught in a dozen years ago. Sure, it's a challenge to teach such a diverse group, but I love it—the diversity adds richness to my life and the curriculum. It's diversity that makes teaching so much more rewarding today than in the past."

While Dewey (1944) might be surprised at the great diversity found in today's typical classroom, he would not be surprised that teachers find this diversity enriching and rewarding. Believing that learning can occur only through free exchange and communication with others whose views and lives differ from one's own, Dewey celebrated and honored diversity: "The intermingling in the school of youth of different races, differing religions, and unlike customs creates for all a new and broader environment" (p. 21).

While Dewey celebrated diversity, he also celebrated unity. The school, he pointed out, offered children a balanced environment and a common subject matter. Because it did so, education would accustom all to a "unity of outlook upon a broader horizon than is visible to the members of any group" (p. 21). This assimilative force, along with an emphasis on the things that bind people together in cooperative human pursuits, would prepare children to be citizens in a democratic society and a global world. Today's standards for social studies continue to endorse Dewey's premise of celebrating unity and diversity. "During the early years of school, the exploration of the concepts of likenesses and differences" takes place (National Council for the Social Studies, 1998, p. 1).

A school environment that celebrates both diversity and unity is built on a foundation of deep respect for all individuals and groups (Copple, 2003; Garcia, 2003). To create a classroom that incorporates deep respect for individuals and groups means you must first understand several things:

- Your own attitudes, values, and ideas about others
- Children's attitudes, values, and ideas about others
- How attitudes toward others are learned

Attitudes and values, which direct and guide behaviors, are the foundation for celebrating diversity. But as a teacher, you need more than just an understanding of your own attitudes and the attitudes of children. You must also be familiar with concepts key to learning to celebrate diversity:

- Understanding interconnectedness and interdependency
- Knowledge of the similarities that unite people of diverse cultures, experiences, races/ethnicities, and nations
- Skills in resolving interpersonal conflict that will later serve as the base for working together with others

The school environment celebrates diversity.

WHAT ARE YOUR ATTITUDES?

Celebrating diversity has much more to do with your attitudes toward and knowledge of others than with preparing and eating foods common in other cultures, hanging pictures of children from a variety of cultures on the wall, or celebrating the holidays or customs of others. These activities may be important in helping children value others, but they are the bare minimum (d'Entremont, 1997; Okagaki & Diamond, 2003).

What is critical—and far more important than these superficial attempts at valuing diversity—are your own feelings, knowledge, and attitudes toward those who differ from you. These attitudes determine how you behave toward and treat children and their parents.

One Head Start teacher found it very disturbing that parents sent their girls to Head Start in frilly dresses and the boys in little three-piece suits, often complete with a clip-on tie. So she told the parents, "Do not dress your children like this. It's better if you send children in old clothes." After listening to the teacher tell parents over and over not to dress children in fancy clothes, a cook at the center took the teacher aside and informed her that she was denigrating the parents, their values, and their behaviors. Head Start parents, the cook explained, dressed their children the way they did because they had deep respect for Head Start and high hopes for their children's success there. They wanted their children to achieve and to respect the school and their teacher. Therefore, they dressed their children in fancy clothes.

To really respect diversity means you will need to examine your own attitudes and values toward those of different classes, cultures, or races and ethnicities (Okagaki & Diamond, 2003). Ask yourself these questions:

1. Am I constantly striving to gain more knowledge and increase my skills in human relations education?

2. Do I approach human relationships with understanding and compassion, both in my verbal and nonverbal communication in the classroom and when relating with parents? Do I ask parents about their goals for children and really listen?

3. Is the point of view I present free from bias? Can I put aside my belief system to honestly think about the beliefs of others?

4. Do I create an atmosphere of warmth and acceptance in the classroom? Do I ask children and families to share songs and stories from their culture, putting them in the role of expert? Are signs and labels in English and in the children's home languages?

5. Do I provide freedom to create? Do I provide many opportunities for children to make choices and decisions on their level?

6. Do I encourage children to look at problems from various points of view? Do I encourage divergent thinking?

Respect starts with and is manifested in your behaviors. You might begin with the following actions:

- Make time for communicating with families, and listen carefully to what families and children say. If you do not understand what the parent is saying, ask another question or repeat what you think the parent has said, asking, "Is this what you mean? Am I correct in understanding . . . ?"

- Develop two-way communication. Ask families to tell you what their goals are for their children, to talk about how they raise their children and what their family preferences are. In turn, describe your goals for their children, your philosophy, and your methods of teaching.

- Observe and become a cultural ethnographer, seeking information about children's languages and cultures (Garcia, 2003; Marshall, 2003), perhaps by visiting children's homes and neighborhoods and becoming familiar with the culture and ways of the community.

- Be attentive and open to negotiation if a parent brings a concern or complaint to your attention. Keep in mind that assertive communication—when you tell the truth and care about the listener—is the most effective form of communication (National Association for the Education of Young Children, 1998). Let the parent know you hear her. With total sincerity, repeat her statement to you: "Understandably, you are worried about . . ."

- Put the information you gathered on children's linguistic and cultural heritage in writing so it becomes as important as all the other things you write down (Garcia, 2003).

- Learn how to pronounce children's names as they are pronounced in their own family.

- Plan to work cooperatively with parents to achieve the goals of human relations education. Make your classroom a caring community of learners and include children's families in that community.

- Open your classroom to parents, welcome them and their attitudes with respect, and establish a system of open communication.

- Ask families to express their goals and objectives for their children's learning about others: "What multicultural understandings do you want your children to learn this year?" "What do you think is important for them to know in the future?" "How do you think they should be taught these things?" "What do you want them to learn about people from other lands?"

- Help families and the community explore their own attitudes and feelings about others through group discussions, meetings with resource persons, or individual conferences.

- Use both children's home languages and English in charts and other print materials in the classroom (see Figure 3.1).

Teachers can also examine their attitudes and values toward those who live far from them geographically (New, 1999). Before teaching about another country,

---

- Include children's home languages on signs, labels, and other classroom print materials.
- Learn at least a few words in children's home languages.
- Involve children's families in the classroom.
- Model learning a child's language. One teacher asked Alberto, a child from Peru, to teach her how to roll *r*'s, putting Alberto in the role of teacher. The other children followed, consulting Alberto on ways to pronounce Spanish words.
- Find books that reflect the cultures and home languages of the children.
- Build security for language learning by snuggling up several times a day for a private read-aloud with one or two children who speak the same home language.
- Talk one-to-one with children about things that are important to them.

Figure 3.1 For children who are just learning English.

ask yourself what you really know and feel about the country. Because children will model you and copy your attitudes and values, ask yourself the following:

1. What have I read about each country? Did this reading present an accurate point of view? Was it current? Was it written by someone of that nationality?
2. Am I familiar with any of the country's films or filmmakers? What do I know about the art of the country?
3. What do I know about the religious customs of the country? The government? The economy? Is my current information up to date? Is it free from stereotypes?
4. Are my background materials relevant to the culture as a whole, or do they represent just one minute portion of the people?
5. Have I talked to anyone who is a native of the country or who has lived in the country for some length of time?

But conflicts do occur. Beliefs about child rearing and how children should be educated differ between cultural groups. For example, many families believe children should be spanked and will tell you openly, "Spank her hard if she doesn't listen." Obviously, you are not going to spank a child, yet you must respect the families' views of child rearing. Bredekamp (2003) suggests thinking about the goals of families. When parents ask you to spank their children, they are really saying they are afraid their children will not achieve in school. Instead of agreeing to spank a child, you can communicate to parents that all children will behave appropriately and learn.

Familes from many cultures revere teachers as authority figures. These families often shower teachers with gifts. One school created two rules about gifts: (1) you cannot accept gifts; (2) you cannot reject gifts. To keep these rules, the gifts of parents to teachers were used to benefit the entire school. In this way parents' traditions of giving presents to teachers were respected, but no teacher personally accepted a gift (Bredekamp, 2003).

HOW CHILDREN LEARN ABOUT OTHERS

Once you have examined your own attitudes toward others, you need to develop an understanding of how children learn about others. Children's awareness of others begins early. By two years of age, children have the ability to identify ethnic distinctions and perceive similarities and differences among persons based on physical characteristics, clothing, language, and political orientation (Allport, 1952; Goodman, 1952; Ramsey, 2003).

Children do not appear to be comfortable with differences. By the age of two-and-a-half, signs of pre-prejudice—of discomfort with physical differences—may appear (Derman-Sparks, 2003). This discomfort has been related to children's thought processes. Children may respond negatively to those who differ from them because of their preoperational, egocentric thinking. Able only to see the world from their

Children learn how to value, or devalue, others.

own perspective, young children may see racial or ethnic differences as something to be feared rather than celebrated. As children age, however, and their thinking becomes more abstract and rational, they seem more accepting of others. Second graders, for instance, recognize differences in people but have little emotional reaction about it, while younger children, 2- or 3-year-olds, often do.

Others believe that early negative ideas of others stem from the home or the culture at large. It's true; children's values and attitudes are internalized directly from parents. To survive, children must win their parents' approval by meeting their parents' expectations and by taking on their parents' attitudes and values.

Society at large also teaches children how to value diversity. Culture is, after all, a human-made part of the environment. From television, the media, churches, and other societal institutions, children learn how to value or devalue others. Perhaps because of its diversity or inherent values of democracy, our culture seems to teach children to value others. Children in our nation express greater friendliness and open-mindedness to foreign people than do children in some other nations, perhaps because of our immigrant heritage or our greater exposure to television, books, films, and travel. Research has shown that children in the United States are more open and friendly toward foreign people than are children in ten other nations (Lambert & Klineberg, 1967; Pellowski, 1969).

Regardless of how they are learned, ideas about others seem to have their roots in the period of early childhood (Kowalski & Lo, 2001; Teichman, 2001). Thus, learning to celebrate diversity must be part of every early childhood curriculum and program (Copple, 2003).

To begin teaching children to celebrate diversity, you should understand the following principles:

1. The manner in which the concept of own group is taught to children, and ultimately learned by them, has important psychological consequences. The process of establishing the concept apparently produces an exaggerated and caricatured view of one's own nation and people. Thus, the stereotyping process itself appears to start in the early conceptions that children develop about their own group. Only much later, from ten years of age on, do children start stereotyping foreign people.

2. Early training in national contrasts appears to mark certain foreign groups as outstanding examples of peoples who are different. The researchers noted a strong cross-national tendency for American children, even 6-year-olds, to refer spontaneously to the same foreign groups as people who are not like them (Lambert & Klineberg, 1967).

3. Early training in contrasts appears to leave the impression with children that foreign people are different, strange, and unfriendly. According to the researchers, children stressed the differences of foreign people, which suggests that these children were generally suspicious in their orientation toward foreign people.

4. Early training in national contrasts also affects children's self-conceptions. Children in certain nations think of themselves in racial, religious, or national terms. Self-concepts of certain groups of children reflect what seem to be the culturally significant criteria used in their training to make distinctions between their own group and others.

5. Parents and other significant people in a child's environment transfer their own emotionally toned view of other people to the child by assigning specific attributes to members of particular groups during the period of cognitive development when the child has not fully differentiated one group from another or his own group from others.

KEY CONCEPTS

Social scientists have identified several key concepts that contribute to children's ability to celebrate diversity in the preschool-primary curriculum:

- *Interconnectedness and interdependency.* As our world becomes increasingly diverse and international contacts become common, the human experience becomes a globalized phenomenon. Today, children's learning, growth, and development are continually influenced by their interactions with others.

- *Multiculturalism.*   The human experience is diverse and multicultural. Although children are quick to recognize differences in people, it's more difficult for them to recognize that people everywhere have the same needs, feelings, and concerns.
- *Conflict resolution.*   Early on, children can learn to handle conflicts with others without aggression or violence. These early experiences can be extended to understanding how nations work together to settle differences without using force or violence.

Interconnectedness and Interdependency

We need to live with others, and others need to live with us. Young children will not be able to understand how our nation relies on other nations for trade and commerce, and they certainly will not understand the political and cultural interdependency of all nations. Regardless, teachers can foster in young children a basis for developing the concept that every part of the world is interdependent.

Interdependency begins early for humans because infants depend on their parents for care. Parents, to be parents at all, depend on their infants. Within the context of the home, children experience the idea of interdependency and interconnectedness.

Once in the preschool-primary classroom, young learners can examine and explore their connectedness with and interdependency on others in a variety of ways (National Council for the Social Studies, 1998). These might include the following:

- Live pets, which require food, care, and attention, give children concrete experiences with the interdependence of living things.
- Each child can tell the class something she can do well or likes to do for the class. These statements can be recorded in a booklet or on an experience chart.
- A pictorial chart, showing ways in which children can help one another, can be an ongoing project, with pictures added as new ways of helping are developed.
- Children can be involved in activities that require working together, such as setting a table, cooking simple foods, caring for a garden, or building a piece of large equipment. Each child can be responsible for a specific part of the group project.

Experiencing dependency, however, is not enough. Teachers need to help children construct ideas of dependency and interdependency. Some teachers begin by using the word *dependent*. As children care for pets, teachers say, "The guinea pig is dependent on you. It cannot live without you." Or when working together on a cooking project, caring for a garden, or constructing a large piece of equipment, teachers remind children of how dependent they are on each other: "We're depending on you, Jose, to stir the eggs." "Hold that wood still; we'll depend on you so we can hammer the nail here."

Live pets give children concrete experiences with interdependence.

When children are familiar with the concept of dependency, they can be introduced to the idea of interdependency: that they are dependent on others and that others are dependent on them. Immediate classroom activities and events demonstrate this idea to the children. As children return toys and materials to their proper places, leave the easels ready for the next painters, pick up coats that have fallen from hooks, or help one another button painting smocks, describe what children are doing: "Thanks, we're dependent on you to . . . and you're dependent on others to do the same."

For children in the primary grades, class activities such as small-group work and community meetings (Vance & Weaver, 2002), in which issues and ideas are openly discussed, can foster children's awareness of their interconnectedness as well as teach them the skills necessary to live and work with others. During group meetings, problems can be solved, children recognized for their contributions to the group, and explicit feedback given on how children are working together as a group.

Trips through the school to observe the interdependency among faculty and staff can foster children's ideas of the concept. A trip to the office or the cafeteria to identify workers and their tasks acquaints children with the idea of how connected one individual is to many others.

Literature and factual books can clarify or expand children's ideas of dependency and interdependency. *Frog, Duck, and Rabbit* (Gretz, 1992), a story about how three animals work together to construct a costume, and *The Chocolate Train* (Kornfeld, 2002), about chocolate making, are examples of books that can contribute to children's understanding of interdependency.

Similarities

A focus on similarities rather than differences is recommended for a number of reasons. First, children can already identify differences and are more likely to concentrate on them rather than on how people everywhere are similar. Further, children begin stereotyping other groups by expressing distrust or fear of those who are different.

Focusing on similarities is not simplistic ("We have different-colored skins, but we're all alike"). Instead, it is complicated and complex and emphasizes the fact that humans everywhere share in the human experience (Brophy & Alleman, 2002). This shared human experience and cultural diversity can be woven into all aspects of the curriculum. The emphasis on social and emotional development can be expanded to incorporate the enhancement of children's cultural identity and their awareness, concerns, and respect for other people (Ramsey, 2003).

By illustrating that, regardless of group membership or geography, people are bound together by their similarities, the content of the social studies unites people (Brophy & Alleman, 2002). Children who understand similarities among people are less likely to fear, distrust, and stereotype others. The world over, in all societies, people share the following commonalities:

- Art forms
- Group rules
- Social organization
- Basic needs
- Language

Art Forms

Children who are encouraged to create their own poetry, paintings, dance, literature, or handicrafts can readily understand and appreciate the art of other countries (Seefeldt, 2000). Art from other nations can help children discover people's common heritage. Children can do many of these activities:

- Visit museums to observe the art of many cultures. You can display art from all over the world in the classroom.
- Exchange their paintings, drawings, or creative writing with a school in some other land.

All cultures have music and art.

- Invite foreign visitors to tell folktales from their nations. You can compare the folktales with those of the United States.
- Listen to poetry from other lands—perhaps some haiku from Japan—and dictate their own poetry.

Figure 3.2 suggests how technology can help. Children can reflect their own cultural and racial identity in their own artwork. One primary group of children from El Salvador was taught how to weave. The children first talked with their grandparents, who remembered weaving and told them how it was done. Then they studied pictures of woven mats and went to visit a textile museum displaying weavings from Central America. Back in the classroom, they designed rugs and wall hangings using crayons and markers. The designs were then transferred into line drawings on larger sheets of paper, which were placed in back of a loom. An art teacher demonstrated how to execute the design through weaving.

Using crayons and clay in multicultural skin tones allows children to create pictures and forms of themselves and others in their classroom and school. The natural skin tones of washable paint, crayons, colored pencils, markers, and modeling clay, which can be applied and blended or mixed easily, allow children to express pride in themselves, their families, and their community through their own artistic expression.

Use technology to show children that their own art forms are both similar to and different from art forms in other countries:

- Set up a class e-mail exchange with a class in another country.
- Using digital photography, exchange e-mailed artwork. You might choose a theme, such as *Clothing We Like, Special Food, Butterflies We Know, What We Do in Winter,* and so on. Both classes draw, paint, or construct their ideas about the theme and exchange their artwork through e-mails or a web site.
- Find web resources about art from other times and places. Compare this art to the work the children create.
- In a discussion, compare artwork from other places and times with children's current work.

Figure 3.2 Using technology to unite children.

Group Rules

As children begin to realize that rules are necessary to live together effectively, they can understand how groups function more successfully when the rights of each group member are recognized. Children can do the following:

- Establish their own rules for using playground equipment, allowing people into the housekeeping area, or walking to the cafeteria.
- Use the rules of the school—e.g., walk in the hall, remain quiet while waiting for the bus—to illustrate the rules of a larger community. You can also help them compare classroom rules with their rules at home.
- Explore the rules of the community, such as the traffic rules. Do all communities have such rules? Why?
- Determine what rules the nation has, and compare them to the laws of other lands.

Social Organization

Although the composition of families and social groups changes dramatically from place to place, all human beings live in some type of group or social organization. To comprehend the similarities among social groups, children in primary grades can do these activities:

- Graph their families' composition to show how many different kinds of family units are represented in their classroom. You will want to discuss with the children how these family units are the same.
- Exchange letters with a family in some other nation to learn how it is like a family in this country.
- Invite visitors from other countries to tell about their families, the things family members do together, and how they share work or celebrate holidays.

Basic Needs

Borrowing concepts from the field of economics, you can teach children that people the world over have the same basic needs for food, shelter, and clothing. Children might be able to do these things:

- Examine different shelters from around the world. Ask children, "How are they just like our homes?" "How are they different?" "How many different kinds of homes do we live in?" "How are they alike?"
- Compare the clothing of other nations. Ask, "How is it just like the clothing we wear?" "What things do we use that they do not?" One kindergartner, after comparing shoes from seven different countries, said, "The shoes are different, but everybody has feet."

A unit on bread illustrates how people of different cultures, while having the same basic needs, meet those needs in different ways. After reading the book *Bread, Bread, Bread* by Ann Morris (1989), teachers asked children what kind of bread they ate at home. The names of the different breads were listed and discussed. Samples were brought to school, compared, and tasted. Children made bread and wrote stories about breads, learning that bread is a food that most people have in common, even though the types may differ.

Language

People everywhere communicate both verbally and nonverbally. Verbal communication may involve many languages; nonverbal communication is useful when the verbal communication of others is not understood. Children can learn that both verbal and nonverbal communication skills are involved when they try to express feelings, ideas, attitudes, and knowledge. Following are some suggestions:

1. Give children many opportunities to communicate in the classroom on a one-to-one basis or in large or small groups. Methods might include using a telephone or tape recorder or dictating to the teacher. Draw children's attention to their use of nonverbal communication and extend the concept by introducing Indian sign language or the sign language used to communicate with the deaf, role playing, or dramatizations.

2. Read children the story *Children of the World Say Good Morning* (Martin, 1969a), and teach children to say "good morning" in some language other than English. Read *What Is Your Language?* (Leventhal, 1998), in which a small child from New York City packs his bags and travels around the world, asking, "What is your language?" and learning to say "yes" and "no" in ten languages. This simple book introduces children to the idea that they are part of a worldwide community.

3. Expose children to someone who is speaking another language; you or a visitor might teach the children a few phrases in the language. You could teach a few simple songs and let the children listen to music from other countries.

4. Children in the primary grades enjoy and benefit from having a pen pal. Even kindergarteners can learn about others by exchanging pictures and dictated letters with other young children who live far from them, perhaps using e-mail or the Internet. For help in setting up a pen-pal program, contact the following organizations:

International Friendship League
40 Mount Vernon Street
Boston, MA 02108

League of Friendship, Inc.
P.O. Box 509
Charlottesville, VA 22905

Student Letter Exchange Bureau
215 Fifth Ave, S.E.
Waseca, MN 56093

National Geographic Society
Dept. Geo Mail
P.O. Box 96088
Washington, DC 20090–6088

ePALS
60 Sound View Drive
Easton, CT 06612
Website: *http://www.epals.com*

The written language in stories, poetry, nonfiction books, and other forms of literature is a way of bridging the gap between what children know about others and what they don't. Such books can provide accurate, authentic information about the similarities and differences among people everywhere. They can help teachers open communication and foster environments of understanding and respect. Each year the National Council for the Social Studies and the Children's Book Council offer a list of multicultural books. (See "Resources" at the end of this chapter.)

An element common to communication is that people everywhere have feelings. Children learn to express their feelings positively in the classroom, without hurting others; they learn to recognize that all people have the same feelings. When reading stories about people from other lands, such as *The Story of Ping* (Flack, 1977), you can ask the children, "How do you think the boy felt when he fell into the water?" "How would you have felt?" "Has anything like that ever happened to you?"

One teacher, after reading Aliki's (1987) *The Two of Them*, asked children to talk about love. The children talked about love they receive from adults, how a cat loves her kittens, and so forth. In another lesson, a teacher used two guinea pigs of different colors to demonstrate how things can be alike but different, which led to a discussion of how people can love others who may be different from them and can be friends with others who have a different skin color.

Other classroom experiences give children opportunities to clarify their feelings toward other people and understand the feelings of others. You can ask the children,

"How did you feel when you hit him?" "How do you think he felt?" "How did it feel when they asked you to play with them?" "How did you feel when they called you a name?" You can also help children perceive the feelings of others: "What do you think she was telling you when she screamed at you?" "How do you think she felt?"

RESOURCES FOR LEARNING ABOUT OTHERS

The most effective resources available for children's development of international concepts are the children themselves. Their heritage and backgrounds of experience provide a base from which you can build their knowledge. Teachers, along with children and their families, can explore the ethnic heritage of the children in the class by making charts of the different nationalities represented, discussing the customs of different families, and participating in these customs.

Equally effective resources are people who have lived in or visited other countries or who are citizens of other nations. As visitors to the class, they can illustrate how people everywhere are similar yet do things in different ways. The mere presence of resource persons, however, does not guarantee the development of positive attitudes and understandings. To ensure a positive experience for both the visitor and the children, you need to prepare:

- Know something about the person to make sure that she has more than a cursory knowledge of the country and can talk to children.
- Brief the visitor about the class, and help plan the presentation. Young children become restless when asked only to listen. The visitor might be asked to include some concrete materials or props in the discussion to attract the children.
- Be certain that the children have sufficient understanding of the country. Visitors from Bombay or Rio de Janeiro are frequently appalled when children want to know whether they have refrigerators or cars.
- Prepare the children for possible differences in appearance or language before the visitor comes. Discuss with them how to behave in the presence of a guest. Plan with them about ways to make the guest comfortable: "Who will take her coat? Where will she sit? How will we listen, ask questions, and thank her?"
- Have globes and maps available so children can locate the country.
- Use on-line resources to learn about others.

You can use other experiences to help children recognize cultural similarities. You might suggest specific television shows that offer children insight into other people's cultures, or you might bring in newspaper and magazine articles that clarify children's concepts of others. Reference books, travel posters, photographs, films, slides, and movies are also useful to compare people's similarities. Analyze these materials to make certain they do the following:

- Reflect the many groups in our nation and world
- Do not omit, distort, or present insensitive pictures of any group of people
- Reflect our pluralistic society

Holiday activities can introduce children to pleasant and interesting aspects of other people's customs. Young children enjoy a Japanese Kite Day as they marvel at the Japanese custom of giving children a day off from school to fly kites. An egg tree for an Easter celebration helps children understand and appreciate Slovakian celebrations. Baking and eating hot-cross buns may help children feel close to children in Great Britain.

Tasting other foods from various cultures is useful. Discuss why people prepare the foods the way they do, and find the countries on the map to help children develop an awareness of other people's customs and similarities.

Museums, historical societies, and embassies all offer children concrete experiences with other cultures. Each community will have some type of museum where children can view artifacts from other lands and compare their similarities.

Toys and play are universals in childhood and can be a natural basis for a global education curriculum (see Figure 3.3). Teachers can use toys and play to connect children from all parts of the world. You can provide children with toys made in various countries, such as puzzles from Holland, blocks from Switzerland, dolls from Korea, or games originating in Africa. Children over age 6 or 7 can be introduced to

On-line resources let children reach out to others far from them.

Equip the sociodramatic play area with multicultural cooking tools:

Chopsticks	Woks
Perogi press	Teapots
Rolling pins	Ravioli makers
Graters	Chafing dishes

Figure 3.3 Play with multicultural props.

games that children in other nations play. But teachers need to interact sensitively with children. They may point out that the differences in the dress of dolls reflect the variety of clothes that people wear rather than being costumes or that steering wheels on cars in other countries are on *another* side of the car rather than on the *wrong* side.

Kindergarten children can play with puppets and use them to retell stories. The variations in familiar folktales—such as the variety of ways people around the world tell the story of the Three Billy Goats Gruff and the role of the troll—can be compared and acted out with puppets. First graders can compare toy catalogs from other nations or draw and write their own, and second graders might put on a toy fair in the school library.

SUMMARY

When teachers emphasize the things that bind people together and help children see the similarities among all people, regardless of culture, children learn to celebrate diversity. Your attitudes toward others and your understanding of how children form attitudes play a necessary role in developing respect toward and valuing others.

All people are dependent upon each other, and all people are similar, as evident in the fact that all have language; families and other social groups; systems for provision of food, shelter, clothing, government, laws, religion, and ethics; systems for explaining natural phenomena; rules regarding property; and art forms. Introducing children to the languages, art, and social systems of other peoples is one way to teach them that they are part of a larger community of people, who, though they may differ, share many of the same feelings, needs, and systems. Teachers who are trained to promote cooperative learning, value student opinions, respect the rights and opinions of others, encourage students to reflect on their experience and play with new ideas, and give students some responsibility for control over the learning process may foster many of the learning outcomes that are important in human rights education (Ramsey, 2003; Wardle, 2003).

Extend Your Knowledge

1. Contact the embassies of different countries and request free materials that present current information about the country. Write to "The Embassy of _____, Washington, DC." Some of the materials will be appropriate for use with young children; others will be useful in building your own understandings of other countries.

2. Begin a resource file of children's games from around the world. Teach one game to a small group of young children, explaining the origin of the game to them.

3. Obtain a curriculum guide from your local school system or state department of education. Analyze the guide for stereotypic representations of other people.

4. Within your classroom or college, many nationalities and ethnic groups will be represented. Interview some adults from these groups, asking them what elements of their culture they want young children to understand.

Resources

ArtsEdge, a Kennedy Center web site (*http://www.artsedge.com*), offers on-line curriculum plans. The unit "African Art and Culture"—integrating mathematics and knowledge of Africa, its art, and its culture—offers first through third graders lessons in patterning, symmetry, and the language arts.

The *National Council for the Social Studies* and the *Children's Book Council* both offer a list of children's books and related literacy materials that acquaint children with people and places around the world and throughout time. Go to *http://www.ncss.org* and click on "Notable Social Studies Books for Young People."

The *National Association for the Education of Young Children*'s position paper offers an excellent perspective on how teachers can learn to work effectively with cultural diversity:

National Association for the Education of Young Children. (1996). NAEYC position statement: Responding to linguistic and cultural diversity—Recommendations for effective early childhood education. *Young Children, 51*(2), 4–13.

The *Children's Book Council, Inc.*, offers a catalog of other multicultural books:

Children's Book Council, Inc.
568 Broadway #404
New York, NY 10012

The books listed for older children might be useful reference books as you plan to introduce young children to people of different cultures.

Following are other associations to contact for information on celebrating diversity:

Educators for Social Responsibility
23 Garden Street
Cambridge, MA 01238
Website: *http://www.educatorssocialresponsibility.org*

National Multicultural Education Association
733 15th Street NW
Washington, DC 20262
Website: *http://www.name.org*

References

Aliki. (1987). *The two of them.* New York: Morrow.

Allport, G. (1952). *The nature of prejudice.* New York: Doubleday Anchor.

Bredekamp, S. (2003). Resolving contradictions between cultural practices. In C. Copple (Ed.), *A world of difference* (pp. 59–61). Washington, DC: National Association for the Education of Young Children.

Brophy, J., & Alleman, J. (2002). Beyond expanding horizons: New curriculum directions for elementary social studies. *Elementary School Journal, 103,* 99–114.

Copple, C. (Ed.). (2003). *A world of difference.* Washington, DC: National Association for the Education of Young Children.

d'Entremont, L. (1997). A few words about diversity and rigidity: One director's perspective. *Young Children, 53*(1), 72–73.

Derman-Sparks, L. (2003). Markers of multicultural/antibias education. In C. Copple (Ed.), *A world of difference* (pp. 171–173). Washington, DC: National Association for the Education of Young Children.

Dewey, J. (1944). *Democracy and education.* New York: Free Press.

Flack, M. (1977). *The story of Ping.* New York: Viking.

Garcia, E. E. (2003). Respecting children's home languages and culture. In C. Copple (Ed.), *A world of difference* (p. 3). Washington, DC : National Association for the Education of Young Children.

Goodman, M. (1952). *Race awareness in young children.* Reading, MA: Addison-Wesley.

Gretz, S. (1992). *Frog, duck, and rabbit.* New York: Simon & Schuster.

Kornfeld, J. (2002). *The chocolate train.* New York: Simon & Schuster.

Kowalski, K., & Lo, Y. F. (2001). The influence of perceptual features, ethnic labels, and sociocultural information in the development of ethnic/racial bias in young children. *Journal of Cross-Cultural Psychology, 32*(4), 444–455.

Lambert, W., & Klineberg, O. (1967). *Children's views of foreign peoples: A cross cultural study.* New York: Appleton-Century Crofts.

Leventhal, S. (1998). *What is your language?* New York: Puffin.

Marshall, H. (2003). Cultural influences on the development of self-concept: Updating our thinking. In C. Copple (Ed.), *A world of difference* (pp. 167–171). Washington, DC: National Association for the Education of Young Children.

Martin, B. (1969a). *Children of the world say good morning.* New York: Holt, Rinehart, & Winston.

Martin, B. (1969b). *David was mad.* New York: Holt, Rinehart, & Winston.

Morris, A. (1989). *Bread, bread, bread.* New York: Lothrop, Lee, & Shepard.

National Association for the Education of Young Children. (1998). *Early years are learning years: Building positive relationships through communication.* Washington, DC: Author.

National Council for the Social Studies. (1998). *Expectations of excellence.* Washington, DC: Author.

New, R. S. (1999). Here we call it "drop off and pick up:" Transition to child care, American style. *Young Children, 54*(2), 34–36.

Okagaki, L., & Diamond, K. E. (2003). Responding to cultural and linguistic differences in the belief and practices of families with young children. In C. Copple (Ed.), *A world of difference* (pp. 9–15). Washington, DC: National Association for the Education of Young Children.

Pattnaik, J. (2003). Learning about the other. *Childhood Education, 79,* 204–211.

Pellowski, A. (1969). *Children and international education portfolio no. 6.* Washington, DC: Association for Childhood Education International.

Ramsey, P. G. (2003). Growing up with the contradictions of race and class. In C. Copple (Ed.), *A world of difference* (pp. 5–6). Washington, DC: National Association for the Education of Young Children.

Seefeldt, C. (2000). Art for young children. In C. Seefeldt (Ed.), *The early childhood curriculum: Current findings and theory* (3rd ed., pp. 201–218). New York: Teachers College Press.

Teichman, Y. (2001). The development of Israeli children's images of Jews and Arabs and their expression in human figure drawings. *Developmental Psychology, 37*(6), 749–761.

Vance, E., & Weaver, P. J. (2002). *Class meetings: Young children solve problems together.* Washington, DC: National Association for the Education of Young Children.

Wardle, F. (2003). Supporting multiracial and multiethnic children and their families. In C. Copple (Ed.), *A world of difference* (pp. 33–35). Washington, DC: National Association for the Education of Young Children.

CHAPTER 4

Resources for Learning

The school's job is to begin with the children's own environment whatever or wherever it may be.

Lucy Sprague Mitchell, 1934, p. 16

After you read this chapter, you should be prepared to respond to the following questions:

- o How can teachers use each child's family as a resource for teaching social studies?

- o What resources in and around the school are useful in fostering the goals of the social studies?

- o Why are centers of interest necessary? What is the role of the teacher in establishing centers of interest and supervising and teaching through centers?

- o How do you plan a field trip to use the resources in the community fully?

Suppose you wanted to learn how to swim. Would you read books about swimming and listen to people tell you how to swim? Or would you jump into a pool and, with the guidance of an expert swimmer, learn by doing?

People have long known that humans, whether adults or children, learn best by doing. This is why the social studies curriculum demands that children be able to learn through firsthand experiences grounded in their here-and-now environment. But the here-and-now environment is more than physical. It includes interaction with others, both adults and children, as well as children's actions in the physical environments of the classroom and community.

THE CHILDREN

Children themselves are resources for social studies learning. Each child brings a unique set of experiences and skills to share with others. To enrich the social studies curriculum, children can become involved in many ways:

- Share their experiences by telling others about how they do things in their own families
- Bring in objects, photographs, cultural foods, and stories to share with classmates
- Demonstrate how to make a bridge of blocks, how to paint, or how to make a replica of an Indian pot
- Teach one another how to complete a puzzle, read a map, or sing a song from their culture

THE FAMILY

The family offers a world of resources for the social studies! Think about it: probably all of the content, attitudes, values, and skills included in the social studies could be fostered through study of the family (Helm & Katz, 2001; Seefeldt & Denton, 1997).

Families have a history. Where did each family come from? What stories do they tell about how they got here and where they first settled? Do children's parents tell their children about their own childhood? What about family celebrations?

Geography is also part of families. Find out where each family came from, and locate the country on a map. How did the family travel here? Families move, even within the same city. Make a map, and locate where each family once lived.

What jobs do parents hold? How are tasks divided within the family? What about budgeting? Children find economic concepts meaningful when they are related to their own experiences in the family unit.

Weaving parents into the fabric of early childhood programs is a primary goal of educators. But for social studies learning, parental involvement is even more critical. All types of involvement—informal and formal—bring parents, teachers, and children together and serve as resources for social studies learning and teaching.

Informal Involvement

Here are some simple things that you might do to involve parents in the social studies program:

• Establish an open-door policy. Rather than asking parents to visit only during American Education Week or on special days when they may not be able to take time off from work, encourage them to visit the school any time they can. Parents may find themselves with an afternoon off, an hour or two at lunch, or a few hours free during the morning. Be certain that parents know they are welcome to spend this unexpected free time in school with their children. Arrange a space at the school where parents can meet to chat, relax, or work on a task.

• Send home a questionnaire at the beginning of the year, inviting parents to indicate the kinds of things they would like their children to learn in social studies. It might be a good idea to list several choices, asking the parents to check the ones they like as well as leaving space for their suggestions. Other questionnaires could request suggestions for field trips or visitors to the class.

• Send home a brief outline of each unit or project plan. A page of simple statements tells parents something about their children's activities: "For the next few days, we will study the concept of production. We will visit a store and. . . "

• Children in the primary grades can write a class newsletter. In the letter, you can include plans for parties or field trips, reviews of movies or books the children have enjoyed, or the things they have learned.

• Forward a booklet of children's favorite poems and songs.

• Send home individual notes with children, telling parents about their child's progress—a new skill learned or how the child used new knowledge to solve a problem. Single sentences on the back of a picture or attached to some of the child's work do much to inform parents about the progress their children are making and the things that happen during the school day: "Please notice how well Aletha completed this map. It's a drawing of our playground, and it's quite accurate." "This is the first time John included a base line in his painting; it means. . . " "Toni's ideas are exciting; this story shows imagination and thought."

• After children were familiar with *Brown Bear, Brown Bear* (Martin, 1969), one second-grade teacher put a stuffed brown bear in a backpack along with a journal. Each child took turns bringing home the bear and the journal. The child wrote in the journal about what Brown Bear did during the afternoon and evening in her home. The child then read the journal notation to the class.

• M. S. Gorter-Reu and J. M. Anderson (1998) developed home kits, which include music tapes and idea cards for making simple toys and games at home. Kindergarten and first-grade teachers in Texas and New Mexico have used these kits. Other teachers send home backpacks containing thematically related books with suggestions for their use.

• Give parents your e-mail address so they can keep in touch with you and ask questions. This not only opens communication between parent and teacher but lets both exchange thoughts about children's progress.

• Teachers at the Center for Young Children at the University of Maryland laminate class books created by the children. Children take turns bringing home the books. A sheet in the back of the book is provided for parents to sign and comment on the children's work.

Involving parents in the school's program implies respect for each child and family. To communicate the school's respect, you can do the following:

• Involve parents in the teaching-learning process. Letters telling the parents about the concepts being taught and asking them to extend these concepts at home are useful: "We're learning about traffic safety. The next time you go for a drive, could you point out the traffic signs and explain their meanings to the children?" Parents can also take part in children's homework, not the dreary pencil-and-paper kind but the homework involved in looking for all the tools in the house, counting the number of jobs that family members have, drawing a map of the block the child lives on, or watching a certain television program together. Many preschool programs foster children's cognitive growth by involving parents as teachers of their own children. You could send toys, books, games, puzzles, and other equipment home with the children, permitting parents to take an active part in their child's education.

• Be aware that attitudes are communicated subtly through language use. The term broken home or the comment "he doesn't have a father" imply stereotypical attitudes. Families who have experienced divorce may be more whole after the divorce rather than broken by it; and each child does in fact have a father, who may or may not be present in the home.

• Structure school activities for the parent in general, not specifying the mother or father. This shows your respect for the family unit as it may exist in many children's homes.

• Offer real support in recognizing the time limitations of working parents, and schedule conferences when parents are free to attend.

Formal Involvement

Informal parent-involvement activities often lead to more structured involvement of parents in the social studies program. At first, parents and teachers are comfortable communicating at the day-by-day informal level. As trust develops, parents find they are interested in more structured involvement. Attending group meetings, working with children, and making decisions about the social studies program then take place.

Group Meetings

Parents are interested in seeing photos and videos of their children at school, and these can serve as the focus of a group meeting. One teacher took many digital photos of children participating in social studies activities. At the end of the year, she held a parent meeting and, transferring the digital photos to overheads, showed photos taken at the beginning, middle, and end of the year that illustrated the children's growth in skills and their progression in caring, sharing, cooperative attitudes, and school knowledge.

One school system instituted Family Nights Out. The school provided dinner for families, children, teachers, and the principal. After dinner the children played together while the parents met with a family therapist who led group discussions. Both teachers and parents said they benefited because they got to know one another as equals (Seefeldt & Goldsmith, 1998).

Working with Children

Parent volunteers are needed for field trips as well as on a daily basis. Parents may be able to work with individual children or help groups carry out projects. Some parents may serve as resources when children study various topics and themes.

Decision Making

When parents are involved, they should eventually make decisions about the social studies program. They may help set some of the goals and objectives of the program or decide on topics or themes.

The Transition Demonstration is a national program that follows Head Start children through the third grade with Head Start–like services. In a number of cases, it involved parents in writing an Individual Transition Plan with their children's current and future teachers. Together, teachers and parents shared what they knew about the child's strengths, interests, and learning style and made decisions about the goals they would set for the child for the coming year.

THE SCHOOL

If you want to be a teacher of young children, you must be able to look at the world through the eyes of a child. Take a walk inside the school and on the playground and consider what would interest a child who is 3, 5, or 8 years of age. Look at the playground and pretend you are that child filled with wonder and curiosity. What do you see?

Following the theories of Mitchell (1934), Piaget (Piaget & Inhelder, 1969), and Vygotsky (1986), you can ground a great deal of your social studies in the here-and-now world of the school. To provide children with this type of experience, you can take a number of steps:

- Identify building materials, how they got to the building, and who used them
- Study communication systems—mail, computers, fax machines, cell phones, and telephones

Families are asked to make decisions about their children's learning.

- Care for the school grounds
- Examine various delivery systems for food, materials, and supplies

The people in the school also serve as resources for children's learning. Every member of the school staff has some special skill or background to share with the children. Just observing the staff at work—art, music, and physical education teachers; media specialists, lunchroom personnel, office workers, custodians—puts children in touch with real-world learning. Some staff members might demonstrate a specific skill used in their jobs, or they could invite small groups to observe them complete a specific task. Just as the parents do, the staff might share something from their background with the children—a song, a favorite food, a game, or a custom enjoyed by the person's family.

The teacher is a resource for social studies learning. Your experiences, the different places you have worked, the things you did in college, the places you have visited—all can be used to enrich children's learning by giving them vicarious experiences on which to build concepts. Then, too, the skills, knowledge, and information you bring to your job are potent factors for children's learning. Regardless of the extent of materials available, the teacher's creativity is the most important learning resource in the classroom.

THE CLASSROOM

Even though it is an artificial setting, the classroom can, through careful planning and arranging, become a world for social studies learning. In any developmentally appropriate classroom, children can find water and sand, rocks and mud, woodworking tools, computers, art materials, blocks, books, other children and adults, boxes, foil, animals, and many other resources for learning.

But the careful selection of resources for social studies learning is not enough. Teachers must know how and when to present them to children. Clearly, manipulatives alone have no great educational value unless the teacher knows the materials and can instruct children in their productive use.

Anyone can present children with materials, but good teachers use those materials to lead children to meaningful activity and thinking and to the fulfillment of their educational goals. Good teachers know many things:

- What materials to select, and how and when to present them to children
- When and how to interact with children as they use the materials
- How to extend children's activity and expand their thinking
- When to remove resources, add new materials, or end activities

By creating centers of interest, the teacher arranges the classroom to provide as many opportunities for learning as the home, community, and world do. The teacher arranges clearly defined spaces where children can find equipment, materials, and furniture grouped together for specific purposes and goals (Isbell & Exelby, 2001). Taking on the appearance of a workshop, these interest centers, or learning areas, permit children to make choices about how and what they will learn. The areas of interest enable individualization of instruction as children themselves select the materials to use, decide how to use them, and determine the purposes for their use.

The idea is for children to be actively engaged in meaningful learning, either alone or with others. As children work in these interest centers, they learn social skills, especially cooperation and sharing, and they run head-on into the ideas, attitudes, and values of others.

Children select materials and decide how to use them.

Any number of centers of interest can be located in one room. Decisions about the number and type of centers depend on the goals of the program, interests of the children, and space available.

Deciding on Centers of Interest

Typically, every preschool and primary room should include areas of interest for sociodramatic play, blocks, mathematics, art, library, manipulative play, music, writing, sand and water play, and woodworking. For the social studies curriculum, other areas are planned. These depend on the children's interests and the curriculum (see Figure 4.1).

Depending on characteristics of the community, you might want to create a post office, a gas station, a grocery store, a doctor's office, an airport, or another area to promote sociodramatic play. Or you could set up learning centers of books and slides about children living in a different country. These areas can be rotated and changed, with areas added as needed and removed when no longer in use.

Introducing Centers of Interest

Just setting up centers of interest does not ensure that learning will take place. You need to allow children large blocks of time and the freedom to explore and experiment, and you need to be actively involved with the children as they work in the centers.

Introduce the centers by describing some of the possibilities and limitations and the rules of each one: "Here are the paints, brushes, and paper; this is how you wash the brushes." These kinds of statements give children the adult guidance necessary for them to feel free to assume responsibility and begin to be self-directing.

As children use the interest centers, you can suggest problems for them to solve and interest them in different learning opportunities. As 4-year-olds enter the classroom, the teacher might talk with each child, discussing the possible choices available in the centers and asking him what things he might want to do that day. A group of 5-year-olds can listen to a description of the learning areas, materials, and problems and select the area in which they wish to begin working. Children in primary grades can place their names on a chart indicating the center or centers they will work in that morning. They could also keep their own record of the centers they worked in, whom they worked with, and what they completed.

Types of Centers of Interest

A Place of Their Own

In open classrooms filled with interest centers, it is imperative that children have some place to call their own. Young children seem to feel more comfortable when there is a territory they are sure of. This does not mean that children need a desk of their own or even a cubicle or a locker. Discarded shoe boxes, empty ice cream cartons, or other boxes for their treasures give children the feeling of having their own territory.

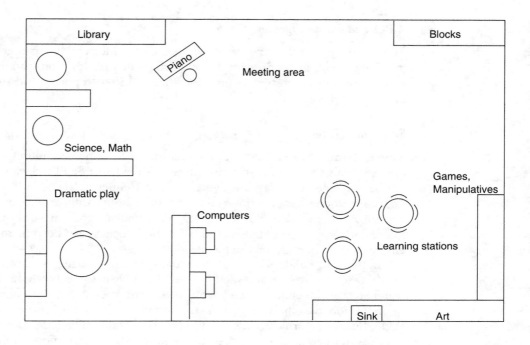

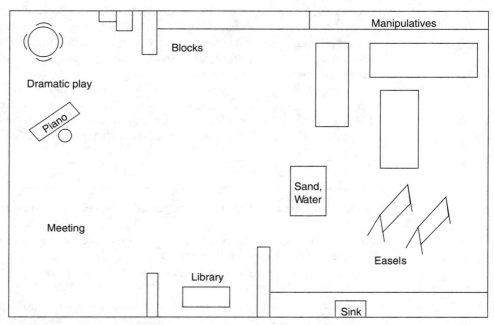

Figure 4.1   Centers of interest.

A Place to Come Together

The specific physical arrangement for the area in which children gather doesn't matter. They might sit on risers or a special rug, but the classroom should have some space for the total group to come together to listen to poetry and stories, discuss events, and share news.

Sand and Water

Sand and water areas are a must for social studies learning. As children play with natural materials, they are constructing physical knowledge. Sand and water centers may not be available every day, but they should be frequent and regular centers. It is not necessary to purchase commercial sand tables; large cardboard boxes, leaky plastic bathtubs, or discarded plastic wading pools make excellent substitutes. Partially filled, flat cardboard containers (12 by 18 by 3 inches) can become miniature sand environments for children's explorations.

In the sand, children can construct roads, tunnels, bridges, cities, farms, airports—anything they have seen and want to re-create. A clean squirt bottle can be filled with water so that the children can keep the sand moist enough for building. Props that might be added to the sand include toy animals, people, shops, cars, airplanes, shells, sticks, feathers, marbles, rocks, or even live land crabs and beetles (see Figure 4.2).

A water center gives children the opportunity to learn more about their earth. You can easily provide water for children's use; small plastic dishpans placed on a plastic or newspaper-covered table are adequate. Other containers might be plastic tubs or buckets, commercial water tables, or plastic wading pools. Children can cover themselves with plastic aprons, and teachers can keep an extra set of clothing handy in case children do become too wet.

Adding objects to water play gives children new ideas and materials with which to experiment. Sieves, funnels, squirt bottles, a piece of hose, plastic spoons, cups, and dishes are all appropriate additions. If children lose interest in water play, adding dishes, pots, pans, and doll clothes to wash renews their motivation.

Relate children's play with sand to the social studies (Barbour, Webster, & Drosdeck, 1987):

❑ Give labels to their sand creations. "This looks like a valley between two mountains." "This is a river, and this is a stream."

❑ Pose problems. "What would happen if rain fell on your mountain? Do you want to try using the sprinkler?"

❑ Motivate building with stories. After reading *Desert Life* (Kirk, 1970), second graders created animals' homes in the sandbox. A first-grade class created a clam flat in their box after reading *One Morning in Maine* (McCloskey, 1952).

Figure 4.2   Sand and the social studies.

Primary children use sand and water to learn more about measurement and volume, make comparisons, identify cause and effect, and problem-solve (Moriarty, 2002). These older children can also observe how things float, sink, and dissolve. Clipboards near the sand and water areas allow children to record their findings.

Blocks

Blocks are one of the most valuable learning resources in the social studies. Block building invites children to work together. Rather than relying on suggestions from the teacher, the discipline of construction itself asks for cooperative effort. Children seek each other's help, working together as they build (see Figure 4.3).

First introduced by Friedrick Froebel (1887), unit blocks were used by Caroline Pratt (1948) in the early 1930s as a primary tool for social studies learning in her New York City nursery school. Smooth, solid, and increasing in size in length only, unit blocks allow children the comfort of repeating forms and predicting results. Although initially expensive, unit blocks are indestructible and are a good investment.

A variety of blocks might be used in addition to unit blocks. Large, wooden, hollow blocks; cardboard blocks; blocks made from wood scraps that have been sanded and smoothed; and blocks made from paper milk cartons stuffed solidly with newspaper and covered with paper are all useful. Storage of blocks is easiest on open shelves, with a place on the shelf for each shape and size. When blocks are stored in this manner, children can see all of the possibilities for constructing and can find the

---

❏ Provide firsthand experiences to be represented through block building. Ask children to observe the school building, the fire station, or a shopping center and speculate on how it was built.

❏ Recognize children's representations. Pay attention to the block configurations with comments and questions such as "How will the truck get in and out?" "Where can the street go?" "Did you see the warehouse?" "This block will balance the others."

❏ Encourage children with a smile, nod, or comment to let them know you support their building.

❏ Add vocabulary. "Shaneka, use the arch." "Put the double block here."

❏ Pose problems. "What will happen if you . . . ?"

❏ Add props. Based on firsthand experiences, add wood animals, people, street signs, cars, boats, planes, trains, and ladders to the block area. Natural materials, pieces of shrubs, stones, wood, plants, shells, and human-made materials such as wire, cables, and ropes motivate block building.

❏ Evaluate their block play. Observe children's buildings, noting their progress and movement from laying blocks out flat on the floor to constructing vertical buildings.

❏ Provide resources.

Figure 4.3 Blocks—the teacher's role.

right block for the right job. Symbols on each shelf, representing the shape of the block to be stored there, help children remember where to return the blocks when they have finished working with them (Hewett, 2001).

A smooth, hard surface is best for constructing. If possible, allow the buildings to stand as long as the children's interest lasts. Encourage the children to add to or rebuild them, thereby extending their original concept and using it in play. If this is not possible, you can set aside an area away from traffic, and with a measure of privacy, for block play.

Children's first block buildings are explorative. Young children begin to build by placing the blocks in rows, making lines across the floor. Later, they start putting one block on top of another, knocking them down, then beginning again. Simple construction is next, with square and rectangular buildings of one level appearing (Hewett, 2001). Children in the primary grades, who have a wider background of experiences, begin to create the things they have observed in the community—the zoo, the airport, an apartment house, a mobile-home park, and the neighborhood. They begin cooperative play, with plans, goals, and purposes; their block play and its resulting structures become increasingly complex, based on group effort and individual ideas.

Literature stimulates primary children to construct many kinds of things with blocks. Together you could read these books:

- Read *The Lot at the End of My Block* (Lewis & Cartwright, 2001). Then children can figure out how to build a house with blocks.

Children's first block buildings are explorative.

- Read *Tunnels Go Underground: A Building Block Book* (Hill, 2000), which engages children in building tunnels with blocks.
- Read *Building an Igloo* (Steitzer, 1995) and try to engineer an igloo with blocks.
- Read *Canals Are Water Roads* (Hill, 1997a) and build canals with blocks.

Children can create their own literature around block building. At the Center for Young Children at the University of Maryland, the 3-, 4-, and 5-year-olds keep block journals. Teachers take digital or Polaroid photos of children's block buildings and paste them in children's journals. Children then either dictate or write about their block building. They describe how they balanced blocks, used unit blocks to build arches, and how the building would be used.

Dramatic Play

Dramatic play encourages children to take on the role of another being and use symbolic thought (see Figure 4.4). Dramatic play has been called a unifying force by which children integrate their social and physical experiences in the external world with their internal mental and emotional processes to produce novel transformations, which children then project outward in symbolic form (Bodrova & Leong, 2003). Sociodramatic play—e.g., children acting like astronauts, mothers, fathers, doctors, or teachers—is important in the development of learning strategies and the skills involved in thinking. In the housekeeping area, children learn to (1) maintain

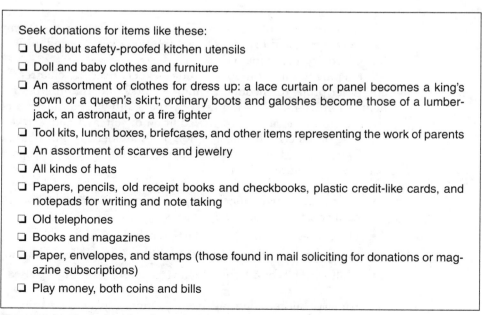

Seek donations for items like these:

- ❏ Used but safety-proofed kitchen utensils
- ❏ Doll and baby clothes and furniture
- ❏ An assortment of clothes for dress up: a lace curtain or panel becomes a king's gown or a queen's skirt; ordinary boots and galoshes become those of a lumberjack, an astronaut, or a fire fighter
- ❏ Tool kits, lunch boxes, briefcases, and other items representing the work of parents
- ❏ An assortment of scarves and jewelry
- ❏ All kinds of hats
- ❏ Papers, pencils, old receipt books and checkbooks, plastic credit-like cards, and notepads for writing and note taking
- ❏ Old telephones
- ❏ Books and magazines
- ❏ Paper, envelopes, and stamps (those found in mail soliciting for donations or magazine subscriptions)
- ❏ Play money, both coins and bills

Figure 4.4 Equipping the dramatic play area.

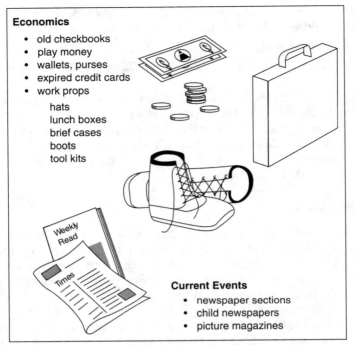

Figure 4.5   Social materials for the dramatic play areas.

a planned sequence of activities, (2) abstract and embody the salient features of a situation or a role, and (3) focus their attention over a period of time on the capacity for objectivity and empathy.

Keeping in mind the social studies experiences the children have had, you can add other props to encourage children to try out still different roles. A trip to the dentist's office might be followed by the addition of a mirror, a chair, and a white shirt; a trip to the airport by the addition of suitcases and a ticket desk; and a visit from the postal clerk by the addition of a shoulder bag and a hat (Vukelich, 1990).

Every area of the social sciences can be reinforced with props in the housekeeping area (see Figures 4.5 and 4.6):

- Economics—play money for purses and wallets, scales for weighing groceries, cash registers, blank receipt books
- History—sunbonnets, long skirts, ranch-hand hats
- Geography—road maps, dress-up clothes for traveling, wheel toys, steering wheel
- Multicultural education—clothing, games, or other objects used in other countries

Primary children continue to enjoy dramatic play. The nature and purpose of this play differ from that of preschoolers. In the primary grades, children can make masks

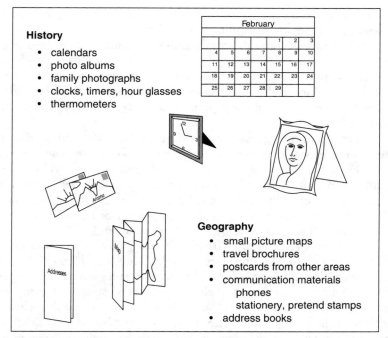

Figure 4.6 History and geography materials for the dramatic play area.

and costumes to act out their favorite stories, assigning parts and rehearsing their roles. Or they can write their own plays, put on puppet shows, or role-play problem situations.

Special Centers

A number of special areas are also required from time to time to foster social studies concepts. The grocery store is well known in kindergarten and first-grade classrooms. Other shops may come and go as children's interests and experiences suggest. Children could use a large packing crate, with a change of signs and the addition of curtains and a few appropriate props, to portray the post office, a card shop, a beauty or barber shop, a hardware store, a gasoline station, a drugstore, a toy shop, a laundromat, or a bank. These kinds of shops are useful only if the children have experienced them and are interested in re-creating the experience. Even if space permits, there is no need for these shops to become permanent additions to the room.

Library

A library area is more than a place to read books. It should be filled with color and beauty: growing plants, a dried-flower arrangement, a terrarium, prints, children's art. Here children can read by themselves or with a friend; they can curl up in a big, overstuffed chair or use a pillow on the floor.

To reinforce children's social studies experiences, you need to offer all types of books at all reading levels appropriate for children's use. Simple reference books, picture dictionaries and encyclopedias, books about various topics studied by the children—all are useful resources for children's social studies learning. Books that show the beauty of language, humor, security, suspense, and excitement are also appropriate.

Keep children interested by rotating the books, selecting those relevant to children's interests or experiences. Too many books at one time can be confusing. Display the books on a table, or arrange them on shelves so children can see the choices available. You can help children sharpen their thinking skills by providing several different books about the same topic (compare and contrast), two different versions of the same story (find similarities and differences), or two identical books (discuss and play riddles: "I see a picture of. . . " "What page am I on?").

The best-loved and most frequently read books in the library are those the children dictate or write themselves. Class booklets, in which children in the class contribute an illustration or a dictated or written story about a class trip, an experience, or a unit topic, give them the pleasure of cooperating in a group project while expressing and recording their ideas. Individually written booklets are also valuable additions to the library corner. The authors of these books grow in self-esteem as others read their books or as the teacher reads them to the class. Class scrapbooks, with photos of the children on a field trip, at work, or at play, are also useful library resources.

Books can be shelved in other areas of the classroom as well. In both the library area and other places in the room, some teachers separate books in plastic crates according to type. Biographies, nonfiction, fiction, concepts, and poetry are stored in separate containers. Some books are arranged in other centers. For example, Lynn Cohen, a teacher in New York, places a plastic container of books about building in the block area, spring books with art supplies to provide children with ideas for their construction, or Mother Goose and baby poem books in the housekeeping area to use to "read babies to sleep."

Writing

Social studies provide a point of departure for children to write and record their experiences and ideas (see Figure 4.7). Children can share their writings with others in the library area, with their parents, or with another class in the school (Schickedanz, 1999). If children's interest in writing lags, you might suggest that they dictate or write a story about how they think it would feel to go to the moon, what they saw on their latest field trip, how they would feel without a friend or about their friend, or some other topic.

In the kindergarten and primary grades, a writing area fosters children's written expression and records their ideas about social studies learning. A shelf set aside for writing materials in the library or art area is all the space that is required. You can provide a can of sharpened pencils; soft-tipped pens in a variety of colors; blank booklets (several sheets of paper stapled together); and an assortment of different

Teachers of primary-aged children can either make a journal for each child by stapling some paper together between cardboard covers or purchase a loose-leaf notebook for each child. Labeling these with children's names and storing them in a plastic bin, along with pencils, markers, and pens nearby, encourages children to record their experiences each day.

Teachers of younger children, those in kindergarten and preschool, also encourage journal writing. Younger children will probably use a combination of drawing and writing, scribbling, and invented spelling to record their experiences, thoughts, or feelings.

Make certain, however, that children do have something to record and are free to write in their journals during the day. Artificially setting a "journal time," when everyone in the class *must* sit and write in their journal, seems to destroy the spontaneity and the need to record only those things that are important and meaningful to children.

Figure 4.7   Journal writing.

sizes, shapes, and colors of paper. These supplies can be available to children who have a story to dictate, write, or draw. You might provide box dictionaries (boxes of cards with words that children can read), chart dictionaries (lists of words that might be needed during a special season or unit of study), and commercial dictionaries.

Art

Every social studies experience can be enhanced by re-creating it, giving it expression through an art activity. As children create, they share materials, sometimes work together in a group, take responsibility for cleanup, and help prepare the materials needed. They are learning and practicing social skills. The very act of creating is emotionally satisfying, for it lets children know they have power and control over materials and things. It is a safe, acceptable way of releasing feelings and expressing ideas.

Through art, children become acquainted with cultures other than their own. Observing paintings from Japan, touching pottery from Mexico, or examining a woven mat from the Philippines, children gain understanding of other cultures. "Who made this?" "How did they do it?" "Why did they make it?" "What does it mean to them?" are questions that might be asked.

An art center is really many different areas containing a variety of materials through which children can symbolize their knowledge and understanding as well as their values and attitudes. Every day, children need to find something with which to draw, paint, cut, paste, model, construct, sew, weave, or build. In addition to all of the materials readily available for children's use, one additional ingredient is required—experience. The secret ingredient in stimulating children's art production, in making it relevant as a learning tool for social studies, is experience. Without experience, children have no ideas to express through art. All of the social studies experiences—field trips, observations, interactions with others—stimulate children's art (Seefeldt, 1995).

The products of children's artistic expression also serve as a tool for learning. By displaying all of their work in a variety of ways, children have the opportunity to reflect on their experiences and learning. These displays also inform adults, school adminstrators, teachers, and parents about what children are learning and doing (Seefeldt, 2002).

Another type of art experience is possible. By sharing an object of art with children, you stimulate ideas for art while introducing them to the cultures of others. You might share a Mexican bark painting with the children, examining how it was made, who made it, and why. Primary-age children can then make their own bark paintings on brown wrapping paper or wooden planks. Many other ideas are appropriate for children in the primary grades:

- A piece of Inca or Pueblo pottery can lead children to finding out who made it and how these people lived, and to making pottery.
- An Oriental brush painting can give children ideas about using their brushes in new ways to achieve different effects.
- Puppets can be constructed to portray the first Thanksgiving, the discovery of America, or other historic events.
- A unit on Indian life can lead to replication of Indian designs and sign writing.
- A model of a farm, a factory, or an airport can be constructed with blocks or boxes.
- At Halloween, a story about masks can lead to making masks.
- Costumes made of brown paper bags and decorations can be constructed for plays and creative dramatics when children act out some historic event.
- Jewelry made of ceramic clay might replicate jewelry made by Mexicans, Spaniards, or American Indians.
- Hats and clothing similar to those worn in another country or time can be constructed.
- Rhythm instruments such as drums, bamboo sticks, and shakers can be constructed to duplicate those used by other peoples.

Drawing and Painting.   Because drawing and painting are symbolic processes, they are uniquely related to the social studies. As children draw and paint, they have the opportunity to clarify relationships among their social studies experiences and bring their own interpretation and imagination to them. Drawing and painting activities contribute to children's social skills by permitting them to communicate ideas, feelings, and experiences and to solve problems.

You can provide a variety of drawing tools. None requires much space, but the organization of the materials should remind children of their availability. A shelf, a tabletop, or even a windowsill can hold drawing materials. For ease of cleanup, each type of drawing tool should be kept in a separate container, either a clear type or one that is labeled with a symbol of the tool.

Easels, already set up, with cans of paint, brushes, and large newsprint stored nearby, are typical but not the only possible arrangement. If easels are not available in the classroom, any type, size, and color of paper; a can of brushes; and a six-pack of paints can serve as painting tools. Children can pick up their materials and begin to paint anywhere in the room or even in the hallway.

Commercial tempera paints are usually best suited for children's painting, for they provide a smooth, bright medium thick enough not to run or drip. An assortment of brushes—wide, rounded, and fine-pointed—can be provided.

Murals are often outcomes of children's social studies experiences. Kindergarten and preschool children do not understand the purpose of working together to create a group project; and even primary children, unless they have had plenty of prior experience, require some introduction to murals. The value of having children work together to create a project enjoyed by the entire class is worth any effort needed. In some fashion, divide the large brown paper used for murals, giving each child a section to paint. This permits children to work by themselves and with a group. After the class has enjoyed the mural, it can be cut apart, and children can take home their own paintings. You might suggest mural themes depicting some social studies topic—transportation, the firehouse, the farm—and each child can do something connected with the general theme.

Constructing. An assortment of odd pieces of junk, such as berry baskets, toilet-paper tubes, cookie containers and other types of boxes, ribbons, string, foil pie pans, and anything that will be discarded, fosters a wide range of creative responses to social studies concepts. Masking tape, hole punches, plastic-coated wires, and pipe cleaners are also helpful additions.

Once the children have joined boxes together with masking tape or wire, they can paint them with tempera that has had detergent or liquid starch added to it to allow it to adhere to a variety of surfaces. Or the entire structure can be covered with a thin layer of papier-mâché and left to dry. Once it's dry, the children can paint the piece with any type of paint.

Sewing and Weaving. Sewing and weaving are important aspects of many cultures. Once children have mastered the techniques of sewing and weaving, they can create banners, flags, mats, and clothing representative of these cultures.

Large, blunt needles and brightly colored yarns are ideal for beginning stitchery experiences. You will need to show children how to thread the yarn through the eye of the needle and how to make a knot in the end of the yarn. Usually, one or two of the children catch on very quickly and can help the other children with the threading and knotting task. The stitchery experience is much more successful if the sewing material is loosely woven. Plastic screening or berry baskets, net potato or onion bags, or burlap with a border of masking tape to stiffen it are useful materials for beginning sewers since the large needles and thick yarn slip easily through the mesh. Tightly woven material does not permit the large needle, threaded with thick yarn, to pass through it easily. Mounting the material to be stitched on an embroidery hoop or stiffening it in some other way is very helpful for young children, enabling them to hold the material more securely.

Primary-age children find an old-fashioned sewing box useful. This box may contain spools of thread, blunt scissors, buttons, fancy lace, patches, and a large sewing needle. Before using the sewing box, children should know how to use needles and scissors safely. A sewing kit allows children to make puppets, clothes for puppets and dolls, or clothing for a play or to mend other items.

Weaving is possible with a large variety of materials. First, children can begin the weaving process with paper. Later you might provide the cut paper and let the children weave with materials they have found during a field trip or nature walk. Once children learn the over-and-under pattern of weaving, they can use it to make decorations, wall hangings, mats, or items of clothing.

Woodworking.   Children have always delighted in the power and sensory pleasure of working with wood. Wood is solid, has weight, and takes up space; and real products can be created with it. A woodworking bench is not necessary for children to have experiences with wood. Any discarded stand, table, shelf, or solid wooden chair can become a woodworking bench with the addition of C-clamps, which hold the wood while children are working.

Tools—strong, sturdy, and real—can be mounted on a pegboard hanging on the wall or stored in a box if space is a problem. You can get softwood scraps from the local cabinet shop, from high school or college industrial arts programs, or from builders. As with other art materials, children progress through definite developmental levels when working with wood. The first experiences with wood are exploratory. Children pound nails into pieces of wood, not joining anything but enjoying the power and thrill of working with real materials. The next stage involves joining two pieces of wood together with no definite plan in mind; sometimes after the pieces have been joined, children will give names to their creations. The last stage involves making plans, deciding on materials to use, and completing the construction.

Many social studies concepts are reinforced as children work with wood. Primary children could work together in committees to build a product the class can use—a rabbit hutch, a shelf, a CD-player stand, or a playhouse—or they can re-create their observations of construction workers, cabinetmakers, or builders. If involved in purchasing the wood and wood supplies, they become consumers as well as producers. Woodworking might also stimulate interest in this type of career or in finding out how things are made and who makes them. Or they could use the skills they've gained working with wood to do other projects:

- Create a model of the Empire State Building with wood after reading *The Empire State Building* (Holland, 1998)
- Construct a dam after reading *Dams Give Us Power: A Building Block Book* (Hill, 1997b).

Cutting and Pasting.   Even the youngest children—who only cut, cut, and cut—enjoy cutting and pasting and making collages. Scissors that do cut, stored point down in a box, and an assortment of things to cut—paper, fabric, ribbons, yarns, gummed papers, felt, feathers—and glue and paste give children unlimited possibilities for re-creating their experiences.

Collage materials are more useful when they are stored by category. Keeping all of the feathers, sticks, pebbles, shells, ribbons, upholstery scraps, and toothpicks in their own boxes enables children to select the materials needed. Returning from a trip to the zoo, one group of kindergartners went directly to the box of rough-textured upholstery scraps and began creating the animals they had seen, with the exception of one child. He ignored the upholstery scraps, picked up the box of toothpicks, and re-created, with all the intricacies of spans and wires, the bridge they had crossed on the way.

Modeling.   Modeling activities are excellent for making objects, folk art, pottery, jewelry, or a character—animal or human—from a well-loved story. Preschool or primary children, without a background of experience with modeling materials, will need time to experiment with clay before actually creating any objects. Teachers may also need to introduce children to techniques of working with clay—such as slipping two pieces together—for children to make objects. When children examine clay products from other cultures or times, you might ask, "How do you think they made this point?" "Feel this seam. They must have joined it here." "What tools do you think they used to make this rough part?" These kinds of questions help children see possibilities for their own modeling work.

Water-based clay can be stored in any airtight container. If it dries, you can add water; and in a day or two it will return to its original pliable texture. Storing clay in fist-sized pieces and keeping it pliable and soft encourages children to use it. Plasticine, because of its oil base, will never completely dry out; however, it is not as pliable as other materials and may be more difficult for young children to handle. A set of oilcloth-covered boards, stored next to the clay container, allows children to take a piece of clay or dough and a board and work in any area of the room (Koster, 1999).

Vicarious Materials in the Classroom

Vicarious experiences cannot replace children's concrete experiences. Learning that results from vicarious experience is often inaccurate and incomplete. Nevertheless, until children can actually walk on the moon or go to a foreign country, they can learn something about these places from others. Looking at photographs, reading, or watching a movie about the moon, children learn something about the moon's nature. The wise use of audiovisual materials, bulletin boards, books, and pictures can help children (1) clarify concrete experiences, (2) refine their perceptions of these experiences, and (3) extend their meanings. A movie filmed during a trip to a bottle factory can be a useful tool for children's learning. Shown after their trip, it enables children to do several things:

- *Recall.*   "Do you remember what that was used for?" "What was the purpose of this tool?" "Let's watch the movie again to find out."
- *Focus.*   "When we see the video this time, be sure to look at how the bottles got into the box."
- *Clarify.*   "Let's check that idea when we watch the CD-ROM."

Then, too, concrete experiences seem to happen so quickly: the moth emerges from the cocoon, the snake sheds its skin, the lights are fixed, the telephone wires are spliced and back in their casing. Children have little opportunity to make accurate observations. Thus, vicarious experiences—a book on electricity, photographs of the telephone system, a movie showing in slow motion a moth emerging from a cocoon—enrich and extend children's actual experiences.

Careful selection of resources for vicarious experience is necessary. Deciding on the resources to use depends on the goals and objectives of social studies. You will want to choose whatever experiences help foster the children's attainment of your goals. Having determined that a specific resource might aid in fostering your goals and objectives, you can ask the following questions:

- How available is the resource? Materials that require mailing time or that are not handy when children's interests demand them are not useful.
- How costly is it? Can a natural material or real experience serve the same purpose less expensively?
- How easily can it be used? Finding space for projectors or changing rooms to see a movie, especially with young children, may require more time and effort than the film is worth.
- How does it fit in with the children's background of experiences? Does it fit logically and provide information on which to base future experiences?
- How will it be used to meet the needs of individual children? Not all resources are necessary for the total group; some might be selected for use with individual children or small groups.

Children's Literature

In today's whole language classroom, children's books are everywhere. For children to respond to literature in ways that are honest, personal, rich, and deep, the books they find in the library, dramatic play areas, science and math corners, and throughout the room must be of the highest quality possible. Only then will children be able to identify and become involved with the major characters of books, learning about people and places far from them (National Council for History Education, 1998). Libraries are very willing to lend teachers armloads of books for a month to 6 weeks at a time. Beautifully illustrated books are available at all reading levels to meet children's interest on any social studies topic.

The power of children's literature depends on the responses children bring to it. Having enjoyed listening to a story read by the teacher or another child or having read special books themselves, children can follow up on this pleasurable experience. To report on the books they have read or listened to, children might do these activities:

- Draw or paint a picture of the parts that they enjoyed most, that frightened them the most, or that were the most exciting.
- Make clay models of an animal, a character, or some object in the story.

The library area—a valuable resource for learning.

- Construct something that was made in the book or that the book was about.
- Act out the story with puppets or with other children.

Social studies textbooks may be useful as well. Instead of ordering one textbook for each child, it may be more valuable for you to have a few copies from each of several different textbook series. When textbooks from various series are available, children can select the book they need and find information about a particular topic or problem of interest to them.

Reference Materials

Feet propped up against the table and with a newspaper open, the 5-year-old boy clearly was trying on the role of father. Intrigued by anything that appears to be adult-like, young children find something appealing about using newspapers, magazines, and other reference materials. It makes them feel grown-up. Taking advantage of this natural interest, teachers can use newspapers and magazines as social resources.

You can gradually introduce the local newspaper to young children. Besides being a useful prop in the housekeeping area, it also contains information that children can use. Certain sections of the newspaper—the picture magazine, sports, or feature sections—are manageable for children.

Some newspapers or magazines are produced especially for children. You can subscribe to these for individual children or obtain a few copies for use by small groups of children. The value of these newspapers depends on how they are used. It is inappropriate to give an entire group of kindergarten or primary children the same paper and make them listen to an adult read it, for any reason. If you make these papers available as they pertain to topics of interest and as incidental resources, they might be useful. In the housekeeping area or on the library table, they can be used independently.

When you have determined that the children understand what constitutes news, you can begin to present articles from newspapers or magazines to teach them to understand individual stories or items. Perhaps beginning with the news story and pictures carried in the local paper, the news chart or board can be expanded to include news of the broader community and environment. You or the children can clip a news item from the paper, tell the class about it, and put it on the board. It is best to begin with local news of interest to the children. A story about and a picture of storm damage, the new shopping center, street repairs, or a new baby at the zoo can arouse children's interest in looking through the newspaper.

You can bring newspapers to the classroom for children to find items to share. First graders might be interested in analyzing the parts of a newspaper. Using several old papers, children could cut out different elements—headlines, news stories, news pictures, want ads, advertisements, weather maps, and comics.

Newspapers are not the only source of news for children. Television and radio are other major sources. To make television news useful for young children, you might do the following:

- Videotape a segment of a major news story to show to the children the next day. This lets them view and discuss current events that might not be available to them or that might be too long to hold their interest. A brief segment from a presidential inauguration, a space launch, or some event from another country would be interesting to children.
- Use a television in the preschool or primary grades so children can watch a segment of some special news event.
- Tape short portions of other events children could listen to. The Martin Luther King, Jr., "I Have a Dream" speech is an example.

As children become interested in the news and aware of current events, they will come into contact with controversial issues as well as tragic events. Some teachers omit all controversy or news of tragedies from the classroom, believing that young children are not mature enough to handle these. Others believe it not only impossible to protect children from these topics but unfair. Nearly every child watches a plane crash or other disaster on TV over and over again and observes grieving families. It would be unfair and untruthful not to discuss this event with children or at least recognize that, having witnessed the event, they may need help in processing and understanding it. Either way, teachers need to approach controversial and tragic events with caution (Levin, 2003).

Before including a news topic for study, assure yourself that the children do have the ability to discuss and explore it. Ask yourself:

- Do these children have the mental maturity necessary to work on this topic?
- What in their backgrounds would enable them to respond to it and understand it?
- Is the issue of real significance to the children? Is their interest high?

You also must be certain that you understand the issue, know its history, and can objectively analyze your own values and attitudes toward the issue. In addition, you will want to inform the parents of your plans to handle the topic with the children. You might ask parents to serve as resources, sharing information they know about the issue. Controversial topics can provide children with a focus for research, encouraging them to find additional information, analyze it, and reach their own conclusions. Watching television news shows and reading magazines and newspapers allow children to begin to build a concept of the importance of being informed citizens.

Audiovisual Resources

Many videos about places, people, and things of interest to children are readily available. As with other resources, you will need to select them carefully and use them with a specific purpose and objective in mind. Short videos, CDs, or portions of longer ones work best since young children cannot attend to vicarious information for long periods of time. If the content of a particular video is of interest to the children but the narration is too complex, you might show it with the sound off, letting the children tell the story in their own words, letting the pictures tell the story, or having the children make up the narration as they view the movie or video.

1. *Before viewing:* Preview any video you select before showing it to the children. You can then give the children a focus for viewing, asking questions or identifying things to look for or things to support their "I thought so's." You can ask the children to predict what they will see. Before the presentation is the time to clarify unfamiliar vocabulary and prepare children for viewing.

2. *During viewing:* Encourage children to talk with one another, ask questions, or make points while the video or movie is being shown. You may want to show it twice: the first time for viewing, the second for discussing; or once for listening and looking, another for looking and telling the story in children's own words. The single-loop film, which preschool-primary children can show without adult help, is useful for individualizing videos and fostering development of a single concept.

3. *After viewing:* A number of experiences can follow a video. Children might not want or need to follow the video with any activity; on the other hand, films often are used to stimulate discussion, ideas, or activities. Here are examples of follow-up experiences:

- Dramatic play, with props added to the play areas reflecting the theme of the video
- Books to read about the topic covered
- Art, music, and rhythm activities based on something seen in the video
- Further study of the topic by observing the environment and interviewing others

Remember, however, that techonolgy can never be the end of learning, only the servant of learning (Postman, 2000).

Video Clips, Slides, and Cameras

Video clips, slides, and cameras are sometimes more practical than videos are. Preschool and primary children can learn to use slide projectors and can view slides individually if the machines can be set up in a corner of the room.

An interesting way to discuss relationships or to solve problems of living with one another in a group is to use slides taken of the children while working and playing. Some slides might be used to illustrate the rules that are necessary when using wheel toys, the swing, or the slide. Others could be used to discuss how to settle arguments or to illustrate cooperative use of materials. All children enjoy seeing themselves, and slides will stimulate language use as well as help children see solutions to problems.

Cameras are perhaps even more useful in recording children's experiences. Digital cameras are especially useful. Prints of the photographs can be made for each child and family. Digital photos can be used on charts, to document children's learning, or to paste in individual books or a class scrapbook.

CD Players, Tape Recorders, and Television

CDs, used with or without a listening jack, are also available to reinforce children's social studies concepts. Some recordings offer children the opportunity to listen to the music of children from other countries or regions. Students might listen to folktales recorded by Native Americans, songs and music from Hawaii, the sound of African musical instruments, or the music of Appalachia. The value of this type of listening lies in children's responses: singing, dancing, making instruments, or recording their own folk songs.

Singing the folk songs of a culture, especially in the language in which they were written, children are transported in spirit to this culture and, in the process, feel a kinship with its people. Listening to music recorded in a particular culture serves the same purpose (Klein, Surback, & Moyer, 2003).

After the Communists overtook Hungary in the 1950s, Kodaly, a Hungarian philosopher and musician, created a national music curriculum. He believed that if the Hungarian people could sing and share the experience of their music, they would continue to be united and connected with their culture until they could once again experience freedom. During the Velvet Revolutions in Eastern Europe, as the Soviet Union was breaking up, a news program showed the Hungarian people in Freedom Square celebrating their freedom by singing the folk songs of their country. Listening to their national anthem and songs, one could only conclude that music can transmit a culture and hold people together (Seefeldt, 1993).

Tape recorders are readily available, inexpensive, and nearly childproof. Children can tape reports or interview school personnel or their parents. You might even tape the sounds of the children. A tape of the sounds of a factory, recorded during a field trip, lets children review and remember the trip. Taping stories the children love allows them to listen to them again and again. Some teachers use the tape recorder to leave messages for the children, such as a news item, a surprise that will happen during the day, or some directions to follow. Children can develop strong listening skills through use of a tape recorder.

Occasionally, a television program or a news show can be useful as a resource for children's listening. When some event will be televised—the visit of a king, the arrival of a new animal at the zoo, a space launch—a television could be placed in the classroom to allow the children to witness the event. Young children will want to listen and watch for only a brief time, just long enough to satisfy their curiosity.

Few television shows in their entirety are appropriate for viewing by young children. Investing 20 or 30 minutes in the vicarious experience of a television program is not an efficient use of time. However, children can be guided to view specific shows at home with their families to gain information about a specific topic, find out the meaning of a term, or just enjoy a program related to their interests.

Computers and CD-ROMs

Computers are now part of nearly every early childhood program. They are useful for developing computer literacy and introducing content. Numerous CD-ROMs are available for primary-age children to use as resources for social studies learning. They include encyclopedias as well as other reference materials. Many publishers are now releasing CD-ROMs that link with the Internet. An example is DR Multimedia's *The Jolly Post Office* (Wilson, 1997–1998), which can be used to promote computer literacy as well as teach content.

Developing Computer Literacy. Children are becoming competent in the use of the computer, just as they are learning to use tools such as the telephone and the television. Two skills are needed to develop computer literacy: learning how to turn the computer on and off and learning to type. Children can master these skills easily as they play with computers.

Children can master keyboard letter-matching tasks after a few weeks. Within 2 months, most children are easily able to select options from menus and read prompts related to the operation of particular programs. Even among different programs, the framework for using the computer is often similar. Within this meaningful context, children became adept at reading the language they needed to control a new environment.

Teaching Content. When programs are carefully selected to meet specific goals of the curriculum, computer-assisted instruction can increase achievement in vocabulary development, mathematics, and prosocial development (Hesse & Lane, 2003). If they know how to use technology, children and adults can create their own programs. By focusing on specific content, these programs give children the tools to publish their own books; practice skills; and publish on-line versions of their stories, drawings, and songs (Blagojevic, 2003).

Children are competent computer users.

Selecting Programs.   Software must be evaluated in the context of developmentally appropriate curriculum goals. In selecting computer programs, ask yourself the following:

1. Can more than one child use the program at a time?
2. How can I arrange the computer area to promote child-child interactions?
3. Will the program be used only for computer-assisted instruction of the practice, or rote learning, type? How does the program differ from typical workbooks or worksheets?
4. Is the program designed to develop high-order thinking skills such as judging, evaluating, analyzing, or synthesizing information?
5. Does the program require some action on the part of the child, such as drawing, moving things, or writing?

Additionally, you will want to examine the program for accuracy as well as for the values it presents. Some computer games emphasize war and violence and do not portray women and minorities in visual representations. You will want to consider the quality of the program in terms of color, sound or voice quality, animation, and other technical elements.

Packages are becoming available touching on every school subject, including the social studies. Teachers also have found they can adapt some computer games for classroom use. These programs have been integrated into the classroom in several ways:

- To introduce a new unit
- To offer enrichment

- As a reward
- To regulate the pace of individualized work
- To foster thinking skills

On-line Resources.   Many on-line resources can enrich young children's social studies learning. The program Journey North provides one example of units and theme learning available on the Internet. Other on-line resources put children in direct contact with other people in different parts of the country and the world. While building a knowledge base about others, these resources can challenge children to understand the lives of others more fully and to advocate for equality of opportunity for all (Berson, 2001).

On-line resources can provide needed information about a myriad of social studies topics. Some teachers routinely ask children to find information by accessing *http://www.ajkids.com*, where children can ask the virtual host, Jeeves, about any social studies topic.

Pictures

Pictures mounted on a bulletin board or available for children to handle, sort, feel, or carry with them as they play are a valuable social studies resource. You can use them to begin a discussion; as a take-off point for role or dramatic play; or to give information about people, places, or things far from the child's immediate environment. But the primary purpose of picture reading is to develop thinking skills. For pictures to be valuable, they must be read as thoughtfully as the printed page is read. When problem solving provides the motivation for reading pictures, children use them to discover clues about land forms and climate, economic development of an area, relationships of work to environment, cultural likenesses and differences, density of populations, characteristics of historical periods, and so on.

Children do not automatically learn to use pictures to solve problems in this manner. Young children should not even be asked to read pictures until their experiential background indicates readiness. Although most young children have had these experiences, it is important to begin with real objects and events before asking children to interpret the symbols of a picture or a photograph. Pictures are symbols that stand for some object or event; and children require many experiences in classifying, comparing, and contrasting real objects and events before they can interpret a picture representing them.

The first stage in picture reading involves naming the objects that appear. At the beginning level, ask questions that require children to name, list, or tell what they see in the picture. Unless children have had a great deal of experience with oral language and obtaining meaning from symbols, they cannot be expected to do more than simply name the objects that appear in a picture.

The next stage in picture reading is interpretive. Having mastered the ability to describe or name what is in the picture, children can then begin to interpret or discuss what is happening. This is followed by the ability to predict what might occur. Only after repeated experiences, increased maturity, language development, and a background of experience in creative thinking can young children use their imaginations to create a story when given a picture as a stimulus.

Teachers can ask questions to stimulate picture reading. Beginning questions revolve around knowledge: "What do you see?" Next, comprehension questions—"Why did this happen?"—seek to elicit a response that indicates an understanding of the conditions or trends included in the picture. Application questions demonstrate the use of an abstraction in a concrete situation: "What will he do?" These questions search for responses that demonstrate children's ability to identify elements, relationships, or organizational principles or the ability to put together elements and parts to form a whole that is not clearly identified in the picture: "Do you think he did the right thing?"

Not all children will see the same thing in a picture, nor will they interpret the picture in the same way. These differences in perception can lead to small-group discussions and later to critical, analytical thinking. Picture reading is not easy for children, and teachers sometimes become discouraged with the process and look for other methods that seem easier for both children and teacher. Work, effort, and repeated experiences with picture reading are required before the process is entirely successful. You do need to encourage children's development of picture-reading skills, accepting the level of skill they bring to the task and continuing to use pictures as a resource for learning.

Bulletin Boards and Displays

Bulletin boards and displays are one way for children to organize their thoughts and reflect on a social studies experience. By arranging materials on a table or creating a bulletin board, children have the opportunity to classify information, to find some way to record their ideas and experiences and label them (see Figure 4.8).

Set the stage for involving preschool and kindergarten children in constructing a display or bulletin board by asking each to make a contribution to the display. Popular topics might include a bulletin board titled "We Are in Kindergarten." Each child draws a self-portrait for the board, which is later labeled with the child's name and other information. Other boards might be "Ways We Travel," "Machines in School," "Clothes We Do Not Wear," or "Our Friends."

Primary-age children may take more responsibility for the boards and displays and will be better able to begin coordinating their work as members of small groups. They can select a theme and decide what will be included and how things will be displayed. Displays and boards might be created around themes of "Fire Fighters," "The Supermarket," and "Recycling in Our Neighborhood" to illustrate and explain content of interest or things that children have learned through some social studies experience.

Commercial Materials

Commercial kits and materials are available for teaching social studies concepts. Before investing in commercial kits, you will want to evaluate them:

A kindergarten class released 1,000 ladybugs in the class garden.
Two children painted pictures of the garden with hidden ladybugs.

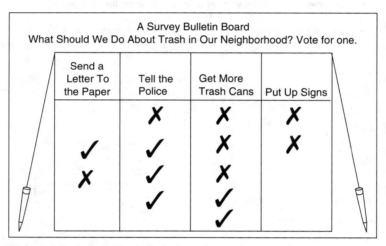

Figure 4.8 Interactive bulletin boards.

- Observe children using similar materials to get an accurate idea of how appropriate they will be.
- Talk with teachers who have used the materials to obtain other information about children's reactions to them. Ask if the children were able to use the materials independently, how interested they were, if the materials held their interest, how many ways the materials could be used, and if they helped to accomplish stated goals.
- Answer the question "What else is available that would accomplish the same purpose for less money?"

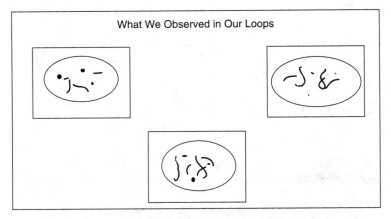

A class took yarn loops outside and observed what they found inside the loops when they placed them in different areas on the playground.

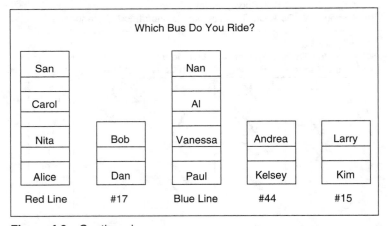

Figure 4.9   Continued.

FIELD WORK

In the lovely northern Italian city of Reggio Emilia, children in the city-run child-care centers leave their centers frequently, taking trips into their community. They run in the poppy fields, sit on the stone lions guarding a building in the town square, go to the supermarket, and walk in the rain. On these trips children observe, and they work. They measure, feel, compare and contrast, and keep records. Like teachers in Reggio Emilia, teachers in the United States have always valued taking children on excursions into the community. Field work and social studies seem to go together. Field work has many benefits:

- It extends children's knowledge of their environment, providing them with firsthand experiences that would not be possible to implement in a classroom.
- It acquaints the children with their immediate environment and orients them to it by developing concepts of direction, maps, and spaces.
- It provides contact with adult models in the social world, increasing children's knowledge of the world of work.
- It allows children to use scientific methods as they gather information, observe the environment, and draw conclusions.
- It unifies children, providing a common core of experience for them to play out, problem-solve, share, and discuss.
- It promotes parent involvement by taking children to visit one another's homes or the places where their parents work or by going to the same places they go with their parents. A field trip also involves parents as participants.
- It stimulates new ideas and new learning by enlivening children's interests and posing new questions that demand answers.

Types of Field Work

"There can be no general list of trips recommended for kindergarten or first grade. Each environment furnishes its own particular trips. Each school, each teacher, must find trips within his own environment which fit each group of children. Each year the trips fit into an integrated program" (Mitchell, 1934, p. 23).

It is up to the teacher to identify, locate, and evaluate the possibilities for field work within a community and to decide what type of work is best suited for the children. Lucy Sprague Mitchell would probably have chosen walking trips through children's immediate school and neighborhood environments. Other types—split-group, repeated, those for a specific purpose, and WOW trips (described later in the chapter)—can be taken as well.

Walking Trips

Perhaps the most valuable trips are walking field trips that can be taken once or twice a week in the school building, the school yard, or the neighborhood. There is much to see and learn within walking distance. These trips can be planned ahead by you or the children or can arise spontaneously as the children's interests dictate.

Split-Group Trips

Some trips will involve the total class, with the entire group visiting the library, the firehouse, or the florist. Other trips might involve a committee or a small group of children who are vitally interested in some specific place. Once children become accustomed to waiting their turn to go on a trip, and the trips are frequent, there is no difficulty in planning committee trips.

Repeated field trips help children assimilate knowledge.

With a volunteer adult, a committee can be sent to purchase a goldfish for the class or a soup bone to make "stone soup." Or the three children interested in engines can be allowed to go to the corner garage to observe a mechanic at work. On some total-group trips, the class can be divided into committees, with each having a specific purpose or a goal to fulfill. One group might be asked to investigate where the fire fighters sleep, another what they eat, and another to find out the answer to a question about fighting fires. On purchasing trips, each group of children can purchase a separate item.

Repeated Field Work

Why not return to a place? Children can gain from visiting the same place again, learning something new from each trip. Young children, excited about being away from their familiar classroom, often do not see everything or focus on the specific idea or purpose of the trip. Returning to the same place gives children a sense of mastery; being familiar with the place, they feel secure, competent, and safe enough to risk new learning.

Specific-Purpose Field Work

You can plan field work to fulfill specific purposes. A trip can be taken to observe all of the round things inside and outside the classroom, to record the sound that feet make on different materials in the building, or to find out the name of the street on which the school is located.

WOW Trips

Once or twice a year, perhaps as a culminating activity or a traditional school trip, you might plan a WOW experience, with all of the parents involved. Trips to the zoo or the circus and end-of-the-year picnics are WOW trips. These trips are relatively unimportant for children's learning; their value lies in involving parents and in providing the excitement of doing something new and different at school.

Planning Field Work

The longest, perhaps most important, part of field work includes the hours the teacher and the children spend getting ready for it. Just the thought of dealing with a group of young children away from the confines of the classroom can terrify an inexperienced teacher; yet once the teacher knows the group, this problem seems minor compared to the difficulty of planning meaningful trips: those that provide a continuity of experiences and field work for the children. In planning for valuable field work, you must do the following:

1. Survey the community to learn what is available, where places of interest are, whom to contact, and what places welcome children. One teacher discovered a broom factory, one of only a few still in existence in the country, just a block from the school. Another teacher made a card file of places of interest in the community, recording the telephone number, contact person, safety factors, and special things of interest for children.

2. Have a clear idea of the purpose of each trip. Writing a list of objectives for the trip helps you clarify the purpose and internalize your goals. Check the history, geography, and civic standards and select goals from those elements.

3. Attempt to provide continuity among and between trips. Education is a continuous experience, and field trips should ensure the continuity of that experience rather than interrupt it.

4. Think in terms of a simple field trip and work. The world is so confusing to the young child that a simple trip to help the children understand their world might be more valuable than a complicated one.

5. Use the children's play to direct your planning. Observing the children at play, you can note their interests as well as misconceptions that might be clarified with a trip. If children are interested in transportation, a trip to visit a gas station might be more appropriate than a trip to a zoo. A teacher can also observe what ideas need to be extended or enriched and can plan trips accordingly.

6. Make a survey of the children and their parents to find out places the children have already visited, things parents would like their children to see and do, or places the children would like to know more about.

7. Consider the time of day, week, and year. It is wise to take walking trips when the children are fresh—early in the day or after a nap. You can plan returns to coincide with snacktime, lunchtime, or rest periods. The weather and seasonal conditions will also affect the type of trip planned.

Before Field Work

Establish the goals and objectives for a trip and field work, and assure yourself that the trip will provide the children with a continuity of experience that is built on their backgrounds of interest and experience. You then begin the actual planning for the trip:

1. Visit the place first, checking for safety hazards, noting special needs for clothing or supervision, checking bathroom facilities, and confirming arrangements with the contact person.

2. Notify the parents that their children are leaving the school building. A blanket statement, given at the beginning of the year in a handbook or at a parents' meeting, can inform parents that their children will be going on many walking trips. Notices can still be sent home informing parents about the exact nature of the trip; however, they need to know that some trips will be spontaneous—walking in the rain, finding ice puddles, or looking for the rainbow. For more involved trips, permission slips prepared according to the dictates of the school board will need to be sent home, signed, and returned.

3. Discuss the trip with the children. Ask children what they know about where they are going. Record their answers. Have children list things they want to know while on the trip. Write their questions on a chart. Later you can cut the questions into strips and give one to each child to ask while on the trip.

4. Provide the children with a background of experiences. Stories, props for play, video clips, pictures, or slides of the place to be visited give children a foundation on which to build their new experiences.

5. Review simple safety rules with the children. Definite standards of behavior can be established for field trips. It is important to review these standards with the children as well as with the adults going on the trip. When adults and children are certain about what is expected of them, trips are safer. Some rules might be recorded on a chart.

6. The teacher will want to involve as many adults as necessary for a safe trip; plan for emergencies; and include supplies such as tissues, adhesive bandages, and drinkable water.

Field Work

The teacher must provide skillful and tactful guidance during the trip. The interest of the group will be somewhat restricted by the trip's location and activities, yet you may still need to focus children's attention on the goals of the trip and the work they have to do as well as keep them together as a group.

During the trip, you can do the following:

1. Encourage singing of marching songs to keep children together.
2. Repeat some of the safety rules: "Remember to stop at the corner." "Always stay on the sidewalk."
3. Follow a map, showing the children their present location, where they will turn, and how they will return to the school.
4. Tell the children again what they will see.
5. Let the children take their own time, observing things that are of interest to them, making discoveries, asking questions, and discussing the things they see.
6. Help the children to observe, identify, and recognize different things in the environment. Empty paper-towel or toilet-paper tubes were given to one group of

children on a nature field trip to use as field glasses or telescopes, which helped them focus on specific things in the environment.

7. Give children clipboards with assignments to complete. Divide the paper on the clipboard into four sections. For example, on a trip to a hardware store, the four spaces on the paper were labeled "Flowers," "Not Flowers," "Plant Food," "Tool." Children were instructed to write and draw a corresponding object.

8. Take the chart with the list of questions children decided to ask. Cut it up before the trip. On the trip, give a question to each child to ask. Have two children serve as recorders, writing the answer to the questions. Or the child who asks the question could also record the response on another sheet of paper on her clipboard.

9. Take pictures of the children or make tape recordings to use in the classroom for recall and discussion.

After the Trip

For very young children, the time immediately following a trip will be for resting and refreshment or some other relaxing activity. Young children may not be immediately ready to recall their experiences and may be too fatigued to react. Sometime later, you can provide follow-up activities, which increase the value of a field trip. Through these activities, children can reconstruct their experiences, use their memory, relate events to ideas, use language and creative expression, and become involved in dramatic play with others.

Discussions.   Some discussion of the trip and the work children did can take place. The children should have the opportunity to tell about their impressions of the trip and raise questions. They might dictate or write a thank-you letter or a story about the trip. You can use this time to help them clarify their ideas and concepts and recall their experience. "What do you think the scale was for?" "Why did the people wear uniforms?" "How many types of beans did we see?"

Play.   After a trip, you will want to add props to the housekeeping or play corner that will help the children act out their experiences. Pieces of hose after a trip to the fire station, gardening tools and equipment after a trip to the florist, and various hats and uniforms all encourage children to replay the trip.

Additional Experiences.   You can structure additional experiences to reinforce the goals and purposes of the trip. Often the trip is the stimulus for a unit or more complete study of a concept. Vicarious experiences such as reading stories, seeing movies, listening to a resource person, and viewing slides have more meaning after a trip.

Creative Expression.   You can provide opportunities for creative expression after a trip. Make blocks available for constructing and give the children paints, clay, and other materials for creating. Make books of the things you saw on the trip. Each child makes a page of the things that impressed him the most. These are stapled between two pages of construction paper and laminated. Music, dance, and dramatics are also encouraged.

Increasing Knowledge. Depending on the type of field trip taken and the goals of the trip, you can structure activities that will enable you to determine the effectiveness of the trip and to increase children's knowledge:

- A discussion of near and nearer, left and right, far and farthest will help children understand time-space relationships.
- You might construct bingo games using the words children have noted on the trip.
- You and the children can use riddles: "I'm thinking of something we saw on the trip. It was made of metal and was red and white."
- Play absurdity games: "I put my mail in the supermarket. What is wrong?"
- Follow the trip route on a map, using a toy car or model of a person.
- Give the children pictures of houses, stores, workers, or whatever they saw on the trip to play with and sort into categories.

SUMMARY

The world is available for children's learning. Become an astute observer of the environment and use all the resources you can find to foster children's learning. Children and their parents, as well as the school staff, can serve as resources for the social studies. The school building and the classroom provide children with many opportunities for learning social studies concepts.

The classroom should contain a quiet space for each child, sand and water, and centers of interest. The class should have centers for blocks, dramatic play, housekeeping, a library, writing materials, and a varied selection of art materials.

Other materials are also useful. You can select textbooks, children's literature, reference materials, audiovisual resources, computer programs, and pictures to foster specific concepts. Real objects aid in re-creating the natural environment and are vital to the social studies; things for children's manipulation and experimentation are best. You can also use bulletin boards, learning stations, and commercial materials as resources.

The field trip is the cornerstone of the social studies. You can plan several different types of field trips for the year. Children learn best through actual experiences, and these trips offer a rich resource for the social studies.

Extend Your Knowledge

1. Walk in and around a school building. List all of the possible resources for children's social studies found within the building and the block around it.
2. Make a floor plan of a primary classroom designed for children's learning. Include as many interest centers as space allows, but plan carefully for the arrangement of each.
3. Observe an activity or work time in a kindergarten and a primary classroom designed for open education. How do the activities differ in each room? List the

social studies experiences the children have during this time. How many skills, attitudes, and concepts do you see children using or reflecting?

4. Make a card file of children's literature that relates to history, geography, economics, or international education.

5. Begin a resource collection of your own. Include pictures and reference materials for yourself and for children's use. Begin to collect posters, photographs, and other materials you believe would be useful for teaching social studies.

Resources

The National Institute of Education (NIE) has a website, NIEOnline (*http://www.detnews.com.nie*), that offers teachers weekly lesson plans for children 5 to 7 years old. The plans revolve around using multiple forms of newspapers to foster literacy, mathematics, and other knowledge. Professional books offer teachers many ideas for integrated learning through the use of resources.

LET'S FIND OUT is a 32-issue, theme-based newsletter for young children that supports the early childhood curriculum and active learning projects. With accompanying mini-books and take-home activities, LET'S FIND OUT is a great introduction to newspapers. It is available in Spanish and English.

Website: *http://scholastic.com.classmag/let'sfind.htm*

Professional books offer many ideas for using childrens' here-and-now world as their learning environment:

The Power of Projects (Helms & Katz, 2003) describes how to plan projects based in children's here-and-now learning environment.

Early Learning Environments That Work (Isbell & Exelby, 2001) provides detailed descriptions of innovative, functional, and beautiful room arrangements.

Creating Rooms of Wonder (Seefeldt, 2002) provides teachers with suggestions for creating social studies dioramas and displaying children's work.

References

Barbour, N., Webster, T., & Drosdede, S. (1987). Sand: A resource for the language arts. *Young Children, 42*(2), 20–26.

Berson, M. J. (2001). Promoting civic action through online resources: An emphasis on global child advocacy. *International Journal of Social Education, 15*(2), 31–45.

Blagojevic, B. (2003). Funding technology: Does it make a difference? *Young Children, 58*(6), 28–34.

Bodrova, E., & Leong, D. J. (2003). Chopsticks and counting chips: Do play and foundational skills need to compete for the teacher's attention in an early childhood classroom? *Young Children, 58*(3), 10–17.

Froebel, F. (1887). *The education of man* (W. Hailman, Trans.). New York: Appleton.

Gorter-Reu, M. S., & Anderson, J. M. (1998). Home kits, home visits, and more! *Young Children, 54*(3), 71–80.

Helm, J. H., & Katz, L. (2001). *Young investigators: The project approach in the early years.* Washington, DC: National Association for the Education of Young Children.

Hesse, P., & Lane, F. (2003). Media literacy starts young: An integrated curriculum. *Young Children, 58*(6), 20–27.

Hewett, K. (2001). Blocks as a tool for learning: A historical and contemporary perspective. *Young Children, 56*(1), 6–12.

Hill, L. S. (1997a). *Canals are water roads.* New York: Carolrhoda.

Hill, L. S. (1997b). *Dams give us power: A building block book.* New York: Carolrhoda.

Hill, L. S. (2000). *Tunnels go underground: A building block book.* New York: Carolrhoda.

Holland, G. (1998). *The Empire State Building.* New York: Raintree/Steck Vaughn.

Isbell, R., & Exelby, B. (2001) *Early learning environments that work.* Beltsville, MD: Gryphon House.

Klein, A., Surback, E., & Moyer, J. (2003). Teaching across cultures in an international seminar. *Childhood Education, 79,* 340–346.

Koster, J. B. (1999). Clay for little fingers. *Young Children, 54*(2), 18–22.

Levin, D. E. (2003) *Teaching young children in violent times: Building a peaceable classroom* (2nd ed.). Cambridge, MA: Educators for Social Responsibility; Washington, DC: National Association for the Education of Young Children.

Lewis, K. , & Cartwright, R. (2001). *The lot at the end of my block.* New York: Hyperion.

Martin, B. (1969). *Brown bear, brown bear.* New York: Holt, Rinehart, & Winston.

Mitchell, L. S. (1934). *Young geographers.* New York: Bank Street College.

Moriarty, R. F. (2002). Helping teachers develop as facilitators of three- to five-year-olds' science inquiry. *Young Children, 57,* 20–25.

National Council for History Education. (1998). *NCHE recommendations.* Westlake, OH: Author.

Piaget, J., & Inhelder, B. (1969). *The psychology of the child.* New York: Basic Books.

Postman, N. (2000). Will our children inherit only the wind? *Theory and Research in Social Education, 28,* 580–586.

Pratt, C. (1948). *I learn from children.* New York: Harper & Row.

Schickedanz, J. (1999). *Much more than the ABC's.* Washington, DC: National Association for the Education of Young Children.

Seefeldt, C. (1993). Learning for freedom. *Young Children, 48*(3), 4–10.

Seefeldt, C. (1995). Art—A serious work. *Young Children, 50*(3), 39–66.

Seefeldt, C. (2002). *Creating rooms of wonder.* Beltsville, MD: Gryphon House.

Seefeldt, C., & Denton, K. (1997). The family as a resource for learning. In S. S. Beck and B. Hatcher (Eds.), *Learning outside of school* (2nd ed., pp. 81–89). Olney, MD: Association for Childhood Education International.

Seefeldt, C., & Goldsmith, N. (1998). Family night out: A new way to involve low-income parents. Here's how. *Elementary School Principal, 16*(4), 1–4.

Steitzer, U. (1995). *Building an igloo.* New York: Holt.

Vukelich, C. (1990). Where's the paper? Literacy during dramatic play. *Childhood Education, 66*(4), 205–210.

Vygotsky, L. (1986). *Thought and language* (Rev. ed.). Cambridge, MA: MIT Press.

Wilson, L. (1997–1998). Technology in the classroom: Testing the water before surfing. *Childhood Education, 74,* 116–117.

PART TWO

THE PROCESSES OF SOCIAL STUDIES

CHAPTER 5

Self, Others, and the Community: Social Skills

The development of social competence is a central feature of preschool programs, and research suggests its importance to later school success.

National Research Council, 2001, p. 185

After you read this chapter, you should be prepared to respond to the following questions:

- How do behavioral, Freudian, and social-cognitive theories explain the development and growth of social skills?
- What factors affect social development?
- Why is children's sense of self—their self-concept—important to the development of social skills?
- How do schools foster children's self-concept?
- What skills are involved in prosocial behaviors?
- How do children make and keep friends?

Thumb in mouth, Shawn stands watching Scott, Carol, and Ann build with the blocks. Taking his thumb from his mouth, he asks, "Can I play?"

"No! Only us can build with blocks."

Shawn sighs, then sits at a table and watches a group of children pasting pictures into scrapbooks.

"I'm the mother," Claress informs the group playing in the housekeeping corner. She then proceeds to direct the children in their play until, one by one, they leave and find something else to do.

"Andrea, Andrea," the girls call, "come and play store with us."

Smiling and nodding, Andrea takes Marcia by the hand and joins the others, saying, "Marcia's going to play with us too, okay?"

Young children enter an early childhood classroom with a wide range of social skills. But once in a classroom, they face the daunting task of learning to relate effectively with adults and children, most of whom are strangers. Not only are new and perhaps different social skills required, but children will be asked to give up some of their individuality for the good of others and the group.

Nevertheless, children will learn necessary skills, attitudes, and values as they live. The small democracy of the early childhood program is designed to support and foster social skills and knowledge children need not only to participate in democracy but to continue to work to change and improve that democracy in the future. In the democratic society of the classroom, social skills are fostered daily as teachers plan opportunities for children to interact with one another, lead and follow, select leaders, vote, and resolve their own conflicts (Bronson, 2000).

Valued and respected within the democracy of an early childhood program, children, in turn, are able to respect others, both those who are similar to themselves and those who differ. The rights of the individual are continually balanced with those of the group. Freedom of speech and thought are fostered. Dissenting voices, even when in the minority, are respected. Children are expected and taught to assume responsibility for themselves and participate to the fullest extent possible in the working of the group.

The entire early childhood program and curriculum are designed to foster children's social skills; but the skills that enhance children's abilities to learn, make decisions, and develop as competent, self-directed citizens are more meaningful and useful when developed within the context of the social studies (National Council for the Social Studies, 1998). Through the social studies, children form the foundation of a healthy self-concept, developing the skills of communicating, sharing, cooperating, and participating in a social group.

SOCIAL SKILLS DEVELOP

Differences in the ability to relate with others depend in part on children's maturity. Although most 3- and 4-year-olds are moving from parallel play to beginning associative play and can manage one playmate at a time, others prefer solitary play and are not yet ready to relate to others. By age 5, children generally have developed a special friend and will be able to visit this friend on their own. By the time children are 6 or 7, most can take turns, negotiate, and cooperate to keep play going; and they begin to form peer groups.

THEORIES OF SOCIALIZATION

Children enter the preschool-primary classroom with a wide range of social development and skills. Researchers have advanced a number of theories to explain why children differ in their ability to relate effectively with others. Among them are behavioral theories, those based on Freudian psychology, Erikson's theory, and more current social-cognitive theories (Bronson, 2000).

Behavioral Theories

Behavioral theory has its roots in the philosophy of John Locke (1690), who believed that children arrived in the world as blank slates. By educating a child through a series of rewards and punishments, adults wrote on the slate.

Historically, behaviorists have believed that learning comes about because a person receives a reward, or reinforcement, for an action or a correct response (Skinner, 1974). Children are conditioned by a series of stimuli and responses, and learning results from the conditioning provided by adults and the environment. Children learn from having their needs satisfied—or not satisfied—by another person or environmental factors. When a child's behavior is followed by something pleasant or some type of reward or reinforcement, the child will repeat the behavior. If a child's behavior is followed by something unpleasant or ignored, the behavior will eventually disappear.

Using the idea that reinforced social behaviors will increase, teachers make certain that children's interactions with other children are positive and rewarding. Teachers arrange the room with sufficient materials to enable children to interact pleasantly, without being frustrated by lack of space or materials. Children are praised and reinforced for prosocial behaviors. A child who shares or cooperates and is praised will continue to share and cooperate.

On the other hand, behaviors can be extinguished. Inappropriate or undesirable social behaviors can be eliminated simply by ignoring them, although sometimes this is a difficult task. For example, many 4-year-old children like to spit. The child who is spit on screams and cries; the adults admonish or punish the spitter. This serves the

The entire program is designed to foster children's self-concept and social skills.

same function as attention; thus, the child spits again. When teachers ignore the spitter and focus their attention on the child who received the abuse, they open the possibility of eliminating the antisocial behavior.

Not all social behaviors are learned through a series of stimuli and responses. Behaviorists' studies have shown that children also learn social and antisocial behaviors by observing models. The models may be their teachers or parents as well as the media. By observing people, cartoon characters, or actors receiving rewards for aggressive behaviors, children will model and repeat these behaviors. When prosocial behaviors are observed, these, too, will be modeled and imitated.

By studying the theories and practices of behaviorists, teachers can learn to reinforce children's positive social skills and foster their development. On the other hand, behaviorist techniques are useful in eliminating undesired behaviors. Teachers using these techniques, however, must realize that they are controlling children externally. Children still will need to develop their own internal controls for their behavior.

Freudian Theory

Sigmund Freud's (1949) theories were basically concerned with emotion, motivation, and personality development. He believed that children possess human sexual energy, which is invested in different ways as they grow and develop.

According to Freud, an infant possesses three basic drives: the sexual drive, survival instincts, and the drive of destructiveness. He defined three structures to explain a person's personality. The id is the instinctive structure that infants possess and that drives them to seek satisfaction. As they come into conflict with reality as they grow and develop, the ego, or rational part of the being, emerges. Finally, the superego, or moral or ethical part of the being, is developed.

Freud believed that children go through distinct developmental stages. The particular stages called psychosexual stages reflect the development of gratification zones. The oral stage (first year of life) reflects the infant's need for gratification from the mouth. An infant's eating, sucking, spitting, and chewing are not only a need to satisfy hunger but also provide pleasure. The anal stage (second to third year) reflects the toddler's need of gratification from the rectal area. The phallic stage (fourth and fifth years) reflects the preschooler's source of gratification from the genital area. The latency stage (middle childhood) reflects a repression of sexuality, which ends during the preadolescent years at the start of puberty. During the genital stage (teenage years), the adolescent develops a mature sexuality and love relationship, which derives its primary source of pleasure from the genital area.

As the needs at each stage are gratified, the child moves on to the next developmental stage. Freud maintained that if too much or too little gratification occurs at any stage, the person becomes fixated at that stage. He asserted that the reasons for different personality problems such as alcoholism, depression, compulsiveness, overaggression, and promiscuity are the result of a person's fixation at one of the stages.

Erikson's Theory

A follower of Freud, Erik Erikson (1963) developed a theory focusing on the ego and what it means for human development. Like Freud, Erikson believed that each stage of life is characterized by a central problem. Unlike Freud, however, he saw these crises as psychosocial rather than psychosexual. The stages result from social interaction instead of being the product of conflict between inner drives and the need to develop a superego.

Erikson theorized that there are eight psychosocial stages, each of which has a negative and a positive trait:

1. Basic trust versus basic mistrust
2. Autonomy versus shame and doubt
3. Initiative versus guilt
4. Industry versus inferiority

5. Identity versus role confusion
6. Intimacy versus isolation
7. Generativity versus stagnation
8. Ego integrity versus despair

Each of the eight positive psychosocial strengths exists at all eight stages and is related to the others. However, each strength has a critical period for development, and there is a proper sequence to the stages. For a child to develop in a normal pattern of behavior, the positive attribute of the stage needs to be satisfied at the critical period before the next stage is developed. The person's development from a trusting infant to an old man or woman with ego integrity depends on the successful integration of all the stages.

The stages most pertinent for early childhood educators are basic trust versus mistrust, autonomy versus shame, initiative versus guilt, and industry versus inferiority.

Basic Trust

For basic trust to develop, infants between birth and 18 months of age must gradually develop a sense of inner goodness because they feel assured of an outer predictability. The environment must provide consistency, continuity, and sameness of experiences (Copple, 2003; Marshall, 2001). Without this security, children develop a basic mistrust and hostility toward others and the world.

Autonomy

Between 19 months and 3 years of age, toddlers develop a sense of autonomy. As they start to walk, they develop a desire to let go as well as a need to hold on. Children begin to develop a sense of self and pride in their achievements. If they are shamed because of their attempts at letting go and their experiments with the world, they develop a sense of shame about themselves and self-doubt as they function in the world.

Initiative

At the age of 3 or 4, a new stage, initiative, unfolds. At this stage, children can undertake and plan their own activities and do them in cooperation with other children. If the adult world does not offer proper regulations, children may undertake more than they can achieve, thus developing a sense of guilt or failure. On the other hand, if the adult world doesn't permit them to practice developing skills, children live with a sense of failure.

Industry

From 6 years of age until puberty, children develop a sense of industry. At this stage, they become producers of things and users of tools, not the least being reading, writ-

Initiative unfolds—children plan their own activities in cooperation with others.

ing, and mathematics. Children become socially adept as they work beside and with others. One problem that can occur in this stage is that children may develop a sense of inadequacy in using the tools of their world or see themselves as inferior to others. Another danger is overworking so that the child becomes a "conformist or thoughtless slave of his technique" (Erikson, 1963, p. 247).

Social-Cognitive Theories

Children are whole beings. They cannot be divided into parts for physical, intellectual, social, or emotional growth. Social-cognitive theories recognize this wholeness. Its adherents see social-emotional growth parallel to, or even the same as, intellectual growth.

A basic principle of social-cognitive theories is that what happens in one area of growth or development affects other areas (Bronson, 2000). Children who can't make friends, cooperate, or share have difficulty in a group. Unable to relate with others or to make friends, these children may also have difficulty focusing on schoolwork. Likewise, children who have trouble learning may also have difficulty developing social skills. And it's well accepted that emotional problems—perhaps anxiety, learned helplessness, or insecurities—can affect children's ability to learn and achieve.

A child's social behavior is considered within the context of cognitive maturity. A 3-year-old who is scribbling away on a piece of paper continues scribbling with the marker on a neighbor child. The child is not punished because a 3-year-old cannot yet cognitively differentiate that others are not objects but have feelings like herself. Rather, the teacher attempts to teach the child, saying, "Color on your paper," showing her the paper and saying, "Color here. Do not color on other children." By evaluating children's social behavior in terms of cognition, teachers have a better understanding of what they can and cannot expect children to do at any given age.

Another principle of social cognition is the idea that the individual is in charge of his or her own learning. Although growth stems from the interaction of maturation and experience, the individual must construct social knowledge. Stimulating children to think about social relations and offering them suggestions to enable them to construct knowledge of social skills are viewed as important.

With this framework, teachers guide children to talk about social situations or problems and help them come up with their own solutions. Instead of offering solutions to a child who grabs a toy from another ("Use your words instead of grabbing so she'll know what you want") or offering alternative solutions ("Give her a turn now"), the idea is to develop children's skill in thinking of solutions for themselves. There is no recrimination. Shaming or blaming children for behavior isn't acceptable in a democratic classroom.

Spivack and Shure (1978) developed the cognitive approach to interpersonal problem solving. Inherent in this approach is the assumption that the ability to think clearly paves the way for emotional relief and healthy social adjustment. When children have problems relating socially, teachers ask them what happened, how they felt in the situation, what they did, and what other ways they could act in similar situations. In addition to the scripted learning experiences that form their program, Spivack and Shure maintain that the dialogues teachers have with children informally and in connection with ongoing events are even more important in developing children's social skills.

FACTORS AFFECTING SOCIAL DEVELOPMENT

Children's development of social skills is affected by the nature of their family and early educational experiences (NRC, 2001). Whether in a nuclear, blended, or extended family; a communal arrangement; or a single-parent family, the child learns social patterns and skills within this context. Children find love and security and form attachments with people who protect and care for them.

In the family, children become socialized through interactions with parents, siblings, relatives, and neighbors; once in a school setting, they need new ways of acting, relating, and socializing. Children who have had a strong attachment to a nurturing figure and see themselves as separate from this nurturing figure are ready for a group situation. Children who have not fully developed strong attachments to another person may have a more difficult time adjusting to the complexity of the social system of the school.

The Family

Children who experience the security of loving parents and have strong attachments to their parents are better able to reach out to relate with others. According to attachment theory, children who enjoy a secure attachment relationship with their parents and caregivers use this relationship as a support to venture out and explore their environment (Maccoby, 1993). They reach out to others, return to the caregiver for support, and venture out again, going further into the world of social relationships (Ainsworth et al., 1978). As the child confidently wanders out to test the social waters, he enlarges his social world, expands his social contacts, and is more likely to learn from experience in social interaction.

Parents who are social themselves serve as models for their children. Children may be able to use the image of their parents interacting with others in their own attempts to make and be friends with other children or to cooperate and share. Socially competent parents may affect their children's social skill development in another way. Parents who are secure and competent offer children a model of security from which to build their own social skills.

The nature of parent-child interactions is also related to a child's development of social skills. Children who are raised in democratic families, where reasons are given along with the rules, are more likely to be socially active and open-minded. Such parents explain, "No hitting. If you ask her for the truck instead of hitting, she'll give it to you," or "We always say thank you to someone who does something for you," or "In church, we sit quietly during the sermon so others can hear. If you want to, you can write in your notebook or take a puzzle with you so you don't disturb the others." These parents are more likely to have children who cooperate, share, and initiate social activities.

On the other hand, parents who are more authoritarian, who demand obedient, conforming, and dependent offspring, may have children who are never really comfortable exploring the world for themselves. Often, these children fail to develop the ability to relate effectively with others throughout their life (Dorsey, 2003).

Gender differences play a role as well. In one study, fathers' negative attitudes toward child rearing predicted behavior problems in children (DeKlyen et al., 1998). Fathers' warmth and control have also been related to better academic achievement for children, and interactions with nonpaternal men can result in more prosocial behaviors toward peers (Coley, 1998).

Role of Culture

The characteristics of culture also affect children's developing social skills (Wardle, 2001). Teachers who take the time to observe and know the culture and community in which children live are better able to build on its strengths or work to mediate its potential negative effects on children's social development.

Children who live in violent or unsafe communities may be fearful and withdrawn when in the classroom. Those exposed to domestic abuse, gang violence, and petty or not-so-petty criminals do not feel safe or secure. Their feelings of insecurity will interfere with their total development, especially social skills development.

Children who experience violence in their community will need to find the following in the preschool-primary classrooms (Gross & Clemens, 2002; Slaby et al., 1995; Wallach, 1995):

- Meaningful relationships with caring and knowledgeable adults
- Schedules and environment that are as consistent as possible

- Structure and very clear expectations and limits
- Many opportunities to express themselves safely in play, art, and stories and storytelling

All of us are affected socially and emotionally by violence, wars, threats of wars, and terrorism (Avery et al., 1999). During these frightening, sad, and uncertain times, even children who live in relatively safe environments are exposed to a great deal of violence.

Some children and their families have been directly and deeply affected by war and terrorism. Even children with no direct contact with war, however, can be deeply affected. Children who witness violence or have been personally affected by violence will express their needs, grief, fears, apprehensions, and thoughts in different ways (Rosen, Rahay, & Rosenbaum, 2003). Some may withdraw, become irritable, or stop eating or sleeping; others may act out. It's important for teachers to take their cues from the child. Support each child as an individual while providing all children with the following (NAEYC, 2001):

- Make sure routines are kept, that children know and can depend on the structure of the day.
- Accept children's feelings and behviors with support and acceptance.
- Find ways for children to express themselves, whether through outdoor play, running, drawing, painting, building, or telling stories.

Many children view far too much violence on TV or in games, toys, stories, and other media. In schools throughout the nation you can observe children acting out the violence they observe: playing war or superhero and acting aggressively.

Teachers have found a number of ways to help children and their parents cope with the prevalence of violence in children's lives. Teachers and parents discuss the problems of children's exposure to media violence and work to change the media (NAEYC, 2001). They also work with children to do the following:

- They develop the concept of real and not real by informing children about which stories, movies, and television shows are "real" and which are not. They then ask children to determine which shows or movies are factual and which are fantasy.
- They foster the development of critical viewing skills for evaluating media violence.
- They reduce television viewing.
- They ensure that children watch more prosocial television programs.

Role of the School

Once children are in a school setting, other factors affect their social development (Berk, 2001; NRC & IM, 2000). In addition to a child's parents and family, the teacher becomes an agent of socialization. Now the teacher and perhaps the principal set rules, limits, and standards for behavior. Other children also become models, setting new or different standards for social behaviors.

Children model violence they observe.

Entrance into the school society can be difficult for young children (Seefeldt, Galper, & Denton, 1998). Leaving home, unsure of how to manage interactions with this new socializer and with other children, preschool-primary students can find school a miserable experience at first. Many transition techniques have been designed and implemented to ease children's entrance into school. Some schools encourage parents to stay with their children for part or all of the first few days to let the children know they are not being totally deserted. Some schools begin by inviting a small group of children on the first day and adding another four or five each day until the total group has been integrated. This approach allows children to get used to relating to small groups and become familiar with the school and the new social situation before the entire group is present. Home visits by the teacher or school visits by parent and child help ease possible stress.

The dichotomy of socialization—developing a strong sense of individuality while learning to become a member of a group—is ever-present in school. Children must retain their individuality, yet they must give it up by putting the welfare and interest of the group before their own. At school, they find they must share not only materials, toys, and time but also the attention of the teacher. Here they learn to cooperate, see others' viewpoints, and work together for the common welfare.

The school's role during these early years is twofold. First, school experiences must focus on strengthening the child's self-concept and feelings of individuality. Children who feel good about themselves can make the difficult, complex adjustments necessary for group living. Having aided the child's development of self-esteem, the school then uses this strong sense of self as the basis for guiding children into positive group experiences where they can learn the skills necessary for living in a society.

In the school, the focus on social skill development is threefold, revolving around the development of the following:

1. *Self-concept*. Children's feelings about themselves are the foundation from which they learn to relate to and communicate with others.
2. *Prosocial skills*. Being able to cooperate and share are necessary for forming solid relationships with others.
3. *Making and keeping friends*. Children who relate to and communicate with others, sharing and cooperating, are those who are accepted by their peers and can make and keep friends.

SELF-CONCEPT

"I'm not big now, but I'm growing. I can ride a bike and run and jump and skip, and next year I'll learn to read, too," answers Domingo when asked to tell about himself. Domingo's answer reveals his attitude about himself—not very big but growing, an "I can do" attitude, and an attitude that says, "I will grow, I will learn, I can do it!"

Self-esteem, self-identity, and self-concept—educators use these terms to denote the totality of meanings, feelings, and attitudes that children maintain about themselves. *Self-concept* refers to cognitive activity: children's awareness of their own characteristics and of likenesses and differences between themselves and others (Marsh, Craven, & Debus, 1998). *Self-esteem* refers to children's regard for and feelings about themselves. *Self-identity* has a social connotation; it includes awareness of group membership.

Whatever definition or terminology they use, scholars have long recognized the importance of feelings of self-esteem in human behavior. As a theoretical construct, the self has been an object of interest since the 17th century, when René Descartes (1646) first discussed the cogito, or self, as a thinking substance. Throughout the ages, prominent theorists and researchers have recognized the importance of feelings of self-esteem in human behavior. Theories of Sigmund Freud (1949), Carl Rogers (1961), Abraham Maslow (1969), and others have been directed toward understanding the conduct of human beings by examining the feelings and beliefs that individuals hold about themselves.

The theories of these scholars differ greatly. However, amid the diversity, some assumptions are basic to all theories of self. One assumption is that self-esteem begins to be established early in life and is modified and shaped by the children's succession of experiences with significant people in their environment. Another assumption present in all theories of self is that self-esteem has a predictable effect on behavior. The theories also hold that self-concept, self-esteem, or self-identity is multifaceted: children's self-concepts about their social, academic, physical, and other facets may differ (Marsh et al., 1998).

Finally, theories of the self generally agree that an early childhood program can foster children's self-esteem and build the foundation for future relationships with others (NICHD Early Childcare Research Network, 1998). Teachers can structure the classroom and respond to children in ways that contribute to their feelings of general identity, their physical and academic self-competence.

General Identity: Names

People's names make them unique (see Figure 5.1). Using children's names in the classroom fosters their sense of esteem. When you use a child's name, you are saying, "I know you, and I respect you." Teachers may encourage children not only to call one another by name but also to use the names of teachers, volunteers, and assistants. In this way, children learn that each person is an important individual and that each is different from the other.

"I can't say my last name, but I can show it to you," says Michael, leading the teacher to a piece of plaid fabric, mounted and framed. "My last name begins with *Mc*, and that's my sign." First names come naturally to the children and teacher, yet you do not want to neglect children's family names. Children might, as Michael did, find out the history of their last names, the places on the map where the names originated, or what they mean.

Very young children might be encouraged to learn their parents' first names. Understanding that their mothers and fathers have their own names helps children see their parents as people in their own right. In the classroom, you might do the following:

- Use children's names in songs, and substitute their names in stories, poems, and games.
- Write the children's names on objects that belong to them.
- Make up news stories using the children's names: "Susan has new shoes. They are brown."
- Purchase a stamp pad and rubber stamps with the children's names individually imprinted on each. Children just learning to read their names enjoy these stamps.
- Place two stacks of name cards on the game table for the children to play with. Children can sort through them and find their own name, all the names they can read, or any names that are alike. Depending on their age, they can classify the name cards according to boys, girls, friends, or initial or final sounds.
- Take snapshots of the children, and mount them on cards with their names. As the children become familiar with the pictures and names, cut the names from the cards. Then the children can match the names with the pictures.
- Make bulletin boards using children's names. One might be, "We are in kindergarten. There are 15 children," with the children's self-portraits and names below.
- Make a name picture book. Place a photo of each child on a page. Then the child or you writes her name under the photo and a sentence about what she likes.

Do's

1. Recognize the differences in names among Vietnamese, Cambodian, Hmong, and Laotian children.
2. Learn to pronounce their names clearly, correctly, and in the Southeast Asian way. For example, Nguyen Van Thu is pronounced "wen van tu" (Vietnamese). Sok Phoung is pronounced "sawk poong" (Cambodian).
3. Teach children to write their names in the American way.
4. Respect the "special" quality of given names.
5. Recognize that the family name is placed first as an emphasis of a person's roots.
6. Determine if the family has chosen to "Americanize" the use of the family name. If so, call the child by his or her preferred name.
7. Respect the child's choice of name.

Don'ts

1. Assume all Southeast Asian names are used in the same way.
2. Call a child "Nguyen," "Chan," or "Sourivong," as it is improper to address a child by the family name.
3. Neglect to show children the differences in writing names in the American and Southeast Asian ways.
4. Treat names as unimportant.
5. Minimize the importance placed on the family's roots.
6. Assume that all Southeast Asians will prefer the use of their given name only. Instead of being called Mr. Van, the father may want to be called Mr. Nguyen.
7. Change the name in an effort to Anglicize it. For example, don't call Vinh Vinnie or Nhung Nancy.

Figure 5.1   What's in a Southeast Asian name?

Source: From "What's in a Name? In Particular, a Southeast Asian Name?" by Robert D. Morrow, 1991, *Young Children, 44*(6), p. 23. Copyright 1991 by National Association for the Education of Young Children. Reprinted by permission.

The Physical Self

Children, as physical beings, have attitudes about themselves involving their physical body. How that body moves and interacts with objects, how children think they look, the kinds of skills their bodies can do—all influence self-esteem. Self-awareness is thought to originate when infants begin to discover themselves and their environment by flinging their hands about and learning what is part of their bodies and what is not. Sensations of cold, hunger, and warmth all work together to help infants learn about body and self. During the entire sensorimotor period, children use their bodies to learn about themselves and their world.

Recognize the importance of children's physical selves to the development of self-esteem:

- Take many photos of children for scrapbooks, bulletin boards, or gifts.
- Talk about differences in skin color. The California Tomorrow Project (1999) recommends obtaining paint chips and having children find chips that match their skin color. Children can be taught that they have different skin colors because of different amounts of melanin inside their bodies.
- Provide all kinds of mirrors for children to use—full-length, hand, magnifying—and give children feedback as they look at themselves: "You have dark brown eyes." "Look at your shoulders." "Where are your eyebrows?"
- Keep records of children's height and weight. Cash-register tapes or long strips of paper, exactly the heights of the children, help them see how tall they are. Make certain you are sensitive to children who are taller or smaller than others.
- Measure other parts of the body, such as hands, feet, ears, thumbs, and noses, with arbitrary measures such as hands and feet.
- Make a graph with children's names on one axis and skin, hair, or eye color on the other. Discuss differences in skin, hair, and eye color.
- Play games that emphasize body parts—Looby Loo or Simon Says.
- Provide large- and small-muscle equipment for children to climb in, through, over, or under and to manipulate with their fingers and hands.
- Make booklets or charts of things children can do. A booklet called *I Can Run* could begin with the main sentence "I can run," which then serves as the basis for other pages in the book: "I can run quickly; I can run slowly or angrily or happily," and so forth. Children can illustrate each page. Similar books could be titled *I Can Jump, I Can Bend* or *Climb* or *Stretch* or *Hop* and so on.

A vital part of the child's physical self is gender. As children mature, they become aware of sexual differences. This awareness is often apparent in frank discussions while using the bathroom or in detailed drawings of self. A confident and aware teacher treats discussions and questions with respect and is ready to help clear up misconceptions (Chrisman & Couchenour, 2002).

Teachers and parents must recognize the importance of sexuality and its relationship to children's positive or negative feelings about themselves (National PTA, 2002). Adults working with children should use proper names for genitals, talk frankly about the differences between boys and girls, and encourage children to take on the roles and feelings of others during sociodramatic play.

Adult attitudes toward sexuality are important to children's self-esteem. For many adults, the topic of sexuality produces guilt and anxiety as well as positive feelings. Adults who infer in subtle ways that certain behaviors are bad may create anxiety or shame in the child. Positive feelings are aided by a teacher who understands and accepts the child's sexuality.

Gendered cultures develop during the preschool years (Gunnar, 2003). Promoting unbiased attitudes and values toward gender and gender roles requires you, the teacher, to examine your values and prejudices. Women's movements have made our nation aware of society's part in assigning rigid gender roles early in life. For example, the statement "He's all boy" reinforces behavior in boys that would not be tolerated in girls. You can help children become aware of their own sexuality without assigning them stereotyped gender roles:

- Be certain that the block, woodworking, and wheel-toy areas do not become boys' centers and the housekeeping area a girls' center.
- Dismiss or call together children with red shoes, blue socks, buckle shoes, zipper jackets, green eyes, and so forth, rather than dividing the group by boys and girls.
- Provide male and female models in a variety of job situations.
- Ask the boys to help clean up, cook, wash tables, and do other tasks often stereotyped as women's work.
- Find stories to read portraying men and women in various occupations not assigned by gender role.
- Challenge children when they make statements such as "Boys can't do that" or "That's not for girls" by giving information and facts to correct their stereotyped thinking.

Self-Efficacy

Crucial to children's self-esteem is the belief that they are capable individuals who can set goals for themselves and achieve them. Children can have good concepts of self and realistic self-esteem yet not be able to succeed in school or life because they lack the ability to believe that they are capable (Bandura, 1997). Self-efficacy, like self-concept and self-esteem, is highly related to children's later academic and social success. Children who know they can learn to read and write are those who are able to set goals for their learning and, if they fail, to try again. Schools provide children with many opportunities to experiment with ideas and materials and time to gain some kind of mastery.

You can help children perceive themselves as learners and enhance their self-efficacy through activities such as the following:

• Provide toddlers and very young children with equipment they can handle by themselves. Low coat hooks and small tables and chairs permit the youngest child to achieve some sense of mastery over self and the world. Juice can be prepared in small pitchers so 3-year-olds can fill their own glasses. In the bathroom, small fixtures and towels and soap placed within children's reach help them be in control. Children feel they are competent when they can care for their own needs.

• Allow kindergarten and primary-grade children to continue developing a sense of mastery and self-control by encouraging them to master mechanical things, includ-

Self-efficacious children know they can do and learn.

ing the record player, the slide projector, or the filmstrip projector. Learning to use the computer also fosters children's sense of competence.

• Expand primary-grade children's understanding of the world. As children learn to read and gain information through books and other written materials, knowledge of their immediate environment, obtained through field trips and direct experiences, is expanded to knowledge of the larger community and the world.

• Provide plenty of raw materials. Raw materials force children to do the following:
  • Set a goal. "What will I do with this?"
  • Make plans to achieve their goal. "I'll tape these two pieces together."
  • Monitor their progress toward achieving their goal. "That didn't work; I'll try. . ."
  • Experience the feelings of joy and pleasure that come from achieving a goal. "I did it. I knew I could."

Assessing Self-Concept, Self-Esteem, and Self-Efficacy

As you do with any other skill, you want to assess children's growing self-esteem. Standardized tests designed to assess self-concept are available. But even if you use a standardized measure, you will still want to assess children's growth through in the following ways:

1. *Observation.*   Observing children, you can record how well they are (a) working with others, (b) entering into group play, (c) trying new activities, and (d) growing in their overall ability to relate to others.

2. *Interview*.   Children enjoy talking about themselves. A few questions, such as "What makes you smile?" "How do you feel when . . . ?" "Who are your best friends?" "What makes you angry?" "What will you do when you grow up?" "What do you do when you can do anything you want to?" will give you insight into children's self-concepts.

3. *Self-reports*.   Helping children make self-evaluations is another way of estimating self-concept. You might help children make booklets titled *Things I Learned in Kindergarten, Things I Need to Learn, My Best Subjects Are. . . , I Need to Work Harder On. . .* Other booklets or creative writing might be titled *My Three Wishes, Things I Do Not Like, My Angry Book,* A *Book of Me,* or *My Family.*

RELATING TO OTHERS

With a strong sense of self, children are ready to learn to live in a group. Basic to living with others is the ability to communicate.

People live in a community by virtue of the things they have in common. Communication is the way through which people come to possess things in common. Without communication to ensure that participants have a common understanding to secure similar emotional and intellectual dispositions, there could be no community, no group with which to relate (Dewey, 1944, p. 4). Certainly, the ability to communicate, verbally or nonverbally, is essential before children can learn the social skills required of them to live in a group. Dewey believed that social life was identical to communication.

Communicating

Not all communication is verbal. Like adults, young children are quick to read the meaning of touching, gestures, smiles, sounds, facial expressions, and ways of moving. "Don't be scared," one second-grader told another on the way to the engineer's room. No one had said a word about being frightened of the experience, yet one child sensed fear of a new experience in the other by reading nonverbal signals.

Communication, however, is not always easy. With limited language ability and background of experiences, young children have trouble communicating verbally. Communication also demands the ability to put one's self into the role of another. Effective communication, and hence social relationships, depends on children's ability to see how another person feels and to take into account the other's needs.

Researchers have long studied how and when children learn to consider the ideas, feelings, or emotions of others. John Flavell's (1979) early work suggests that understanding the thoughts of others requires (1) an understanding that there is a perspective other than one's own—that not everyone sees, thinks, or feels alike; (2) a realization that an analysis of the other's perspective might be useful; (3) the ability to carry out the analysis needed; (4) a way of keeping in mind what is learned from the analysis; and (5) knowledge of how to translate the results of analysis into effective social behavior—that is, in terms of getting along better with the person whose viewpoint is under consideration.

By age 3, children seem to understand that other people are happy at parties but can be sad at other times (Lillard & Currenton, 2003). Four-year-olds and even some 3-year-olds can participate in dramatic play in which they take on the roles of others (see Figure 5.2). Everyone familiar with young children has observed them acting like parents, doctors, teachers, horses, babies, or firefighters. This type of play is particularly valuable. It helps children to understand their world, sort out the roles they observe, and understand how they fit into the scheme of things. Dramatic play that occurs spontaneously and without interference from an adult is perhaps the best way for children to learn to see the viewpoints of others, eventually learning to take on the roles of others.

Dramatic play is a highly symbolic and cognitive as well as social activity (Bodrova & Leong, 2003). By taking on the roles of others, children become less egocentric. They use language and symbols and hold images in their minds for long periods of time, acting as if the blocks were trucks, the boards were streets, or the boxes were tables. Dramatic play's involvement of other children makes it valuable in strengthening social skills.

Creative dramatics offer children yet another opportunity to learn the skills involved in taking on the roles of others (Bodrova & Leong, 2003; Rowland, 2002). In

---

Teachers Nell Ishee and Jeanne Goldhaber have a special bin for books that lend themselves to children's playacting. In this bin, kept near the area where children act out stories, are

Assorted Versions of Traditional Folk Stories

"The Three Little Pigs"

"The Three Billy Goats Gruff"

"Stone Soup"

"Old Mother Hubbard"

Other Books

Caps for Sale (by Esphyr Slobodkina, 1940, New York: HarperCollins)

The Carrot Seed (by Ruth Krauss, 1945, New York: HarperCollins)

In the Night Kitchen (by Maurice Sendak, 1970, New York: HarperCollins)

The Runaway Bunny (by Margaret Wise Brown, 1942, New York: HarperCollins)

Figure 5.2   Stories for reenactment.

creative dramatics, children act out, by themselves or with others, the role of another person, animal, or thing. In the preschool-primary classroom, creative dramatics begins with rhythmic activities: children act like leaves or snowflakes or move like animals. Pantomime is another beginning step in creative dramatics and role playing. Without using words, children can show the group how to do something they do at home, at the beach, in a store, or at school and let the group decide what the action represents.

With rhythmic and pantomime activities serving as a base, children can be asked to act out nursery rhymes or entire stories. Younger children need something that has parts for all. "Humpty Dumpty," "Jack and Jill," or "Little Nancy Etticoat" are excellent for beginners. One child can be Humpty Dumpty, and all the others can be the king's horses and the king's men. All the children can act out the parts of either Jack or Jill while the rhyme is being read, and all can become Nancy Etticoat.

Children in kindergarten or the primary grades can wait to take turns or act as the audience. The folktales "The Three Billy Goats Gruff," "Goldilocks," and "The Three Pigs" are good beginnings for creative dramatics, but many other stories are appropriate for children to act out. Eventually, children learn the process of taking on the role of another as they mature and grow.

Children's growth in role-taking ability is related to their cognitive growth and general maturity. Direct teaching of role taking is not effective for preschool-primary children. But children can be given experiences that will provide them with opportunities to practice and develop role-playing skills. You can help children grow in taking on the roles of others by using the following strategies:

- Ask children to imagine how someone else feels, to speculate: "How do you think Roberto felt when you called him that?" "How would you feel?" "Have you ever had someone say something to you that hurt you?"
- Help children to connect their own feelings with the things they are involved in, with things that happen to them: "How did you feel when . . . ?" "Why were you angry?" "Did it make you feel good when . . . ?"
- Communicate to the children your understanding of the context of children's experiences, what children are feeling and the reasons for it: "You feel very angry now because you didn't get to paint." "You're happy because your block building is tall and sturdy." "You feel sad because they didn't ask you to help them with the house."

Role play is a technique that can be used to help children take on the view of another. As children role-play, they have a chance to gain insights into the feelings of others, think about alternatives for action, and explore the consequences of their actions.

Children can be given what-if problems and situations to act out. Young children have great difficulty placing themselves in unfamiliar roles or in roles of others. Their egocentricity does not allow them to see another's point of view; therefore, all what-if problems should be real and related to children's own experiences. You might say: "Nancy, what if Steve took your car while you were looking for a place to park it?

Steve, you pretend to take the car; Nancy, what would you do? What other ways could you act?"

Here are some other kinds of questions you might ask children about real situations: "What if you are waiting for your turn on the slide and someone pushes ahead of you?" "What if you want to play in the housekeeping area, but children there say no, you can't come in?" "What if there is only one wagon, but two children want to ride in it?"

Effective communication demands the ability to receive and produce language. Once children have some verbal skills, communication becomes easier. Parents and teachers of young children often remark how much easier and pleasanter it is to work and live with preschool children once the children can express their needs, wants, and ideas verbally and understand the language spoken to them. Once children have language, they no longer need to hit, bite, scream, or cry to communicate with others. Once they can express ideas and communicate through language, many frustrations are eliminated. Language is a useful, safe, and effective way to communicate feelings, ideas, and thoughts.

Listening and Speaking

Listening is a major way in which children learn language. Listening skills, so essential to learning to communicate with others, are critical for all learning. Once children can listen to others, they can begin to see others' viewpoints, learn from others, and expand their world.

Most often, young children's listening experiences will result from their interactions with others, based on their activities and mutual explorations. If children are asked to listen to others, you should make certain they are comfortable, that outside distractions are kept to a minimum, and that the activity or speech is interesting to listen to.

Almost every school experience involves listening. In relation to social studies, children will listen to records, stories, and visitors to the class as well as to one another. The classroom provides occasions for individual children to speak in front of a group. When a 5-year-old loses a tooth, prepares to move to another school, or creates a lovely painting, that child will want to tell the entire group about the experience. These speaking and listening experiences gradually evolve into group discussions.

In one first-grade classroom, a teacher instituted a community meeting. The goal of the community meetings was to create a community in which children lived and worked together, taking the perspectives of each other and embracing diverse viewpoints. Usually the children chose the topic. One hot topic was taking turns. Another time a group of children had a difficult time accepting the small parts they had in a play and wanted to talk about how children were given parts. Sometimes, however, the teacher selected the topic.

Group discussions are not easy for young children. Their ability to listen and attend to a topic while in a group and then offer their opinions about the topic cannot be rushed. Gradually, children will learn the process of holding and continuing a group discussion. Teachers can help children develop this ability by using statements that guide discussion:

- "Sekai, we are talking about the crane operator now. Can you save your book till later?" or something similar to keep the discussion focused on a topic.
- "Roberta, you were talking about your trip. Next, you can tell us what you did at Betty's house," to prompt children to keep track of what they were talking about.
- "Let Bettina finish what she is saying; then we'll listen to you," to encourage children to listen.
- "Speak a bit louder so everyone can hear you," or "Tell us again what you saw on your trip," to help the child who is speaking to hold the attention of the audience.

Perhaps the most pleasant listening and speaking experiences revolve around children's literature. Listening to a good book read by the teacher, a parent, or an older child is one of the most pleasurable experiences a child can have, and one that can teach children social skills. Many social studies books are available, some beautifully illustrated, that tell children about the past, places far away, or their personal lives and experiences. It would be difficult not to find books specifically suited for any group of children.

When you read books to individual children or small groups, you have opportunities to recognize the ideas of each child, talk about the illustrations, ask and answer questions, go back and read a favorite page one more time, or even skip less-interesting parts and go on. Children can chime in, singing the repetitive phrases, reciting the last line, or telling their version of the ending. You can use stories to stimulate children's interest in a topic, for information, or for summing up a topic or a unit. Stories can be read before nap, after lunch, during activity time, or during a regularly scheduled story time that is planned each day and occurs without fail. During this time, children, stretched out on the floor or clustered around the teacher, enjoy the group experience of listening to a story. One teacher calls this time "belly and book time" because his group of 4-year-olds usually stretches out on their stomachs.

Reading and Writing

Just as social studies provides ample opportunities for promoting children's listening and speaking skills, it also provides a medium for children's reading and writing. One first-grade class, troubled by a few children who bullied and teased the others, used a language-experience approach to help solve the problem (Froschl & Sprung, 1999). The teacher began by giving children time and space to talk about teasing and bullying. She used books such as Taro Yashima's (1995) *Crow Boy* as a discussion point. Afterward, the children wrote experience charts: "I feel welcome when . . . ." and "I feel unwelcome when . . . ." Together teacher and students developed classroom rules. As the children discussed the merits of various rules, the teacher listed those that the group had decided to keep.

Children can use writing and reading in connection with social studies in hundreds of ways. Children who are just learning to read and write can express their ideas through invented spelling and drawings:

- Drawings are a precursor to children's narrative compostion. Children who have not fully mastered the linguistic code can express their ideas through artwork coupled with discussions and short, teacher-written messages to augment their drawings (Coufal & Coufal, 2002).
- Practice writing as part of dramatic play. Provide crayons, receipt books, calendars, note pads, and envelopes for children's play. Watch children's play interests. If they are interested in travel play, add tickets and luggage tags. If they play store, add grocery lists, play money, and checkbooks with markers.
- Encourage children to talk about their work and watch as their words are recorded.
- Include many opportunities to draw. Drawing is probably the single most important activity that assists both writing and reading development as well as understanding of others (Schiller, 1995; Seefeldt, 2000).

Children who are 4 and 5 years old can do the following:

- Dictate and illustrate booklets and stories about their experiences. Children might make booklets about the things they saw on a field trip to a popular clothing store, what they know about shearing sheep after watching a shearing, or what they learned during their trip to the post office.
- Tell about their paintings and drawings, watching as the teacher writes their words.
- Dictate letters to firefighters or other community workers, either asking questions or thanking them for a visit.
- Ask the teacher for labels for their buildings, gardens, or other group projects.
- Dictate and record plans for a party or other celebration.
- Dictate their thoughts, ideas, or concerns about a social situation or some other important event in their school.

Children older than age 5 can use reading and writing to do these activities:

- Follow the news.
- Plan and produce their own class newsletter.
- Vote for the name to be given the hamster, the foods that will be shared at a party, or what games will be played.
- Write their own history books and read the books and writings of others about the present and past.

Sharing

Learning to communicate is, in part, learning to share. To communicate, children must share their ideas, take turns talking and listening, and share their time and interest. Learning to share is an important goal of preschool-primary education; the welfare of society depends on the willingness of its members to share.

Children do need to share resources—toys, blocks, materials, equipment—in the preschool-primary classroom. They also need to share the teacher's attention. As children mature, they begin to share in the life of the school, planting gardens, cleaning up the playground, putting on a school play, or decorating the hallway. All these activities encourage children's development of group social responsibilities, resulting in later participation in voting, government, and the concerns of the community and the world.

Everyone finds sharing a little difficult and uncomfortable at first. Each must give up some personal ideas, material, or time, sacrificing something for the good of others. Children have shared with their family and with those in the neighborhood; but once in school, they find they must participate in many other types of sharing and share on a larger scale. When children are part of very large groups, it sometimes seems as if they are called on to share constantly and are never able to have their own needs or desires fulfilled. Their ability to share is closely tied to their total development, especially their social development (McConnell, 2000). As children mature, their ability to share increases. In fact, sharing is a sign of maturity in our culture.

Researchers have identified levels in children's development of understanding what others feel, want, and know:

Level 0 (about age 3 to 7).   Children are aware that other people think differently but either insist "I can't read his mind" or blithely assume that people in the same situation have the same point of view. Even 3-year-olds have some understanding of another's point of view. For instance, studies show that children as young as 18 months are aware that others' desires might differ from their own (Harris, 1989).

Level 1 (about age 6 to 8).   Children realize that two people may see the same situation differently. They become increasingly interested in other people's inner, psychological life (Lillard & Currenton, 2003).

Level 2 (about age 7 to 12).   Now children realize that another person can think about what they are thinking and tune in on their thought processes.

Level 3 (about age 10 to 15).   The child can now think about two different viewpoints simultaneously and sees how one influences the other. Children can step back from a two-person relationship and watch how they and another person interact from the viewpoint of a third party.

Level 4 (age 12 to 15).   Children can now understand the role of society and the usefulness of social conventions.

The ability to share does depend on the development of role taking, but it also involves being able to read other people's emotions. Children have to learn the difference between joy and sadness, anger and happiness, and pain and pleasure in others.

Children seem better able to identify others' emotions in familiar rather than unfamiliar situations. For instance, children are better able to identify the happiness or unhappiness of children at a birthday party than the emotions of people at a summit meeting.

As a rule, children under the age of 4 do not understand motives or intentional acts. They assume that all behavior is intentional, even the actions of inanimate ob-

Children share resources as they work and play together.

jects. Between the ages of 5 and 6, children will begin to distinguish between unintended and intended acts. They gradually become able to differentiate between intentional acts and accidents. Up to the age of 7, children focus on concrete, observable characteristics; by the age of 8, they can begin to focus on abstract traits such as emotions, personality, or abilities.

Fostering Sharing Behaviors

More sharing takes place in classrooms where there is a feeling of security, a model present who shares, an abundance of materials and equipment, and where sharing is taught.

Security

If children feel secure, and if they have enough for themselves, they are better able to share with others. Thus, you need to establish a classroom atmosphere of security. Insecure children are not ready to accept the social techniques of sharing. With young children, small groups with high teacher or adult ratios seem to foster children's ability to share. Small groups allow the following:

• *More teacher-child interaction.* Teachers who have too many children to interact with are frustrated and short-tempered and do not have time to give children the personal attention that says, "You're valued and respected" and "I care for you."

• *Increased recognition.* Children can share their ideas and thoughts more readily; they have more opportunities to take lunch money to the cafeteria, carry the flag, have their story read, play the game the way they want to, or lead the entire group in a song.

• *Feelings of social adequacy.*   Young children just learning to relate to others can find handling relationships with many other children a monumental task. But with only a few others, children feel more adequate and competent in their ability to relate.

• *Consideration of the group context.*   A shy, withdrawn child may feel more secure and able to reach out to others when in a quiet group of children rather than an assertive, aggressive group. Likewise, highly aggressive children may find more security and social acceptance when in a more boisterous group (Stormshak et al., 1999).

Models

Children who observe models sharing appear to be better able to share, and the teacher is the best model. When the teacher is noticeably spontaneous, warm, and responsive, the children show many more sympathetic responses than they do in a group in which the teacher tends to be hard-boiled and unsympathetic to children in distress. Teachers who deliberately try to develop warm friendships with children and who respond freely and openly to children's needs have children who participate more freely in group activities. These children also have higher leadership scores and show more evidence of sharing than do children of teachers who make little or no effort to work closely with individuals or who participate as little as possible in the activities of the group. Conversely, when teachers react negatively to children's antisocial behaviors or enter into conflict with them, children appear to be more aggressive as well as more withdrawn (Birch & Ladd, 1998).

Physical Environment

Children confined in small play spaces with limited equipment and toys are more frequently observed fighting than are those in larger play spaces with an adequate number of materials. With plenty of space and equipment, sharing becomes easier.

You can arrange an environment conducive to sharing even if space is not available. Placing the equipment so that it is readily accessible to children, selecting some things to place on tables, and providing other materials on open shelves invite children to use and share the available materials rather than focus on a single piece of equipment or have to hunt for toys.

Direct Teaching

Teachers teach, and among the things they teach children are the social skills involved in sharing. You can use direct teaching in connection with children's play and social interactions. Children can be taught skills by directed doll play, by practice in solving conflicts over toys, or through direct statements made as they are playing: "We do it this way in school," or "Take two more turns, and then it's Aletha's turn."

Explicit coaching may be helpful, particularly when teaching children to include others with special needs. Successful coaching techniques include the following:

- Clarify the concepts and behaviors that need to be addressed, such as the idea that hitting will not solve the problem.
- Discuss the idea and the behavior with children, and ask them to think about alternative ways for relating with others.
- Practice social skills through role play with others.
- Coach children in the use of concepts and behaviors in real situations (Gillies, 2000).
- Eliminate competitive activities or games. Children exhibit more cooperative behavior when engaging in noncompetitive games or activities (Finlinson, Austin, & Pfister, 2000).

Books are useful when teaching children prosocial behaviors. For example, after reading Aliki's (1987) *We Are Best Friends*, in which a boy makes new friends, the teacher can engage children in discussions of how they could make new friends. One second-grade teacher asked each child to write a personal letter to a friend.

Miriam Cohen's (1998) *It's George*—the story of a boy who is not appreciated by other first graders until he becomes a hero—illustrates a number of ways to make friends.

Cooperating

Cooperating is another skill useful for living in a society. In order to cooperate, children must sometimes give up or share something and become less egocentric—less concerned about themselves and more concerned about the welfare of the group. Adults understand that cooperation is a necessity for the welfare of any society. Chil-

Cooperative behaviors develop as children mature.

dren, especially young children, need guidance and support in learning to cooperate; they must learn to balance the task of developing a strong sense of self with that of learning to become a member of a group.

Cooperative behaviors, like sharing behaviors, develop as children mature. The more social experiences children have had, the better their ability to cooperate. The same kinds of factors that influence sharing behaviors also influence children's ability to cooperate.

Reinforcement

Reinforcing cooperative behavior seems to work. Weingold and Webster (1964) asked two groups of children to work on a mural project. In one group, each child was rewarded for the group product. In the other group, children were told that only the child doing the best job would receive a reward. In the first group, the researchers saw an increase in friendly, cooperative behavior and peer interest. This group's product was also judged to be complete and creative. The latter group worked less on the product and demonstrated more boasting and deprecating behaviors. Weingold and Webster reinforced cooperative behaviors in children and found that these behaviors continued, but cooperating behaviors decreased in those who were punished for not cooperating or ignored when they cooperated.

School Size

The size of the group influences the type of cooperative behavior among both teachers and children. In one study, large centers demonstrated more need for control, scheduled routines, and greater rigidity among adults. Teachers in the larger centers were less free to foster the warm, accepting relationships among children so necessary for both cooperation and sharing (Beaty, 1999).

Competition

Cooperation is the opposite of competition. In many classrooms, competition is fostered because of the belief that it is good for children and consistent with the beliefs of our society. This belief is false. Although competition is natural, teachers try to eliminate it whenever possible. Compemtion has been related to negative social behaviors (Finlinson et al., 2000), destroys group cooperation, and is especially damaging to young children's self-identity as a part of a group.

To encourage cooperation, you need to reduce competition by (1) playing games that do not have winners and losers, (2) remembering that children are individuals, (3) asking all children to take part in special tasks, and (4) complimenting all the children frequently.

Making and Having Friends

"What was the best thing that ever happened to you?" a counselor asked a group of teenagers with disabilities. "One time," replied one of the young women, "I had a friend."

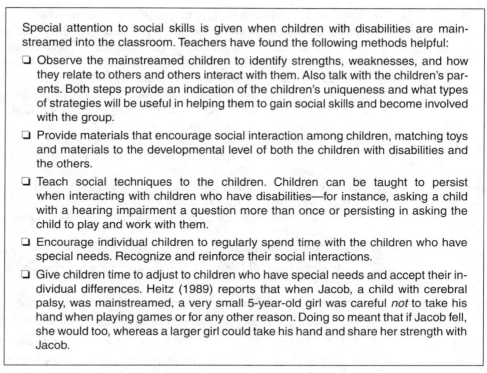

Special attention to social skills is given when children with disabilities are main-streamed into the classroom. Teachers have found the following methods helpful:

❏ Observe the mainstreamed children to identify strengths, weaknesses, and how they relate to others and others interact with them. Also talk with the children's parents. Both steps provide an indication of the children's uniqueness and what types of strategies will be useful in helping them to gain social skills and become involved with the group.

❏ Provide materials that encourage social interaction among children, matching toys and materials to the developmental level of both the children with disabilities and the others.

❏ Teach social techniques to the children. Children can be taught to persist when interacting with children who have disabilities—for instance, asking a child with a hearing impairment a question more than once or persisting in asking the child to play and work with them.

❏ Encourage individual children to regularly spend time with the children who have special needs. Recognize and reinforce their social interactions.

❏ Give children time to adjust to children who have special needs and accept their individual differences. Heitz (1989) reports that when Jacob, a child with cerebral palsy, was mainstreamed, a very small 5-year-old girl was careful *not* to take his hand when playing games or for any other reason. Doing so meant that if Jacob fell, she would too, whereas a larger girl could take his hand and share her strength with Jacob.

Figure 5.3   Helping disabled children make friends.

Everyone wants and needs to have a friend. For young children, having friends and being accepted by peers are critical to their development of a positive self-concept and prosocial skills and are related to academic achievement (see Figure 5.3). Children with friends have many advantages:

- They are accepted by their peers (Bost et al.,1999).
- They seem to adjust more easily to school (Ladd, 1990; Ladd, Kochenderfer, & Coleman, 1997).
- They have fewer adjustment difficulties when teenagers (Parker & Asher, 1987).
- They are better adjusted emotionally and have fewer mental health problems (Parker & Asher, 1987).
- They seem to have higher achievement scores than do children without one or more friends (Diehl et al., 1998)

Making friends is related to other social skills (Dunn, Cutting, & Fisher, 2002). It's hard to say which comes first—social skills or friends. Nevertheless, children who can cooperate and share and who can communicate effectively with others seem to be able to make and keep friends. Children who can cooperate seem to be better accepted by their peers, and those who argue and fight are often rejected by others (Ladd, Price, & Hart, 1988). In one study, children who communicated effectively with others were better liked. These children made it clear to whom they were talking, either by saying the other child's name, establishing eye contact, or touching the child to whom they were talking (Kemple, 1991). They also spoke to one another and were more likely than other children to give a reason for their actions. Instead of just saying, "No, I don't want to play," they explained, "No, I don't want to play house. Let's play office instead—you can be the secretary, I'll be the boss."

Teachers do play a role in helping children to make and be friends, especially by planning and implementing an inclusive classroom, because some research suggests that children with disabilities are less accepted by their peers than other children. Kemple (1991) suggests that teachers begin by observing children who have difficulty making friends. When observing, try to answer these questions:

1. How does the disliked child interact with others?
2. How does the child interact with individual children, small groups, or larger groups?
3. Does the child misinterpret the intentions and cues of other children?
4. Does the child resort to aggression as a means of solving problems?
5. When rejecting another, does the child give a reason or an alternative suggestion?
6. Does the child make irrelevant responses to playmates' communications?

Observing children who have trouble being a friend or making friends helps to pinpoint their problems. Once you identify why children have difficulty, you can choose from a wide variety of approaches to help them (Kemple, 1991). Teachers can use the same or similar techniques used to help children develop prosocial skills. In addition, Beaty (1999) and others suggest the following:

- Organize special play sessions, grouping children who lack social skills with those who are more competent.
- Pair an isolated child with a younger child.
- With an aggressive child, suggest and teach alternative means of resolving conflicts.
- Use role play to help children develop alternative solutions to difficult social situations.
- Assist children who have difficulty becoming part of a group. ("Wendy, you can be cashier.")
- Provide on-the-spot guidance. ("Tell him what you want, Scott.")
- Use skits, puppet activities, or group discussions in which children are presented with a hypothetical situation (e.g., two puppets want to use the same firetruck) and are encouraged to suggest and evaluate a wide range of potential solutions.

- Steer a child who has trouble entering a social group to smaller or more accepting groups of children. Rather than suggesting that a child attempt to enter ongoing play by asking, "Can I play?" a teacher can help the child observe a group, try to figure out the theme, and then think of a role that would contribute to that theme.

You can also help children make friends by enabling them to achieve recognition and prestige in a group:

- Children feel honored and gain recognition from the group when the class makes them a get-well or a birthday book consisting of a collection of pictures and stories by the other children.
- Prestige is the reward for children who can explain to others how to make a clay dinosaur, how to find the way to the principal's office, or how to care for the hammer and saws.
- Children can make friends as the teacher encourages them to work on group projects. Singing songs and playing games together, such as "The Farmer in the Dell," "Ring around the Rosie," and other simple games (really a remarkable accomplishment for young children) help them to feel a part of a group.
- Structuring activities that require more than one child to be successfully completed is helpful. You might arrange for children to plant and maintain a garden, make soup or pudding, bake bread or cookies, create and put on a puppet show, construct a playhouse, paint a mural, or play board games.

Books can also be used. Reading Leo Lionni's (1991) *Swimmy*, in which a little lonely fish teaches others how to work together to scare the big fish away, can be followed by having children make a mural of Swimmy, creating a big fish from many little fish that each child draws and cuts out. E. E. McEwan's (1996) *Whose Hat?* shows adult groups, many of which provide services; and Carol Greene's (1997)*Firefighters Fight Fires* offers children a view of the daily lives of firefighters who live and work together.

Conflict Resolution

"We're sharing" was the reply when two children, scuffling over the same bike, were asked what they were doing. Teachers of young children rarely experience a day without at least one conflict in the group. Whenever young children are together, there will be fighting and arguments. Conflict is healthy, and indeed necessary, for children's growth and development; it is the way they balance becoming individuals with learning to become a part of a group (Levin, 1998). Children's conflicts have several sources:

- *Conflicts within themselves.*   Children cry over a puzzle that is beyond their ability; they wrestle with a decision to paint or work with clay. Or making the wrong decision, they go off to sulk, with thumb in mouth, alone with their conflict.

- *Conflicts with others in the class.*   Children fight with one another over toys or objects, in play, or about an idea.
- *Conflicts outside their personal worlds.*   Mother and father argue over who will take the car or how much money to spend; teacher and aide disagree about the best way to discipline or reward children; and children experience the conflict that occurs in the wider world as they watch strikes, fights, and wars in the movies and on television.

Teachers can use at least two effective ways to handle conflicts that occur when children are together. The first is to validate children's feelings and help them discover ways to express their feelings through nonaggression and without hurting themselves or others. The second is to find ways to keep aggressive feelings from multiplying.

To minimize the normal conflicts in a classroom, you might do the following:

- Help children form close friendships and feel the security of friends. Then they can react to frustrations with less aggression.
- Make clear that aggressive acts are not allowed in the classroom, stopping them when and if they appear. Remember, however, that punishment can serve as a form of frustration and may only increase a child's need to act out aggressively.
- Model for the children ways of meeting frustration without aggressive acts.
- Establish rules, in cooperation with the children, that protect the rights of each individual.
- Remove potentially frustrating situations for the children by preparing the environment with sufficient equipment; providing tasks children can succeed in; and planning a balanced program with opportunities for choices, self-expression, and physical activity.
- Help children to deal with their feelings openly and understand that people everywhere have feelings. Bill Martin's (1969) *David Was Mad* allows children to discuss their feelings of anger without guilt or fear of reprimand and to realize that everyone gets angry. The teacher might express personal feelings to the class—"I was really so angry that happened," or "That makes me feel so happy inside"—and then demonstrate to the class positive ways of handling those feelings. When children begin to see that everyone has feelings, they are better able to relate openly to one another and to feel a oneness with other people in the world.

Even though classrooms are arranged to minimize frustration and conflict, accept the aggression that does occur as an opportunity for teaching. When fights occur, you can intervene and, if necessary, physically separate the children, taking each child by the hand and quietly calming them down. Then, after the children have settled down, follow up with a discussion of what happened and work out a

Aggressive acts are common.

solution with the children. Rather than focusing on who started it or who said what and why or, worse yet, asking children to say they are sorry when they really want to hit harder, explain why the fight occurred and how to handle the situation better (Levin, 2003). You might explain why one child called another a name or took a toy: "He wanted to play with the wagon, and you wouldn't let him have it, so he hit you." "José, if you ask him for it, he might give it to you." "She called you a name because she wanted you to play with her, and you said no." Whatever you say to the children, it is important for you not to make them feel guilty, resentful, or more frustrated, all of which can increase hostility and make peaceful settling of conflicts more difficult.

Teachers need to let children handle some conflicts without interference. Because many conflicts are short, over before they have fully begun, children can handle them without help.

Redirecting children's anger or hostility gives them yet another way to deal with conflict and helps children know that they can be angry but must handle their anger in ways that will not be harmful to others. Words can help: "You really wanted to hit, spit, kick, or whatever, but you cannot hurt anyone here. Tell him how angry you are." Some teachers have found that anger can be dispelled by asking a child to run around the playground as fast as possible, pound clay, hammer nails into wood, or draw or paint a picture.

SUMMARY

Although young children bring a number of skills to the classroom—walking, talking, relating—it is the school's responsibility to ensure the continuation of skill development. The social studies teach map reading, graphing, and cardinal directions; other skills are shared responsibilities with all the school subjects.

The skills most important for the preschool-primary classroom are the social and thinking skills. The social skills of learning who you are and developing self-esteem are prerequisites to learning about others. All children's group activities are social by nature, yet teachers need to plan specific activities and experiences to foster cooperation and encourage social interactions.

Teaching children prosocial behavior involves helping them learn to relate to each other as well learn the communicative skills of listening, speaking, reading, and writing and the social skills of learning to share and cooperate. Because making and having friends are so integral to children's success in school and life, teachers also plan ways for children to accomplish this goal.

Conflicts, however, will occur. Learning how to prevent conflicts and then handling them when they arise is part of a teacher's job.

Extend Your Knowledge

1. Observe 5-, 6-, and 7-year-olds at play. What evidence of cooperation and sharing do you note? How do the ages of the children relate to any differences in their play behaviors?

2. Plan a lesson for developing social skills in a group of young children. Write a complete plan designed to foster the development of the social skill you have selected. If possible, try out your plan with a group of children.

3. Interview several teachers. How important do they consider social skills in their total program? How do they plan to foster social skills?

4. Watch children's cartoon shows for an entire Saturday morning and record instances of violence. Then observe children playing at home or school and record the nature and the number of instances of violence in their play. Analyze your observations, comparing the amount and degree of violence in the cartoons with that of the children's play. Did you observe similarities?

Resources

A World of Difference, edited by Carol Copple (2003) and published by the National Association for the Education of Young Children, Washington, DC, offers teachers a wealth of information on children's developing awareness of others and building inclusive classrooms.

Myrna B. Shure's (2000) *Raising a Thinking Child Workbook: Teaching Young Children How to Resolve Everyday Conflicts and Get Along with Others*, published by Research Press, Champaign, IL, provides teachers with a plethora of problem-solving ideas to teach children cooperative behaviors.

The Peaceful Classroom in Action by Naomi Drew (1999), published by Jalmar Press, Torrance, CA, guides teachers in developing new ways of helping children to resolve conflicts, communicate, and cooperate.

References

Ainsworth, M. D., Belhar, M., Waters, E., & Wall, S. (1978). *Patterns of attachment.* Hillsdale, NJ: Erlbaum.

Aliki. (1987). *We are best friends.* New York: Morrow.

Avery, P., Johnson, D. W., Johnson, R. T., & Mitchell, J. M. (1999). Teaching and understanding of war and peace through structured academic controversies. In A. Raviv & L. Oppenheimer (Eds.), *How children understand war and peace: A call for international peace education* (pp. 161–173). New York: Jossey-Bass.

Bandura, A. (1997). *Self-efficacy: The exercise of control.* New York: Freeman.

Beaty, J. J. (1999). *Prosocial guidance for the preschool child.* Upper Saddle River, NJ: Merrill/Prentice Hall.

Berk, L. E. (2001). *Development through the lifespan.* Boston: Allyn & Bacon.

Birch, S. H., & Ladd, G. W. (1998). Children's interpersonal behaviors and the teacher-child relationship. *Developmental Psychology, 34,* 934–946.

Bodrova, E., & Leong, D. J. (2003). Chopsticks and counting chips: Do play and foundational skills need to compete for the teacher's attention in an early childhood classroom? *Young Children, 58*(3), 10–17.

Bost, K. K., Vaughn, B. E., Washington, W. N., Ceilinski, K. L., & Bradbard, M. R. (1998). Social competence, social support, and attachment: Demarcation of construct domains, measurement, and paths of influence for preschool children attending Head Start. *Child Development, 69,* 192–219.

Bronson, M. B. (2000). Recognizing and supporting the development of self-regulation in young children. *Young Children, 55*(2), 32–37.

California Tomorrow. (1999). *A place to begin: Working with parents on issues of diversity.* Oakland, CA: Author.

Chrisman, K., & Couchenour, D. (2002). *Healthy sexuality development: A guide for early childhood educators and families.* Washington, DC: National Association for the Education of Young Children.

Cohen, M. (1998). *It's George.* New York: Yearling Books.

Coley, R. L. (1998). Children's socialization experiences and functioning in single-mother households: The importance of fathers and other men. *Child Development, 69,* 219–230.

Copple, C. (2003). *A world of difference.* Washington, DC: National Association for the Education of Young Children.

Coufal, K., & Coufal, D. C. (2002). Colorful wishes: The fusion of drawing, narratives, and social studies. *Communication Disorders Quarterly, 23*(2), 109–121.

DeKlyen, M., Biernbaum, S., Speltz, M. L., & Greenberg, M. T. (1998). Fathers and preschool behavior problems. *Child Development, 34,* 264–275.

Descartes, R. (1646/1951). The passion of the soul. In *The philosophical works of Descartes.* New York: Dover.

Dewey, J. (1944). *Democracy and education.* New York: Free Press.

Diehl, D. S., Lemerise, E. A., Caverly, S. L., Ramsay, S., & Roberts, J. (1998). Peer relations and school adjustment in ungraded primary children. *Educational Psychology, 90,* 506–515.

Dorsey, S. (2003). The relation of social capital to child psychosocial adjustment difficulties: The role of positive parenting and neighborhood dangerousness. *Journal of Psychopathology and Behavioral Assessment, 25*(3), 11–23.

Dunn, J., Cutting, A. L., & Fisher, N. (2002). Old friends, new friends: Predictors of children's perspectives on their friends at school. *Child Development, 73,* 621–635.

Erikson, E. (1963). *Childhood and society.* New York: Norton.

Flavell, J. H. (1979). Metacognition and cognitive monitoring. *American Psychologist, 34,* 906–911.

Finlinson, A. R., Austin, A. M., & Pfister, R. (2000). Cooperative games and children's positive behaviors. *Early Child Development and Care, 164,* 29–40.

Freud, S. (1949). *An outline of psychoanalysis.* New York: Norton.

Froschl, M., & Sprung, B. (1999). On purpose: Addressing teasing and bullying in early childhood. *Young Children, 54*(2), 70–72.

Gillies, R. M. (2000). The maintenance of cooperative and helping behaviours in cooperative groups. *British Journal of Educational Psychology, 70*(1), 97–111.

Greene, C. (1997). *Firefighters fight fires.* New York: Children's World.

Gross, T., & Clemens, S. G. (2002). Painting a tragedy: Young children process the events of September 11. *Young Children, 57*(3), 44–46.

Gunnar, M. R. (2003). Gendered social worlds in preschool. *Social Development, 12* (1), 91–106.

Harris, P. L. (1989). *Children and emotions.* Oxford, England: Blackwell.

Heitz, T. (1989). How do I help Jacob? *Young Children, 45*(1), 11–16.

Kemple, K. M. (1991). Preschool children's peer acceptance and social interaction. *Young Children, 46*(3), 47–56.

Ladd, G. W. (1990). Having friends, keeping friends, making friends, and being liked by peers in the classroom: Predictors of children's early school adjustment. *Child Development, 61,* 1081–1100.

Ladd, G. W., Kochenderfer, B. J., & Coleman, C. C. (1997). Classroom peer acceptance, friendship, and victimization: Distinct relational systems that contribute uniquely to children's social adjustment? *Child Development, 68,* 1181–1198.

Ladd, G. W., Price, J. M., & Hart, C. H. (1988). Predicting preschoolers' peer status from their playground behaviors. *Child Development, 59,* 986–992.

Levin, D. E. (2003). *Teaching young children in violent times: Building a peaceable classroom.* Washington, DC: National Association for the Education of Young Children.

Lieber, J., Capell, K., Sandall, S. R., Wolfberg, P., Horn, E., & Beckman, P. (1998). Correlates of young children's interactions with classmates with disabilities. *Early Childhood Research Quarterly, 13,* 67–87.

Lillard, A., & Currenton, S. (2003). Do young children understand what others feel, want, and know? In C. Copple (Ed.), *A world of difference* (pp. 46–41). Washington, DC : National Association for the Education of Young Children.

Lionni, L. (1991). *Swimmy.* New York: Scholastic.

Locke, J. (1690/1964). *An essay concerning human understanding.* New York: Meridan.

Maccoby, E. E. (1993). The role of parents in the socialization of children: An historical overview. *Developmental Psychology, 28,* 1008–1017.

Marsh, H. W., Craven, R., & Debus, R. (1998). Structure, stability, and development of young children's self-concepts: A multi cohort–multi occasion study. *Child Development, 69,* 1031–1053.

Marshall, H. H. (2001). Cultural influences on the development of self-concept: Updating our thinking. *Young Children, 56*(6), 19–22.

Martin, B. (1969). *David was mad.* New York: Holt, Rinehart, & Winston.

Maslow, A. (1969). *Toward a psychology of being.* New York: Van Nostrand.

McConnell, J. (2000). Children's social skills and understanding of others' emotions. *Dissertation Abstracts International, 62*(5-B), 2788.

McEwan, E. E. (1996). *Whose hat?* New York: Shaw.

Morrow, R. D. (1991). What's in a name? In particular, a Southeast Asian name? *Young Children, 44*(6), 23–29.

National Association for the Education of Young Children (NAEYC).(2001). Helping young children in frightening times. *Young Children, 56*(6), 6–7.

National Council for the Social Studies (NCSS). (1998). *Position statements: Social studies for early childhood and elementary school children. Preparing for the 21st century.* Washington, DC: Author.

National Institutes for Child Health and Development (NICHD) Early Child Care Research Network. (1998). Early child care and self-control, compliance, and problem behavior at twenty-four and thirty-six months. *Child Development, 69,* 1145–1170.

National Parent-Teacher Association (PTA). (2002). *Talking with your child about sex.* Chicago: Author (*http://www.pta.org/parentinvolvement/healthsafety/hs_talking_ sex.asp*).

National Research Council (NRC), Committee on Early Childhood Pedagogy. (2001). *Eager to learn: Educating our preschoolers.* Washington, DC: National Academy Press.

National Research Council and Institute of Medicine (NRC & IM), Committee on Integrating the Science of Early Childhood Development. (2000). *From neurons to neighborhoods: The science of early childhood development.* Washington, DC: National Academy Press.

Parker, J. G., & Asher, S. R. (1987). Peer relations and later personal adjustment: Are low accepted children at risk? *Psychological Bulletin, 10,* 357–389.

Rogers, C. (1961). *On becoming a person.* Boston: Houghton Mifflin.

Rosen, T., Rahav, G., & Rosenbaum, M. (2003). Children's reactions to a war situation as a function of age and sex. *Anxiety, Stress, and Coping, 16*(1), 56–69.

Rowland, G. E. (2002). Every child needs self-esteem: Creative drama builds self-confidence through self-expression. *Dissertation Abstracts International, 63*(1-A), 30.

Schiller, M. (1995). An emergent art curriculum that fosters understanding. *Young Children, 50*(3), 33–39.

Seefeldt, C. (2000). Art for young children. In C. Seefeldt (Ed.), *The early childhood curriculum: Current findings and theory* (3rd ed., pp. 201–218). New York: Teachers College Press.

Seefeldt, C., Galper, A., & Denton, D. (1998). Former Head Start parents' characteristics, perceptions of school climate, and involvement in their children's education. *Elementary School Journal, 98,* 339–351.

Skinner, B. F. (1974). *About behaviorism.* New York: Knopf.

Slaby, R. G., Roedell, W. C., Arezzo, D., & Hendrix, K. (1995). *Early violence prevention: Tools for teachers of young children.* Washington, DC: National Association for the Education of Young Children.

Spivack, G., & Shure, M. (1978). *Social adjustment of young children: A cognitive approach to solving real-life problems.* San Francisco: Jossey-Bass.

Stormshak, E. A., Bierman, K. L., Bruschi, C., Dodge, K. A., Cole, J. D., & the Conduct Problems Prevention Research Group. (1999). The relation between behavior problems and peer preference in different classroom contexts. *Child Development, 70,* 196–193.

Wallach, L. R. (1995). Helping children cope with violence. *Young Children, 48*(4), 4–12.

Wardle, F. (2001). Supporting multiracial and multiethnic children and their families. *Young Children, 56*(6), 38–40.

Weingold, H., & Webster, R. (1964). Effects of punishment on cooperative behavior in children. *Child Development, 35,* 12–16.

Yashima, T. (1995). *Crow boy.* New York: Viking.

CHAPTER 6

Attitudes and Values

To value is the act of cherishing something, holding it dear, and also the act of passing judgment upon the nature and amount of its value.

John Dewey, 1944, p. 128

After you read this chapter, you should be prepared to respond to the following questions:

- Why should teaching attitudes and values be part of the social studies?
- How are attitudes learned?
- Which theory of attitude and value formation holds the greatest potential for children's ability to learn the attitudes and values inherent in a democratic society?
- What democratic values and attitudes will you include in your curriculum, and why?
- How can you provide experiences in the preschool-primary classroom that foster full participation in a democratic society?

Social studies educators are virtually unanimous in stressing the importance of addressing democratic values in the classroom: "Citizens who take the office of citizen seriously are in touch with the cultural heritage of the nation. They possess the attitudes and behaviors that support fair play and cooperation. Without a conscious effort to teach these ideals, a free republic will not long endure" (NCSS, 1998, p. 2). Nevertheless, because attitudes and values, which represent the worth or merit that people place on things, excite feelings and expression, and predispose people to behavior and action, there is less agreement about how these values, or even which ones, should be taught.

The controversy over what and how values should be taught stems from the nature of attitudes and values themselves. An opinion is a verbal expression of a belief, but values and attitudes imply an emotional liking or dislike attached to the belief. Values do not exist in and of themselves; they are not things but are reflected in specific value judgments or claims that individuals make.

Listen to and observe children or adults talking about people, society, their government, or religion. Adults yell and argue; children hit, kick, and call one another names as they defend their attitudes and values. It's clear that attitudes and values are emotionally laden, personal, and deeply ingrained.

Because values and attitudes deal with feelings and personal beliefs, many believe that children should learn them in their own homes or churches. Some claim that these institutions should have the sole responsibility for teaching values and attitudes; the school should not be responsible for teaching other people's children what to value or believe.

In a way, there can be no discussion about whether schools and teachers should be involved in teaching children attitudes and values. Even though the development of attitudes and values does occur primarily outside the classroom (CIVITAS, 2003), their transmission to young children in any early childhood program is, in fact, unavoidable.

Everything that occurs in a preschool or primary grade is bound up in, and influenced by, values and attitudes. Just the fact of going to school and learning to read is value-bound in our cultural belief that school is good and all citizens should be literate. The social studies, however—those studies that introduce children to the different ideas, beliefs, and values of other people and cultures—are even more directly related to teaching children values and attitudes. Social studies should provide a setting for children to acquire knowledge of history and the social sciences and to be exposed to a broad variety of opinions, facilitating the formulation, reassessment, and affirmation of their beliefs (NCSS, 1998).

Prerequisite to understanding the role of attitudes and values in the social studies is knowledge of (1) how attitudes and values are learned, (2) current methods and strategies for teaching attitudes and values, and (3) which attitudes and values should be taught in schools for young children.

HOW CHILDREN LEARN

Research suggests that by age 7 children's attitudes and values—their confidence in themselves and others, their ideas of self-worth—are fully formed. This does not mean that these attitudes and values cannot and will not change as children grow, but it does mean that, by age 7, children who say, "I can't," are likely to say, "I can't," as adults. Seven-year-olds who learn to treat others as they themselves would like to be treated are those who treat others with respect as adults.

Research also suggests that attitudes and values are learned in much the same way that knowledge and skills are gained. At least three theoretical views of attitude and value formation have been developed: (1) values and attitudes are modeled, (2) they are reinforced, and (3) they are learned.

Modeling

Young children take on the values and attitudes of those close to them. Because they love their parents and need their parents to love and care for them, young children want to be like their families in every way. Thus, they model the attitudes and values of their families (Bandura, 1997; Nucci, 2001).

Within the family children learn the *shoulds* and *should nots* of social behaviors. They model the norms of the culture and their family. They learn the social conventions of how to address elders, what fork to use when, what is sanctioned, and what is not. But families also model moral behaviors of honesty, hard work, self-discipline, responsibility, and dependability (Prencipe & Helwig, 2002). The moral values and social conventions that children imitate may depend on the type of parenting strategies that families use (Berkowitz, 2000). The type of nurturance and support, kinds of demand, and family democratic processes influence how children learn and develop respect for others and concepts of right and wrong ways to care for others (Schulze, Harwood, Schoelmerich & Leyendecker, 2002).

Families aren't the only significant group in young children's lives, however; teachers are also very important to young children. Children hold their teachers in high regard and have strong emotional ties to them. Because the teacher is an authority figure—one who cares for, protects, and loves them—they are likely to model the teacher's attitudes and values (DeRoach, 2001).

Teachers, like all people, are shaped and influenced by their cultural heritage, racial and ethnic identity, socialization, and socioeconomic and other factors (APA, 2003). Teachers are encouraged, then, to examine their own attitudes and values and how they learned them. Teachers' values and attitudes may affect how they interact with children.

Perhaps one teacher's culture values and teaches children to be totally obedient and unquestioning. Another teacher may value children who work in harmony with

Attitudes and values are learned.

one another and seek interdependency rather than independence. All teachers should try to understand their own attitudes and value systems and learn the origin and meaning of the attitudes and values of children from differing cultures, racial and ethnic groups, and socioeconomic classes.

Children do not live in a vacuum: "All individuals exist in social, political, historical, and economic contexts" (APA, 2003, p. 377). Children experience a variety of social contexts. This includes more than the child's family, school, or peers. It also encompasses the vast social world the child lives in and all the interactions within that society. Surrounded by shopping malls, advertisements, and media messages, children quickly learn to adopt societal values. They imitate the action figures they find in a fast-food meal and observe role models on TV and in the movies. The high prestige of the role models in children's environment make children susceptible to assuming the values and attitudes of these models.

Teachers will want to make certain that the small society in their classroom provides appropriate models. CDs, children's literature, movies, videos, CD-ROMs, and computer software should be reviewed to make sure they offer a balance of gender and racial, ethnic, and religious groups in a variety of roles and situations. Teachers consciously provide role models who demonstrate the values inherent in a democracy:

- The dignity of each individual
- Universal participation in setting and establishing rules
- Freedom of speech and the opportunity to express ideas and feelings
- The right to feel protected and happy
- Participation in society and responsibility for others
- Cooperation and acceptance of one's role in the community

Reinforcement

Reinforcement theory is used to explain how children learn attitudes and values. Behaviorists claim that children and adults learn their attitudes through reinforcement (Skinner, 1948). Responses and behaviors that are rewarded will be repeated. The same process of conditioning is applicable to attitude and value learning. Children who behave in ways consistent with their beliefs and who are reinforced will have the belief strengthened. According to this theoretical approach, teachers should be careful to reinforce democratic attitudes and values. Beliefs incongruent with a democracy should be ignored. Eventually, they should diminish and be extinguished.

On the other hand, one only has to look at the history of Nazi Germany to understand how reinforcement can be used to negate the values and attitudes of a democratic society. In Germany, individuals and groups were rewarded for allegiance to Nazi philosophy. Children were given medals or other rewards for reporting siblings and friends who deviated from Nazi thought. Women who exemplified the physical characteristics of the Aryan race were given special privileges for bearing children of high-ranking German officials. Those children, women, and men who did not conform to Nazi thought and rules were punished or killed.

Learning

Cognitive theory is another view of attitude and value formation. Cognitive theory describes principles of cognitive growth and development, and suggests that cognitive structures influence the formation of children's attitudes. This view sees humans as striving after goals. Thus, humans acquire attitudes and values consistent with these goals.

Cognitive theories of learning moral development are stage theories. Piaget and Inhelder (1969) suggested that children's attitudes and values are consistent with their thought processes.

In Piaget's first stage (ages 0 to 7), children obey rules because they feel obliged to. Piaget called this stage *moral realism*, or the *morality of constraint*, because children obey rules as if they were sacred and unalterable. Right and wrong are simply what authorities tell them, and they believe that everyone views things the same way. They judge the rightness or wrongness of an act on the basis of the magnitude of its consequences, the extent to which it conforms to rules, or whether or not the action is punished. If they disobey, they believe their actions will be followed by a misfortune willed by God or some inanimate object.

The next stage, called *autonomous morality*, appears around age 7 or 8. Children view rules as established but maintained through reciprocal agreement and open to modification when needed. The child's judgments of right and wrong consider intentions as well as punishments. Conforming to peer expectations, considering other people's feelings, expressing thanks, and putting oneself in the place of others guide behavior.

When formal thought develops, about the time of adolescence, children reach an understanding of right and wrong and the place of rules (Goodman, 2000). They can make new rules; understand their purpose; and understand all the consequences that arise from accepting or rejecting the attitudes, values, and rules of a society.

According to Piaget, children's learning of moral values involves maturation and interactions with others. Children's immature cognitive development, or egocentric thought, limits their ability to see things from the perspective of others, and their dependence makes them feel obliged to comply with the demands of others. Moral development requires that children give up egocentric thought as well as their feeling of being obliged to obey adults or the will of others.

Through social experiences, children are challenged to give up some of their egocentrism. Further, as children interact with peers, they find they must reciprocate, which facilitates an awareness of the internal states underlying the actions of others and contributes to the tendency to take other people's intentions into account.

Through these interactions, each person constructs individual moral values. Just as with the construction of intelligence, children come to know moral values only after experiencing, manipulating, examining, and exploring them in many ways over time. Moral values can only come from repeated encounters in which the child is an active participant in making sense of the information.

These repeated encounters should permit children to make choices. By making choices as they interact with others, children can construct a sense of right and wrong. To achieve a reliable sense of right and wrong, children must make choices; it is the task of the parents and school to make this possible. Teachers can provide children with many opportunities to choose and to experience the consequences of their choices. Initially, children might choose what they will play, with whom they will play, and when they will change their play. For children in the primary grades, choices become increasingly more complex and numerous; and the choices adults make for them decrease (Seefeldt, 1993).

Vicarious experiences—listening to stories, reading books, or listening to the voices of others—are another aspect of the cognitive theory of learning attitudes and values. By listening to and reading historical stories, myths, legends, and narratives of the lives of others, children can consider how those people and characters weighed the consequences of a variety of choices. Some believe that the moral power of stories and histories gives children a common reference point and is a way of transmitting traditional values and wisdom to children (NCHS, 1994). Following a story, discussions take place and children gain skills in weighing right and wrong. Primary children can discuss the probable motives, hopes, fears, strengths, and weaknesses of those involved and propose their own solutions to the problems presented in narratives of the lives of others facing and solving moral dilemmas (NCHS, 1994).

WHICH THEORY?

Educators use all of these theories to teach attitudes and values. Historically, reinforcement theory was used to indoctrinate the young with certain values and attitudes. During the 1970s and 1980s, other approaches became popular. They were based on the idea that children do not learn by being indoctrinated into the values of our nation but should be taught to clarify their own attitudes and values by reflecting on the consequences of their actions and searching for consistency between their feelings and actions. Others advocated that children learn by reasoning about morals and analyzing values.

This view is still current. Experts suggest that children do need to have a variety of social experiences that engage them in disputes, conflicts, negotiations, ambiguities, and uncertainties, along with agreement, harmony, and certainties. This variety forces children to develop embryonic attempts to understand the judgments and positions of others and reconcile these ideas with those of their families, school, and others (Turiel, 2003).

Indoctrination

Some believe that attitudes and values should be indoctrinated. In fact, in many classrooms, children are exposed to stories and historical accounts exemplifying what are seen as basic American values and behaviors and then are rewarded and reinforced for expressing and behaving in ways that are consistent with these values (Brophy, 1990). The authors of the national civics standards, *National Standards for Civics and Government* (Center for Civic Education, 1994), also suggest that children should memorize numerous isolated facts, understand abstract concepts, and become indoctrinated in the values of democracy.

Indoctrination does not work, however. Children who experience power-assertive discipline in their homes are more likely than those experiencing indoctrination to express commitment to others or concern about good behavior (Kochanska, Padavich, & Koenig, 1996). Given unlimited amounts of time to spend in drill and practice, teachers may be able to train children to recite the numerous civics standards. But by memorizing instead of learning, children behave like parrots in a circus—able to recite the three branches of government; explain the consequences of absence of government; or name the people representing them at the local, state, and national levels; but comprehending very little (Seefeldt, 1995).

The ability to recite the numerous facts in the civics performance standards has nothing to do with becoming a productive member of a democracy. Research shows that children who have been indoctrinated in civics fail to understand the basic obligations of citizenship in a democratic society; therefore, the standards negate their very purpose (Torney, Oppenheim, & Farnen, 1975). Learning through indoctrination, children are likely to be unable to accept social responsibility as adults or participate in social criticism and more willing to follow whoever is in power without question (Torney et al., 1975). It seems wiser and more democratic to respect young children by teaching them to value their flag, their country, and democracy in ways that are congruent with their development and learning.

Value Clarification

Believing that values are something an individual chooses, prizes, and then acts upon, teachers plan ways for children to explore their own feelings, reactions, and values within a safe and secure environment:

• Teachers encourage children to make choices freely. They plan many choices and child-initiated activities. They give young children information and help them uncover and then examine alternative choices. For instance, a teacher of 5-year-olds might tell them the choices they have for activity time: "Today you can build with blocks, paint at the tables or the easel, work with clay, or play in the airplane. Think about what you want to begin with." A teacher of primary children could ask them to select a book from those on a particular shelf; develop a project from three choices; or decide whether they would like to draw, construct a replica, or make a slide-tape show for a report.

• Teachers ask the children to weigh alternative choices thoughtfully: "If you decide to build with blocks, will you still have time to make your desert garden?" They ask primary children to weigh the consequences of actions: "Is this really important to you?" "What might happen if you use that idea?" "What other choices do you have?" "When might you use that idea?" "What would be good and bad about the idea?"

• Teachers encourage children to consider what they prize and cherish: "Would other children believe that?" "Is that important to you?" "Should everyone go along with your idea?" "Did you do it yourself?" "Are you glad you feel that way?" "Have you felt this way for some time?" "Is this idea so good everyone should feel that way?" "Who else feels that way?"

• Teachers help children to act on their beliefs, giving opportunities for them to express their own ideas and develop repeated behaviors or patterns in their lives.

A secure classroom atmosphere is necessary if teachers are going to lead children to develop and understand their own values and attitudes. School must be a place where children can feel psychologically safe to talk about their feelings and beliefs. Teachers need to listen to children who are expressing their beliefs and ask questions to help them clarify those beliefs. Teachers must respond nonjudgmentally to children's ideas, questions, and responses. Clarifying values dignifies children as individuals while encouraging them to deal with their feelings, attitudes, and values more consistently and maturely (Medda, 1996).

Encourage children to make choices freely.

Value Analysis

Through value analysis, teachers attempt to develop students' ability to make rational and logically defensible moral judgments by teaching the processes of reasoning about moral or value questions (Brophy, 1990). Value analysis is based on the idea that, although moral judgments can vary widely in the extent to which they are rational and logical, the goal of value education should be to help individuals learn to make rationally and logically defensible moral judgments. To achieve this goal, students are taught a set of skills essential to reasoning about moral and value questions that will help them to understand the consequences of particular values, the conflicts that may occur among two or more values, and the reasons for particular value choices.

Emphasizing thinking, value analysis is primarily a cognitive strategy. The process, which begins with identification of the problem or issue, is similar to Dewey's description of thinking and problem solving:

1. *Identify values.* In a given situation, students are asked to identify the values that people in the situation hold. The situation may be something that has happened to the children or may be a story or problem posed by them.

A teacher read a story to the children:

Susan is in trouble. She was supposed to complete all her math problems and give them to her second-grade teacher before recess. Instead of working on her problems, she chose to paint. When she realized her time was gone, she asked Freddy if she could copy his paper. What should Freddy do?

To guide the children in value analysis, the teacher asked, "What problem are Freddy and Susan facing?"

2. *Compare and contrast values.* Pupils can identify the similarities and differences in various people's value choices. Teachers can ask children to determine the values of the same individual in different situations or to determine the values of different individuals in the same situation.

> The teacher asked, "What does Susan think about the problem? What does Freddy think? What does Susan's behavior tell us about what she values? What does Freddy's behavior tell us about what he values?"

3. *Explore feelings.*   By talking about their own feelings, identifying with the feelings of others, and experiencing situations in which new feelings are aroused, children can understand the strong emotional component of their own values and those of others.

> The teacher asked, "Why do you think Freddy feels the way he does? Why does Susan feel the way she does? How would you feel?"

4. *Analyze value judgments.*   Children can provide evidence to support or refute a particular value judgment.

> The teacher asked, "What would happen if Freddy helped Susan? What if Freddy refuses to help? Is there some other alternative?"

5. *Analyze value conflict.*   Presented with value dilemmas, pupils can determine what the conflicts are, what alternatives are possible, the consequences of each, and what alternative might produce the best outcome and why.

> The teacher asked, "What do you think Susan and Freddy should do? Why do you think so? What do you think the outcome will be?"

6. *Test one's own values.*   Testing includes four steps: (a) role exchange (willingness to exchange positions with the least advantaged person in the agreement); (b) universal consequences (if everyone followed the course of action, would the consequences be acceptable?); (c) new cases (are the consequences of the action acceptable in new but similar situations?); and (d) subsumption (does the principle follow from a higher acceptable principle?).

WHAT VALUES SHOULD BE TAUGHT?

Because attitudes and values deal with the *shoulds*—what people should do; the standards they should live by; or the things they should value, endorse, live up to, or maintain—the question of what values to teach is controversial. One person's standards for behavior differ from another's, and conflicts arise. Each parent wants her children to learn a different set of values.

Obviously, teachers will not teach children what religion they should believe in or what political party they should vote for. Those are family preferences. No teacher can tell a child or a parent that the values he holds are wrong. On the other hand, teachers who do not raise questions about values, ask children to examine their own feelings, or promote the values inherent in our democracy may perform a disservice to our democracy by avoiding those topics. If teachers do not actively promote the values of our society, children learn nothing about democracy; rather, they learn that they can do whatever they wish.

The values that do matter, and are worthwhile and even necessary, are those that are consistent with the values of democracy. In schools for young children, the universal attitudes and values consistent with the rights and responsibilities of living in a democracy are those that are taught (Hayes, 2003). Stemming from the Declaration of Independence and the Bill of Rights, these attitudes and values have been described in various ways by the different commissions on the social studies.

According to CIVITAS (2003), the following dispositions of citizens are most conducive to the healthy functioning of constitutional democracy:

- Civility, including respect for others and the use of civil discourse
- Individual responsibility and the inclination to accept responsibility for one's own self and the consequences of one's own actions
- Self-discipline and adherence to the rules necessary for maintenance of the American constitutional government without requiring the imposition of external authority
- Civic-mindedness and the willingness on appropriate occasions to place the common good above personal interest
- Open-mindedness, including a healthy sense of skepticism and a recognition of the ambiguities of social and political reality
- Willingness to compromise, realizing that values and principles are sometimes in conflict, tempered by a recognition that not all principles or values are fit for compromise since some compromise may imperil democracy's continued existence
- Toleration of diversity
- Patience and persistence in the pursuit of public goals
- Compassion for others
- Generosity toward others and the community at large
- Loyalty to the republic and its values and principles

Similarly, the National Council for the Social Studies (1998) suggests that, within the context of the social studies, children learn the value of fundamental rights: life, liberty, individual dignity, equality of opportunity, justice, privacy, security, and ownership of private property. These also include valuing the basic freedoms of worship, thought, conscience, expression, inquiry, assembly, and participation in the political process.

The National Commission on Social Studies in the Schools (1998) believes that civic virtue—American democratic traditions and political institutions; ideals, human values, and achievements; and the understanding and transmission of citizenship—is not just a matter of observing outward forms, transmitted from the old to the young. It is also a matter of reasoned conviction, the end result of teaching people to think for themselves.

By focusing on those values that (1) are congruent with our democracy, (2) are necessary for children to become participatory members of a democratic society, and (3) predispose children to learn, the social studies can meet the intent of the three commissions on the social studies.

Teaching Democratic Values

In an early childhood program, children are not just preparing to become members of a democratic society but actually *are* citizens of a democracy (Dewey, 1944). Daily, they contribute to building and fostering a democratic society and receive the benefits of belonging to this society.

Through every experience in the program, young children learn that they are worthy, valued, and respected. They know that their individual needs and wants will be met and that their freedom of speech, pursuit of happiness, and other rights will always be protected. At the same time, however, they are learning to expand their concerns and give up some of their egocentrism. As members of a democratic community, children develop a sense of shared concern, recognizing that their interests overlap with the interests of others and that their welfare is inextricably entwined with the welfare of others (Boyle-Baise, 2003).

The teacher establishes and maintains the basic principles of democracy in the classroom. The ways in which the teacher establishes control, deals with individual children and their interactions with one another, and teaches all students send a pow-

Children learn they are worthy, valued, and respected.

erful message to children about the values of a democracy. Although there is no one right or wrong way for a teacher to do this, when observing a democratic classroom one immediately becomes aware of how teachers actively support individual worth and dignity while protecting and nurturing the welfare of the total group. In a democratic group, certain tenets are consistently followed:

1. Teachers share control. They do not give orders and expect children to blindly follow their directions. Rather than emphasizing the task or the skill to be learned, teachers focus on how children are feeling, reacting, and interacting with one another (Bredekamp & Copple, 1997).

> A second-grade group was working in the computer room with the computer teacher. One child had difficulty with the program and did not seem to know what to do with the computer or how to solve the math problems. His neighbor turned to him and began to help. "Stop talking now!" said the teacher firmly, writing both children's names on a box on the board, which meant each child might later lose some favored activity or reward. "It's not time for social talk; it's time to do your math drill." The teacher ignored both the fact that one child had no clue about what to do or how to use the computer to practice this particular math drill and the fact that the other child was offering to help.

2. Children make decisions. Being able to make wise decisions is required of participants in a democratic society (Longstreet, 2003). Instead of prescribing the work to be done, how it will be done, and under what time constraints, the teacher lets children make choices about what they will learn, how, and with whom. Cookbook approaches, filling in the blanks, and following prescribed lesson plans are replaced by centers of interest, learning stations, and other materials for learning. Rather than solo learning, group work is fostered (New, 2000).

> "Here are some plastic containers," said a teacher to the first graders, who had been grouped into committees. She gave each group a box of different-sized and -shaped clear plastic containers. "Your group's task is to decide which container holds the most sand, and which the least. You may use the scale, the tape measure, or any other materials in the sand or water tables. Report to me when you have reached a decision."

3. Discipline is firm and consistent but does not revolve around force, coercion, embarrassment, or threat. Already believing that rules come from authority and that being good means following orders, children need to participate in setting and following rules and begin the long process of separating intent from action.

> Jennifer, a rambunctious 5-year-old, always seemed to be the cause of some trouble with the other kindergarten children. She jumped from one group to another, often upsetting what the others were doing. She never seemed to sit still or simply walk from one place to another but jiggled, jumped, and ran around, a perpetual motion machine in action. One day she knocked down Sean as she darted across the room. The teacher took her aside and repeated the process of identifying and labeling for Jennifer her actions and their results: "You are a very active girl. You need to move about a great deal. When you do

so, you hurt others. How can we arrange for you to move around without disturbing the other children?"

4. Freedom of thought and speech are fostered. Children are expected to have opinions and express them. This expectation governs every area of the curriculum (Greenberg, 1992). Instead of giving children sheets of paper on which to color or patterns to trace around for art activities, teachers ask them to express their own ideas, thoughts, and feelings in drawings, paintings, or constructions. In language arts, they are asked to discuss, write, and express what they know and feel and to make choices about how they will learn math and science skills.

A kindergarten teacher, picking up on the children's interest in dinosaurs, asked them to draw their favorite dinosaur. Clifford drew a large scribble, added some legs and horns, and called it a monster dinosaur. Judy laughed at him, saying, "That's not a dinosaur. That's not real; that's just a scribble."

The teacher said, "Judy, this is the way Clifford draws a dinosaur. It's his pretend monster dinosaur. Your dinosaur is a picture of a stegosaurus, Roberta's is a green dinosaur, and Alice didn't draw a dinosaur at all but drew the forest in which they might have lived." This teacher demonstrated for the children that, although they have different ideas and express them in different ways, each individual's expression is valid.

5. Children are never overwhelmed by the power of others. Teachers are not power figures in the classroom, and they do not permit children to govern through power assertions, bullying, or threats.

In a kindergarten, two boys had gained control of the class. They threatened the others with physical violence; took smaller children's milk money; and had on more than one occasion overwhelmed children in the bathrooms, taking their pants off. As a result, the other children refused to go to the bathroom and began giving the two their money and following their demands. Knowing these behaviors could not be permitted to continue, the teacher began a behavior management program with the class and the two boys. She taught the other children how to ignore the boys and some skills for coping with them. At the same time, she began rewarding the two boys for cooperative behavior. She channeled their needs for power in constructive ways by asking them to lead a song, take charge of the blocks, and become monitors. The behavioral techniques didn't solve the problem, but they gave the teacher and the other children a way to regain control without being overwhelmed by emotions. As a result, she was then able to work with the boys on the cause of their behaviors.

6. A sense of community is built. A classroom is a group of individuals. The teacher develops this group into a community by helping them share goals. Even young children can begin to see that they are a part of, and share in, the common goals of their family, their own group of friends, the class, and the school. Not only are children encouraged to see themselves within the context of the total group, but small groups within the total group are fostered (New, 2000).

Common shared experiences lead to common goals. A trip to the zoo leads to deciding on group rules for the trip, which questions will be answered, and which exhibits will be visited. After such a trip, one second-grade teacher arranged for the total group to complete a mural of their experiences. Knowing that a sense of community develops as children work together, the teacher then divided up the group by their interest in birds, reptiles, fish, and mammals and had each group complete a project and then report to the total group. Throughout the process, the teacher helped the children recognize both their own identity and the needs of the group.

7. Teachers model respect for others (DeRoach, 2001). A teacher who cares about and respects each child in the group and each adult who works with the children serves as a model for the children. Teachers model and encourage mutual respect. They let the children know in a number of explicit ways that each is respected and cared for.

"Let me know when you want me to help you with your math." "You be the judge." "It's up to you whether you want to keep this in your book report or not," a second-grade teacher was heard to say to the children. A teacher of 4-year-olds fostered the idea that it is all right not to be competent in everything. Talking privately to a child who couldn't walk the balance beam, she said, "It's okay not to be able to balance—you'll be able to do so as you grow. You do know how to dress yourself, draw, and sing." Overhearing one child laughing at another's sandwich of shrimp and catsup, a kindergarten teacher said, "When you laugh at Sallie's lunch, it upsets her. It's okay if you don't like it, or even if you'd like to try it, but you cannot make fun of what other people like."

8. Teachers elicit respectful, caring behaviors from the children. Teachers are powerful models for children. They not only model respectful, caring behavior, but they explain what they are doing and find other ways to demonstrate respect.

Kathy, a 5-year-old with spina bifida, was mainstreamed in the kindergarten. The teacher not only modeled caring behaviors for the children but was explicit in gaining their respect for Kathy. At times, the teacher casually asked a child to help Kathy with her coat or chair or to reach something. Other times, she paired Kathy with a partner for necessary help.

To enable Kathy to be a responsible member of the group, the teacher found a carpenter's apron with lots of pockets that could be filled with toys and materials. This permitted Kathy to assume some responsibility in cleaning up. At the same time, the teacher provided the same kind of apron for the other children. Thus, even though Kathy was different, all the children could take advantage of cleaning up with an apron.

Political awareness grows from the base of social interactions within the democracy of the preschool-primary classroom. Both formally (through instruction in understanding the rights and responsibilities of citizens in the United States) and informally (through interactions in the classroom and participation in class and school governance that mirror the values and principles of American constitutional democracy), children's political awareness develops and grows (Center for Civic Education, 1994).

Teaching Political Concepts

Political concepts, typically based on children's own experiences, are introduced to children informally. Most are acquainted with the flag, patriotic songs, the Pledge of Allegiance, laws, and rules; you can use this knowledge to introduce political concepts. In addition, knowledge of the voting process and understanding of war and working toward peace can be developed through life in the political groups of the family, the classroom, and the community.

When teachers follow the principles of a democratic society, children experience political concepts every day. They understand that some people are in authority and know that these people make and enforce rules in their homes, schools, and communities. The child's peer group, family, school, and community relations initially expose them to the core of politics, which is power and its use. Children directly experience rules and limitations as givens and behavior as good or bad depending on whether or not it conforms to the rules.

Furthermore, even very young children are aware of politics beyond their classroom. Researchers note that children have become increasingly more politically aware and can talk about many topics from the field of political science, even though their range of knowledge about any one topic is narrow. Gary Allen (1997) found that, in conversation, first graders could recall political knowledge from a news story. Allen also found that first through third graders' knowledge of the presidency and elections became more elaborate during an election year.

In another study, 6-year-olds were found to be aware of and to endorse democracy and free speech (Helwig, 1998). Even though they were relatively young, the children recognized that freedom of speech is an important part of human activity that must be secured against general intrusion by any form of government. The study concluded that children can consider basic issues of rights and justice and that these can and should be introduced into the curriculum during early childhood.

Even 4-year-olds can identify and accurately label pictures of political symbols, such as the flag and the president and his wife. Connell (1971) noted that, before the age of 5, children's political concepts are made up of bits and pieces of information collected from home, school, and the media. These concepts typically reflect young children's lack of ability to synthesize information as well as their lack of cognitive development. Their political concepts are "full of political figures, cartoon characters, familiar figures of fact and legend that jostle each other with splendid promiscuity" (p. 11). At age 5, children seem to have concepts that reflect their personal knowledge of political symbols, such as the flag and certain songs and stories.

Around the age of 5 or 6, children understand that the world has two groups of people—special and nonspecial—with those in power being considered special. The special people in power are also viewed with benevolence. Children see authority figures as benevolent people who will care for each of them personally. This perception is a result of children's cognitive ability or their emotional needs for safety and security.

The visit of Hillary Clinton, the former first lady, to a kindergarten classroom exemplified children's beginning awareness of politics and political symbols. To prepare for the visit, the teacher asked the children to tell what the president does and what the first lady does. They responded that the president "gives money to good guys and puts bad guys in jail," "takes care of us," and "works for us." They said that the first lady "shares with people," "likes to farm," and "takes care of children."

In their study of children's political understanding, Robert Hess and Judith Torney (1967) found that young children's involvement with politics begins early, with strong emotional attachment to the president. Children seem to think of the president personally—as someone who would help them if they telephoned him or went to him in person with a request.

By age 7, children's political concepts, partially as a result of changes in their cognitive abilities, also seem to change. Concepts are now more accurate, and a political consciousness develops. Children can construct a simple idea of government and the political world. They seem to have a store of ideas but continue to draw randomly from it. They do not yet distinguish among levels of government; when asked what political figures such as mayors, congresspeople, and presidents do, they say that all those people do the same thing.

Connell (1971) concluded that children, even by age 7, do not reproduce the communications that reach them from the adult world; they work them over, detach them from their original context, and assemble them into a general concept of what government is all about. However inaccurate and incomplete children's political concepts are, they form the base for children's later development.

From the research on children's political learning, we can reach the following conclusions:

1. Concepts of politics begin in early childhood, and the process of development is continual.
2. Basic attachments and identifications are among the first political concepts acquired.
3. Children view political authority figures as positive, benevolent, and personal.
4. Feelings and affection develop before knowledge.
5. Not until late childhood can children distinguish between different political roles and acquire basic factual information needed to map out their political world.

Flags as Symbols

Children as young as 6 years old seem to recognize the importance of flags. Under age 6 or so children know that a flag designates a place or country, but they are not aware that flags carry explicit symbolic meaning (Helwig & Prencipe, 1999).

Hess and Torney (1967) found that children see the flag as something belonging to a class of objects, such as stars, and do not think of it in connection with a country until around 12 years of age. You can help children develop a concept of the flag when you do the following:

- Ask the Veterans of Foreign Wars, American Legion, or other patriotic group to demonstrate the proper ways of handling and caring for the flag.
- Arrange for the children to participate in displaying the flag.
- Encourage children to design flags for the classroom. They can design flags that mean time to come in, time to clean up, or story time. Or they can design a class flag, deciding on design, color, and meaning.
- Ask children where they see the flag. Have them construct a booklet called "I See the Flag," drawing pictures and stories of the flags they see in their neighborhood and community.
- Read stories about Betsy Ross and the history of the flag. A book for older children is *The Flag We Love* (Ryan, 1996). Children of all ages enjoy Nancy Caudill's (1995) *Did You Carry the Flag Today, Charley?*
- Start primary children on a research project about the flag. They can find out why the flag is sometimes called the "stars and stripes" and how and why the flag changed over the years. In their research they can find out why the flag first had 13 stars, then 20, and finally 50.
- Help primary children research other flags. These can include the flag of their school, their county, their state, and other states.

The Pledge of Allegiance

Written in 1892 by Francis Bellamy, associate editor of the magazine *The Youth's Companion* and vice president of the Society for Christian Socialists, the Pledge of Allegiance was created to celebrate the 400th anniversary of America's discovery. Since then, the debate over whether or not students should be required to recite the pledge in school has been ongoing (Seefeldt, 1989).

From 1937 to 1943, there was constant litigation, with rulings both upholding and rejecting the constitutionality of requiring students to salute the flag and recite the Pledge of Allegiance. In 1940, the U.S. Supreme Court ruled that a state could require all children to salute the flag. The Court reversed itself in 1943 and held that the flag salute required by state law violated the religious beliefs of Jehovah's Witnesses and could not be compelled.

This holding remains today. No one, whether child or adult, may be compelled to salute the flag. Requiring children to recite the pledge is therefore a violation of fundamental constitutional rights and freedoms. Totalitarian countries impose political orthodoxy upon their citizens by mandating displays of allegiance; the United States does not.

Recital of the pledge may be opposed for other reasons as well. For most children, the ritual of the pledge is meaningless, done without thought. As such, it does not foster love of country or patriotic attitudes and values.

As with other political concepts, children construct their own knowledge of the pledge by putting together things they know with the unknown, in splendid capriciousness. Thus, they recite, "one nation on the windowsill," "with liberty and jelly for all," and "I pledge allegiance to the flag, of the United States of American, and to the Publix [the name of a Southern food-store chain] for which it stands."

Further, children have no clear idea of what the pledge is. "It's like a song, I guess," explains a 7-year-old. "No, I think it's a prayer," said another child. Asked what they think about when they say the pledge, a great many children confess, "I think about going out to play" or "about sitting down" (Seefeldt, 1989).

Because the pledge holds little meaning, reciting it is more an act of indoctrination than patriotism. These rituals establish an emotional orientation toward country and flag even though an understanding of the meaning of the words and actions has not been developed. These seem to be indoctrinating acts that cure and reinforce feelings of loyalty and patriotism (Torney, Oppenheim, & Farnen, 1975).

Ritual acts of indoctrination do not promote patriotism; rather, they have the opposite effect. In fact, frequent participation in patriotic rituals has been associated with lower scores on knowledge of civics and less support for democratic values. Rather than using the pledge as a form of nonsensical indoctrination, try introducing children to its meaning:

- Reserve saying the pledge for special days—Earth Day; Lincoln's, Washington's, or Martin Luther King, Jr.'s birthday; Flag Day or other holidays—so that children learn that it has a special meaning and importance.

- Invite members of a scout troop to class to demonstrate their flag ceremony and recite the Pledge of Allegiance. The scouts might explain the meaning of their actions and tell what the flag means to them.

- Sing patriotic songs, or read poems or stories about the flag that may be more meaningful to young children. "This Land Is Your Land," "Yankee Doodle," and "Flag of America" are examples of songs that children can enjoy and can understand.

Patriotism

Patriotism involves much more than daily recitation of the pledge or even recitation of the pledge on special occasions. Children must first learn who they are and how they fit into their own immediate community. Only after children develop individually, in relation to family, school, neighborhood, and community, can they begin to gain an understanding of their country.

Explorations into the school community might be a first step. Children develop pride in being members of the school community. They share in caring for the school, keeping it clean as well as decorating its halls with artwork or participating in events such as picnics or parties. Children can also observe the work of the many people who serve the school. They see the diversity of jobs, the variety of people, and the need for mutual cooperation.

With this base of understanding, children can then take neighborhood field trips and explore the larger community. Here, too, they observe how people are interdependent and begin to see that they and their school are small parts of a larger world.

You can't take children on a field trip through the nation, but you can give children experiences that will enable them to begin to comprehend its size, magnificence, and diversity. Some of these experiences will necessarily be vicarious; but many can be concrete, with each planned to help children develop knowledge of their country.

The pleasurable, sensory experience of eating is one way to acquaint children with their country. When children eat oranges from Florida, they can locate Florida on a map and learn something about why oranges grow in Florida and not in Chicago. Or they could eat avocados from California, peaches from Georgia, potatoes from Maine, cherries from Michigan, or pineapples from Hawaii. It is also fun for children to plant the seeds from the foods. Then they can make comparisons between distant places and their own community.

The best resources are the children themselves. They can find out where they were born and where their parents and grandparents were born and lived. Primary children can locate these places on a map, or they can bring photos or props illustrating life in different areas of the United States.

Civic Participation

The ability to be responsible for oneself and to participate fully in the welfare of the group is an asset in any society; but in a democratic society, it is a requirement for citizenship (Morgan & Streb, 2001). *The National Standards for Civics and Government* (Center for Civic Education, 1994) indicate that, by the end of grade 4, children should have developed the following skills:

- Capacity to influence policies and decisions by working with others
- Ability to clearly articulate interests and make them known to key decision and policymakers
- Ability to build coalitions, negotiate, compromise, and seek consensus

The disposition to work for the common good and participate in joint efforts begins early in life. For young children under the age of 7 or 8, participation begins when they assume responsibility for themselves. Rooms for 3- and 4-year-olds are arranged not only to permit but to promote children's responsibility for their own dressing, toileting, and washing. These very young children may begin to assume responsibility for others and the group by joining in small groups for brief discussions, dictating thank-you notes or other letters, or listening to stories and singing songs. With adult assistance, 3- and 4-year-olds can participate in setting tables, serving food, cleaning up after play and work, or caring for plants and animals that belong to the group.

Early on, children learn to participate in enabling children with special needs to function fully in the group (Copple, 2003). In one group of 4-year-olds, the children casually and regularly helped Kathy, a girl with spina bifida, by handing Kathy her crutches, helping her on with her coat, carrying things for her, and waiting patiently for her as they played.

Primary children participate in other types of group activities. They can plan together and divide responsibilities. By sharing ideas, children in the primary grades can solve problems and make plans for their own learning. Children who are given responsibilities they can fulfill within the group are learning to participate in a democratic society.

Learning to live and participate within a group means setting rules and following them (CIVITAS, 2003). Children should take part in establishing rules in the class. They can contribute to the rules for woodworking, block building, use of the bathrooms and water tables, and so forth. Other rules are made for them. All must participate in a fire drill; and because there is little opportunity for them to contribute to the rules of the drill, they can use this occasion to discuss why it is important to follow certain rules, why rules are made, who makes them, and how they are made. Children can also become aware of other rules they must follow: the traffic laws, rules for riding the bus, and rules at home. These questions might be discussed: "What would happen if no one followed the rules?" "Do you think everyone should obey traffic rules?" "Why?"

Experiencing rules and discussing their purposes can help children realize that rules are made to protect them and others. Children should also realize that they have the responsibility to follow the rules, to make rules that are needed for living within a group, to change rules that no longer function to protect them and others, and to adjust the rules to fit changing situations (Nolte, Harris, & Harris, 1998).

Children's ideas should move continually toward conventional knowledge. They should be moving away from the following:

- Perceiving rules as coming from "on high"
- Thinking of rules as unchanging
- Perceiving people as powerless before the law
- Being egocentric, self-centered, and indifferent to others

They should be moving toward these goals:

- Knowing that rules and laws are established by people
- Realizing that rules and laws are always changing
- Understanding that they have control over their own lives
- Being empathetic, socially responsible, and considerate of others

The values of participating in a democratic society extend to the wider community as well as to the classroom. Even very young children can be introduced to the idea of serving others. "I don't want to go," a 6-year-old said when asked if he wanted to go visit the elders in a nearby nursing home. "But I'm going! You see," he said, "sometimes it's good to do things for other people. I don't like it, but I'm going because the old people like to see us little kids."

Serving others is part of being a productive member of a society. Even though a primary developmental task of young children is to feel secure and safe and to know that adults and their community will protect and serve them, young children can be introduced to the concept of serving others. Within the family, children are taught to care for siblings and help their parents. Two-year-olds are able to fold diapers, entertain the baby, and help set the table. Three- and four-year-olds assume more of their own care by helping their parents put their toys away—and even their laundry. They can also accompany their parents to visit or bring food to elderly or ill neighbors.

Once in primary grades, children are taught to serve their peers as well. Some learning occurs as children model their teachers, who demonstrate how to care for other children, or children may be asked to care for others directly: "Ask Cassidy to join you," or "Hold Bryan's hand while we're on the trip."

Children may also learn to serve the adults who care for them: "Help Ms. Jones [the aide] to set the tables," or "Ms. Jones needs two helpers to mix paints." "Who will sweep up the sawdust, wash the clay off the tables, or pick up the scraps on the floor?" teachers ask, adding, "We want to help Ms. Smith, the custodian, so she won't have as much work to do." Other times children may cook something for the lunchroom workers or present a painting or a thank-you note to the director or principal of the school.

Knowledge of the community is necessary to expand children's service of others in the broader community. Children can interview community workers to find out how they can help with their jobs. Firefighters, police officers, and other community helpers are more than willing to involve children in serving the community. During a visit to a first-grade class, one firefighter told the children that they could help by asking their parents to check their smoke alarms each Halloween. By doing so they would help keep their family safe, which would help firefighters do their jobs. Several parents reported to the teacher how grateful they were for this instruction; when they checked their smoke detectors, they found out that the batteries were dead.

Primary-age children, like the 6-year-old who articulated his good feelings about doing something for others, can serve others in their community. Depending on the community, neighbors who need help, or the agencies and associations serving others, children can be involved in a number of ways. One primary group took on the task of picking up trash from an elderly neighbor's yard next to the school. Another group made name tags from old greeting cards for a community organization. Others have written get-well letters, read their favorite stories on tape to give to hospitalized children, and selected books to give to Ukranian children learning to speak English.

Five-year-olds in one community wrote joke books and distributed them to children in waiting rooms of nearby medical facilities and doctors' offices. Parents and children waiting to see the health-care provider found the books relaxing, and the 5-year-old helpers learned that the process of helping others gives the helper a lasting sense of pride and satisfaction.

Voting

"I voted!" The right to vote and make choices for ourselves is one of the most valued rights and privileges of living in a democracy. The habits and procedures involved in voting can be an appropriate part of children's early educational experiences (Figure 6.1).

Children gradually learn the concepts of voting and majority rule. Teachers can use these first steps:

- Ask children to make choices and explain the reasons for their choices.
- Let children experience the consequences of their choices. One 5-year-old was observed putting blocks away while the rest of the class watched a video clip. When asked why he wasn't watching the clip, he said, "I decided to keep building. Now I have to clean up and miss the video. It's logical consequences."
- Graph children's choices so children can talk about them.
- Give children two choices, with all children getting their choice. (Decide to make chocolate or vanilla pudding; then graph how many children made chocolate and how many made vanilla.)

Figure 6.1   Learning to vote.

When we vote, we accept that the majority will is followed. Because of their egocentric thinking, young children cannot understand the concept of winning and losing. Nevertheless, this does not mean that children cannot start the process of learning to vote. Children who have made many choices for themselves and experienced the consequences of those choices can gradually learn to accept the consequences of the vote.

To begin, structure voting experiences in which each child can have his or her way. For example, children can vote to make either gelatin or pudding, with each group being allowed to make what it chooses. Or the class may be divided for games, those voting for Simon Says playing in one area of the room and those for Looby Loo in another area (Seefeldt & Galper, 2000).

The right to vote is one of the most valued rights of living in a democracy.

Or you could read the poem "The King's Breakfast" from *Now We Are Six* (Milne, 1955) and try butter or marmalade on pieces of bread. After tasting both, the group votes on whether or not the king was wise. Chart how many children voted for marmalade, like the king, and how many for butter.

While studying babies and their growth, a group of 4-year-olds tasted baby cereal and regular cereal. Then they voted for which cereal they liked best. The resulting graph indicated that every child was in agreement: they liked regular cereal, not yucky baby cereal.

After a number of experiences with voting, the entire class may follow the will of the majority. The class could vote and follow the will of the majority as they decide on any of these issues:

- Rules for clean-up time
- Use of towels in the bathrooms
- Specific equipment they want to purchase for their class or school
- Whose turn it is to complete a specific task
- Who will lead the group for the day
- What safety rules will be followed on a field trip

Children in the primary grades can begin developing ideas of local, state and national elections. When elections take place, ask families to take their children with them as they vote (Figure 6.2). In the classroom try to make the idea of voting as concrete as possible:

- Find books about voting, cooperation, and democracy. One class read *A Picture Book of Benjamin Franklin* (Adler & Wallner, 1991). The primary-age children then talked about the themes of the book: equality and cooperation.
- Create a voting box for the class so children can role-play voting after observing their families vote.

In November send a note to children's families:

Part of our curriculum is teaching children to make wise choices. We ask children to vote and make decisions about many things in the classroom. You can help us build children's understanding of the voting process by taking them with you when you go to vote.

When you go to vote, talk to the people outside the polling places and let your children examine the buttons and materials that are handed out. Inside, have the children examine the sample ballot and the voting machine. If you can, take your child into the booth when you vote. Explain that you are voting and making choices about who will represent you in our government.

Figure 6.2   Families vote!

These ideas are introductions to voting, not actual involvement in a national or local vote. Still, they can be the foundation for building the concept that not everyone holds the same opinions.

Teaching Peace, Understanding War

While it is necessary to teach children to celebrate diversity and learn tolerance, it is not enough. Even though they are very young, children in preschool-primary classrooms must begin the work of learning how to build a culture of peace. This work, like all their learning, begins with themselves and their here-and-now experiences.

In the typical preschool-primary classroom, opportunities to teach peace abound because fighting and conflict are a way of life for young children. Some researchers estimate that young children, with their egocentric thought, engage in a fight every few minutes (Levin, 2003).

Young children are highly affected by violence and wars. Many children have been personally involved in wars because a parent, a relative, or a neighbor is serving or has served in the military or because a relative or a family friend is experiencing war. Even for children who are not personally involved in war, far too often it is a very real part of their lives. Reserchers suggest that children experience a variety of adverse effects in reaction to wars. Both boys and girls appear to exhibit more behavioral problems and higher levels of anxiety when a war is taking place, with girls in particular exhibiting higher levels of anxiety and more behavior problems (Ronen, Rahay, & Rosenbaum, 2003)

It is well known that children are exposed to violence daily through the media. Even parents who monitor their children's television viewing find they cannot shield their young children from viewing violence in commercials for movies, upcoming TV shows, Saturday morning cartoons, computer games, or news coverage. Many researchers believe that the violence and fighting children witness through the media are observed and modeled (Teaching Tolerance Project, 2003). Violence marketed to children through the dolls and other toys that replicate the superheros children view on TV or in movies further channels children into imitating violence they have seen on the screen (Carlsson-Paige & Levin, 1998).

Couple the amount of violence children witness with their immature thought and their need to feel powerful or in control of their lives, and children's violent play is explained (Teaching Tolerance Project, 2003). By pretending to be a Power Ranger, a Teenage Mutant Ninja Turtle, or whatever warlike action figure is popular at the time, children feel and experience the power they do not otherwise have (Caulfield, 2002). Boys appear to exhibit more acts of empowerment when playing with war toys, while girls exhibit more acts of connectedness (Caulfield, 2002). Some observers believe war play is a natural and safe way for children to express normal aggression and, as such, is necessary. Others see war play as a way for children to handle fear of war or make sense of wars they observe in the media.

Just as children have always played war, teachers and parents have always struggled with how to respond to war play. Should teachers permit or ban war play? Should they redirect it—and how?

Early childhood educators also question whether or not to ban war toys from the classroom. Following are some suggestions (Levin, 2003):

- Banning war toys or or play rarely works. Rather than banning violent play, try to help children work things out.
- Avoid films, books, and games that glorify violence. Provide toys and books that support peace.
- Ensure safety for all children.
- Model positive, nonviolent behavior.
- Promote creative and imaginative play rather than imitative play. Observe play, and use the information you gain to help children move to more creative play. In Reggio-Emilia, Italy, teachers have used children's interest in monster play to teach myths.
- Address children's needs while trying to reduce violent play.

If you think children are playing war as a means of handling their own fears then you might try these approaches:

- Consider and talk about fears. Respect the fact that children are fearful, and give them strategies for coping, but do not embellish their fears.
- Give children accurate and appropriate information. Nothing is as bad as not knowing the truth. Know what and how much truth will help children at this time. Tell children in words they can understand.
- See that children develop mastery over themselves and their world. Put them in control as much as possible.
- Emphasize cooperative play and positive, nonviolent behaviors.

Obviously, any war play that intrudes on the rights and safety of others must be stopped. Even when war play is not out of hand, it can be redirected. Rather than focusing on the game or the war toy, teachers might concentrate on children's feelings. An openness to their own feelings, and an acceptance of feelings, might take away the child's urgency for making use of war games.

You can't even think about teaching children about war, peace, or violence without first understanding children's thinking (Carlsson-Paige & Levin, 1998). The following strategies can help uncover children's ideas about war and peace:

- Try to take the children's point of view when you listen to them talk about war.
- Consider a child's general cognitive development and understanding.
- Think about how children will transform what they hear about war in their own unique ways.

Because of their immature sense of social morality, young children seem to accept or favor war and violence more than older children do. Girls seem less likely to become interested in war, warlike games, or aggression than boys are; boys, during interviews, referred to war more frequently. Six-year-olds demonstrate a greater hostility to others than do children of other ages, and children in the third and fourth grades rate wars as more glamorous than do children of other ages. Children's concepts of peace are somewhat less tangible than their concepts of war are. They are usually absent; when present, they are associated with interpersonal peace and absence of personal conflict.

SUMMARY

Democratic attitudes and values are taught in the preschool-primary classroom. Children gain attitudes and values through modeling, reinforcement, and learning and have been taught through indoctrination, programs of value clarification, and value analysis.

Each preschool-primary classroom serves as a small laboratory in which children live the values of democracy. In a democratic classroom, teachers share control; children make choices; freedom of speech and thought are fostered; children's rights are respected, and they are not overwhelmed by the power of others; a sense of community is built; and teachers serve as models of respect for others. Through their interactions with others within a democracy, children will also learn political values, especially those of patriotism, participating in a democracy, and learning to learn.

Extend Your Knowledge

1. Teaching attitudes and values means you must first understand your own belief system. As an individual, take some time to consciously scrutinize your own attitudes and values. Next, in your class, engage in a full and open discussion of values and attitudes. You might begin with one of the following topics:
   a. Competition is part of our society, and children should be taught to compete as early as possible.
   b. Every child needs two parents to develop his or her own full potential.
   c. War toys should be banned from preschools.
   d. Boys should be encouraged to play with dolls.

2. Observe in a classroom. Record any observations of teachers' modeling of democratic values. What instances can you find of teachers sharing control with children, respecting each child, encouraging children to speak freely and have opinions, and fostering children's willingness to participate in the workings of the group?

3. The fact that you are in college suggests that you have developed an attitude of learning to learn. How did you develop that attitude? Who was your model? When do you think this attitude developed? Did any of your experiences in early childhood education foster this attitude?

Resources

The Center for Civic Education and CIVITAS offer a variety of teaching resources and aids:

- *The National Standards for Civics and Government*
- *CIVITAS: A Framework for Civic Education*
- *American Legacy: The U.S. Constitution and Other Essential Documents of American Democracy*
- *Comparative Lessons in Democracy*
- *Morality of Democratic Citizenship*

You can order *The Constitution Papers* (available on CD-ROM), a complete research tool on the U.S. Constitution, dozens of state constitutions, historical documents, and selected speeches from American history for your own use.

Both the Center for Civic Education and CIVITAS can be reached at the following address:

Center for Civic Education
5146 Douglas Fir Road
Calabasas, CA 91302–1467
Phone: (800) 350–4CCE
Fax: (818) 591–9330
E-mail: sales@civiced.org
Website: *http://www.civic.org/catalog_intro.html*

You may also be interested in materials about tolerance:

Teaching Tolerance Project
Southern Poverty Law Center
400 Washington Avenue
Montgomery, AL 36104
Website: *http://www.splc.org*

References

Adler, D. A., & Wallner, J. W. (1991). *A picture book of Benjamin Franklin*. New York: Holiday House.

Allen, G. L. (1997). Children's political knowledge and memory for political news stories. *Child Study Journal, 27*, 163–177.

American Psychological Association (APA). (2003). *Guidelines on multicultural education, training, research, practice, and organizational change for psychologists*. Washington, DC: Author.

Bandura, A. (1997). *Self-efficacy: The exercise of control*. New York: Freeman.

Berkowitz, M. W. (2000). Early character development and education. *Early Education and Development, 11*, 55–72.

Boyle-Baise, M. (2003). Doing democracy in social studies methods. *Theory and Research in Social Education, 31,* 50–70.

Bredekamp, S., & Copple, C. (1997). *Developmentally appropriate practice in early childhood programs* (Rev. ed.). Washington, DC: National Association for the Education of Young Children.

Brophy, J. (1990). Teaching social studies for understanding and higher-order applications. *Elementary School Journal, 90,* 351–419.

Carlsson-Paige, N., & Levin, D. (1998). *Before push comes to shove: Building conflict resolution skills with children.* New York: Redleaf.

Caudill, N. (1995). *Did you carry the flag today, Charley?* New York: Holt.

Caulfield, M. J. (2002). The influence of war play on cooperation and affective meaning in preschoolers' pretend play. *Dissertation Abstracts International, 62*(11-A), 3683.

Center for Civic Education. (1994). *National standards for civics and government.* Calabasas, CA: Author.

CIVITAS. (2003). *A summary of CIVITAS: A framework for civic education.* Calabasas, CA: Center for Civic Education.

Connell, R. (1971). *The child's construction of politics.* Melbourne, Australia: University Press.

Copple, C. (2003). *A world of difference.* Washington, DC: National Association for the Education of Young Children.

Dewey, J. (1944). *Democracy and education.* New York: Free Press.

DeRoach, E. F. (2001). *Educating hearts and minds: A comprehensive character education framework* (2nd ed.). New York: Corwin.

Goodman, J. F. (2000). Moral education in early childhood: The limits of constructivism. *Early Education and Development, 11*(1), 37–54.

Greenberg, P. (1992). Practices pertaining to respect, rights, responsibilities, and roots in any classroom. *Young Children, 47*(5), 10–17.

Hayes, G. (2003). Whose values do we teach? *Delta Kappa Gamma Bulletin, 63*(3), 55–57.

Helwig, C. C. (1998). Children's conceptions of fair government and freedom of speech. *Child Development, 69,* 518–521.

Helwig, C. C., & Prencipe, A. (1999). Children's judgments of flags and flag-burning. *Child Development, 70*(1), 132–143.

Hess, R., & Torney, J. (1967). *The development of political attitudes in children.* New York: Anchor.

Kochanska, G., Padavich, D. L., & Koenig, A. L. (1996). Children's narratives about hypothetical moral dilemmas and objective measures of their conscience: Mutual relations and socialization antecedents. *Child Development, 67,* 1420–1436.

Levin, D. E. (2003). *Teaching young children in violent times: Building a peaceable classroom* (2nd ed.). Cambridge, MA: Educators for Social Responsibility; Washington, DC: National Association for the Education of Young Children.

Longstreet, W. S. (2003). Early postmodernism in social education—Revisiting "decision making: The heart of social studies instruction." *Social Studies, 94*(1), 11–15.

Medda, M. E. (1996). Classrooms where children learn to care. *Childhood Education, 72*, 72–74.

Milne, A. A. (1955). *Now we are six.* London: Denton.

Morgan, W., & Streb, M. (2001). Building citizenship: How student voice in service-learning develops civic values. *Social Science Quarterly, 82*(1), 154.

National Center for History in the Schools (NCHS).(1994). *National standards for history for grades K–4.* Los Angeles: Author.

National Commission on Social Studies in the Schools. (1998). *Charting a course: Social studies for the 21st century.* New York: Author.

National Council for the Social Studies (NCSS). (1998). *Expectations of excellence.* Washington, DC: Author.

New, B. (2000). An integrated early childhood curriculum: Moving from the what to the how. In C. Seefeldt (Ed.), *The early childhood curriculum: Current findings and theory* (pp. 265–288). New York: Teachers College Press.

Nolte, D. W., Harris, R., & Harris, R. (1998). *Children learn what they live: Parenting to inspire values.* New York: Workman.

Nucci, L. P. (2001). *Education in the moral domain.* Chicago: University of Chicago Press.

Piaget, J., & Inhelder, B. (1969). *The psychology of the child.* New York: Basic Books.

Prencipe, A., & Helwig, C. C. (2002). The development of reasoning about the teaching of values in school and family contexts. *Child Development, 73*, 841–856.

Ronen, T., Rahav, G., & Rosenbaum, M. (2003). Children's reactions to a war situation as a function of age and sex. *Anxiety, Stress and Coping, 16*(1), 59–69.

Ryan, P. M. (1996). *The flag we love.* New York: Charlesbridge.

Schulze, P. A., Harwood, R. L., Schoelmerich, A., & Leyendecker, B. (2002). The cultural structuring of parenting and universal developmental tasks. *Parenting: Science and Practice, 22*(2), 151–178.

Seefeldt, C. (1982). I pledge. *Childhood Education, 58*(5), 308–311.

Seefeldt, C. (1989). Perspectives on the pledge of allegiance. *Childhood Education, 65*, 131–133.

Seefeldt, C. (1993). Learning for freedom. *Young Children, 48*(3), 4–10.

Seefeldt, C. (1995). Ready to learn, but what? *Contemporary Education, 66*, 134–139.

Seefeldt, C., & Galper, A. (2000). *Active experiences for active children: Social studies.* Upper Saddle River, NJ: Merrill/Prentice Hall.

Skinner, B. F. (1938). *The behavior of organisms.* New York: Appleton.

Teaching Tolerance Project. (2003). *Starting small: Teaching tolerance in preschool and the early grades.* Montgomery, AL: Southern Poverty Law Center.

Torney, J., Oppenheim, A. N., & Farnen, R. F. (1975). *Civic education in ten countries: An empirical study.* New York: Wiley.

Turiel, E. (2003). *The development of social knowledge: Morality and convention.* Cambridge: Cambridge University Press.

CHAPTER 7

Thinking and Concept Formation

Thinking is a way of learning.

John Dewey, 1933, p. 15

After you read this chapter, you should be prepared to respond to the following questions:

- What processes are involved in thinking, and how do teachers foster them?
- What is concept formation, and why is it an important part of social studies?
- What are key concepts?
- How do teachers nurture concept formation?

Eighteen-month-old Shawn is playing with her toys on a rug. As she pushes blocks around, piles them up, and knocks them down, she stops to take a sip of juice from a plastic bottle her mother has given her. She drops the bottle, and juice spills out on the rug.

By accident, Shawn puts her hand on the wet spot on the rug. The wetness puzzles her. She looks at her hand, at the rug, sensing a problem. She feels the rug once more. She looks at her hand, the bottle, and feels the rug again. Shawn takes her bottle, drinks from it, then looks back at the rug. Once again, she feels the wet spot, appearing to formulate tentative solutions to the problem.

Next Shawn tests her hypothesis by deliberately spilling some juice on the rug and feeling the new wet spot. She does this again, feeling the wetness she's just created on the rug, and once again feels the original spot, collecting additional data. A large smile appears on her face, and she grabs the bottle, drinking the remaining juice as if satisfied by her conclusions.

At one time, educators believed that critical thinking was possible only for older students or an exceptionally bright younger child. Today, however, we know that young children like Shawn use all of the same processes involved in adult thinking. They question and sense problems (identify a wet spot on the rug), locate information (feel the rug and the wet spot), see relationships between ideas and things (spill some juice on the rug), organize and summarize information, and reach conclusions (decide that the juice caused the wet spot).

Observe children at play, and you will find that they do independently question and sense problems (Figure 7.1). Children question constantly; and according to researchers, this questioning is the initial step in thinking. If the goal is to teach chil-

Thinking children solve problems.

Children sense a problem.
   Observe
   Notice
   Wonder
   Question

Children explore and investigate.
   Observe closely
   Ask questions
   Collect information
   Organize information

Children test ideas.
   Try things
   Do things differently
   Interpret collected information

Children reach conclusions.
   Discuss
   Reflect
   Express ideas through drawing, writing, movement

Figure 7.1   The process of inquiry.

dren to think, then teachers should encourage them to question and to identify a problem—one that is their own, not the teacher's.

Young children also locate and collect information in connection with their play. "I found a feather," squeals a delighted child. Another looks up into the tree and asks, "Which bird lost the feather?" Back in the classroom, they try to find a reference book about birds to identify the one that the feather came from. They also see relationships between ideas and things and begin to generalize. "This paint is just like mud—it slips around." By 4 years of age, children can relate an experience to something that has happened before or will occur in the future. After the age of 5, children begin to relate their ideas to the ideas of others by listening and through books and other media. From a simple generalization that mud is like paint, children increase their ability to draw generalizations about the things in their world, connecting one fact or concept to others.

Children begin to classify their world and organize information during infancy. They learn that some things are for sucking; other things are not. Some are food; others are not. By the time children are toddlers, they use words as a means of categorizing their world. They also infer, solve problems, and reach conclusions. These abilities are one of the highest forms of thinking. Children 4 years old and younger solve problems daily: "Sit up on the seesaw. Then we can make it go up and down." By 5 years of age, problem solving extends beyond personal experiences into the classroom, the school, and the community.

PLANNING THINKING EXPERIENCES

Teachers can foster children's thinking in the preschool and primary classroom by providing children with meaningful, integrated, and interesting experiences (NRC & IM, 2000). Effective teachers take the time and care to identify resources that families, communities, and children have to offer. These resources have the potential to provide children with firsthand, meaningful experiences that are of high interest to them.

Experiences that stem from children's here-and-now world promote thinking because they (1) are firsthand, (2) involve others, and (3) are filled with language.

Firsthand Experiences

The younger the child, the greater the need for firsthand, sensory experiences. Through the primary grades, children must find plenty of opportunities to touch, taste, move about, take apart, and put together again (Sousa, 2000). Through these sensory experiences children absorb information about the nature of their world and develop perceptions about heavy/light, smooth/rough, and soft/hard. Raw materials such as paints, blocks, sand, and water provide children with the opportunity to solve problems, make decisions, and think (Brodrova & Leong, 2003).

Dewey (1944) called for more "stuff" in schools and encouraged teachers to use raw materials so children could develop the ability to think. He believed that raw materials, such as wood, clay, and paints—without any predetermined end or goal for their use—push children into thinking (Bronson, 2003; Prawatt, 2000). Given blocks, sand, water, and boxes, children must figure out what to do with the materials, how they will do it, and when they have achieved their goals. They will have to monitor their own thinking and doing. When children are failing to achieve a goal, they must decide whether to adjust their actions and change their plans. When they reach their goal, which they alone have determined, they experience the joy of achievement and the satisfaction that comes from thinking (Brown, 1997).

Experiences Involving Others

Experiences to foster thinking must involve others. Throughout the day, while working in centers, arguing on the playground, or discussing a story in the classroom, children are expected to interact freely—talking, discussing, arguing, and negotiating. Through these naturally occurring interchanges, especially when playing, children are challenged to adjust their egocentric thought, assimilating and accommodating different points of view (Brodrova & Leong, 2003). If they are to get along at all, children must consider the ideas, thinking, and wishes of others. Through this informal give-and-take, children are forced to deal with the perspectives of others and build a foundation for understanding that there are different ways of looking at the world (Prawatt, 2000).

Vygotsky believed that social activity was the generator of thought.

Vygotsky (1986) maintained that this type of social activity is the generator of thought. He believed that individual consciousness is built from outside through relations with others: "The mechanism of social behavior and the mechanism of consciousness are the same" (p. ii). Whether working with others in centers or playing outside, children have an opportunity to build this social consciousness.

Experiences Requiring Language

Experiences make the need for language real and necessary. "Children not only speak about what they are doing, their speech and action are part of one and the same complex psychological function" (Vygotsky, 1986, p. 43). Through talking, arguing, discussing, listening, reading, and writing, children clarify and expand on their experiences.

Experiences and activities give children something to talk about. When children are given the freedom to talk, their informal conversations and interactions "contribute substantially to intellectual development in general, and literacy growth in particular" (Dyson, 1988, p. 535). Children converse informally as they work together on a puzzle, rotate the eggs in an incubator, or build with blocks. More formal conversations take place during group times. Teachers encourage children to tell how they completed a project, how they found their way to the nurse's office, or why they think the fish died. Plans for the day or the party next week may be discussed. As children talk, listen, and discuss shared experiences, they gain insights into one another's perceptions of the experiences—how others view the world.

Writing is also used to communicate. Children can write or dictate invitations and thank-you notes. They can write notes to another class and dictate and send letters to siblings, grandparents, and parents. Children can also e-mail other classes far away who are studying the same concepts. They can then compare their findings and ideas with those of others.

Experiences demand expression. Langer (1942) believed that humans were born with an urgent physiological need to express the meaning of their experiences in symbolic form—a need no other living creature has. As children think about their experiences, they develop images, feelings, and ideas about them. Expression can take any number of forms. Children may draw or paint a picture about their experience, describe it in dance, tell about it in words, or dictate or write down their ideas.

Teachers can use literature and reference books to extend and expand firsthand experiences so children have a richer mental model of their world and the vocabulary to describe it. Stories may be read aloud several times a day. The entire range of literature, from poetry and folktales to the encyclopedia, helps children sum up and clarify ideas gained through firsthand experiences (Whitehurst & Lonigan, 1998).

FOSTERING THINKING PROCESSES

Setting the stage for thinking is necessary but not enough. Teachers also need to recognize and foster the processes involved in thinking: questioning and sensing problems, locating information, organizing information, interpreting, reaching conclusions, and making generalizations.

Questioning and Sensing Problems

Children are full of questions, at least when they are outside of school. The same type of questioning should abound in preschool-primary classrooms. This is not the old-fashioned kind of questioning in which teachers asked children to recite the "right" answers or questioned them to "test" their knowledge. Rather, thinking begins when children themselves sense a problem and pose a question to try to understand reality.

It is not always easy to think of a question. Think back to your own experiences, perhaps after a professor ended a lecture by asking, "Are there any questions?" only to be met with silence. In this situation, there were no questions because no one in the class had an idea, understanding, or knowledge of content. Without knowledge or understanding, there was nothing to question. Then, too, suppose you had a question about the lecture but felt uncomfortable asking it because everyone would recognize your ignorance and might laugh at you.

Children, as well, must have some knowledge, information, or content to sense a problem or ask a question. In a classroom filled with materials for learning—sand, water, blocks—and a teacher who uses the child's here-and-now world in the broader community as a resource for learning, questions will arise. Rooms should be arranged with centers of interest and materials within the centers juxtaposed to challenge students to ask, "Why?" "How?" "What if?"

It is not enough to have a rich environment to stimulate questioning. A psychologically safe environment is also necessary. A child may have a question or sense a problem, but may not feel free to ask it. Children's questions must be accepted and not seen as frivolous or attempts to challenge authority. In classrooms where children are respected and teachers themselves question and ponder, children feel safe and are free to question (Figure 7.2).

Locating Information: Field Trips

Young children learn about their world and themselves through observation; nearly every social studies activity includes observing. By encouraging children to use all their senses, you can strengthen their observation skills.

Field trips are especially useful in fostering observation skills. Whether a trip is within the school building, school yard, or immediate community, children have opportunities to gather information through the senses (Seefeldt & Galper, 2000). You might plan different types of field trips to make children aware of the information they can gain through the senses.

A Feeling Trip

Plan a trip to discover the different textures in the school building or classroom or outside the school. Children can take large pieces of newsprint and blunt, chunky crayons with the paper removed to make "rubovers" of the textures they find. Placing the paper over the texture of a tree trunk, sidewalk, screen grating, or concrete block, children rub over the paper with the side of their crayon, actually feeling the differences between rough and smooth, and observe the texture that appears on the paper. Back in the classroom, children can discuss the textures they noted, observe

---

Teachers can model questioning techniques by frequently asking:

Why? What if? How come? Explain. . . . Give reasons. . . . Prove. . . . Which? Account for. . . . Tell the meaning. . . . Why is that important? Tell why you agree. . . . Why do you disagree? Show me how. . . . Can you think of something else? What is the difference? What is the same? Why did this happen? What happened? What would happen in? Which would you rather? What would you say if someone told you . . .? How do you know?

Figure 7.2   Modeling questions.

other textures in the room with their hands and eyes, and try to incorporate rough-ness and smoothness into their drawings and paintings.

Children can use feeling-observation skills for collecting information on other field trips. You might ask children to feel the smoothness of the fire truck or the roughness of the truck's tires on a trip to the fire station or to observe textures of the environment on a trip to a farm. Trips within the school building, the immediate neighborhood, or the larger community become more meaningful when children are aware of the information they can obtain through the sense of touch.

A Smelling Trip

Children could take a trip to notice how useful the sense of smell is in gathering in-formation. Smells of the office, cafeteria, gym, outdoors, street, or different stores can be observed and discussed. On the trip, children can be helped to distinguish be-tween observations and inferences: "What do you smell?" "Now, what do you think that smell means?" "What are the cooks making?" "You think you smell bread, but can you be sure that it is unless you see it for yourself?" Children can complete their observations and test their inferences by seeing and tasting the bread.

The sense of smell can be used to make continual observations about, and gain information from, the environment. As they try foods from other cultures, children can be asked to smell the food before tasting it or to use smell to identify plant life in the neighborhood.

A Looking Trip

Children can take other trips to strengthen the sense of sight. Ask them to look for different colors, shapes, and sizes they notice within the school building or even a room of the building. Encourage them to describe what they observe specifically—naming things as tall, thin, wide, narrow, shiny, low, bright, or tiny instead of the usual big or small.

Extend children's ability to look by providing them with inexpensive cameras. You can solicit donations from a local business or ask your school to keep a supply of inexpensive cameras and film available for all classes. Inexpensive digital cameras work well because you can print numerous copies of the photos and send them to children's families via e-mail.

Remember, too, it's not necessary for each child to have her own camera because children can take turns. Show them how to look through the camera and frame what they are photographing. Using clipboards, have children take notes about what they took pictures of and why. When the photos are developed, they can be mounted in scrapbooks, on charts, or just left on a table for children to sort through and talk about.

A Hearing Trip

You could arrange a field trip just for listening. "What sounds do you hear in the room? In the hallway? In the cafeteria? In the gym? On the street? In the supermar-ket?" Take along a tape recorder to capture some of the sounds. Have the children

Children use all their senses as they observe things in their environment.

listen for information by asking them to stand still, close their eyes, and name the things they hear. Back in the classroom, children can listen to the tape and recall the sounds they heard. They might draw pictures of the sounds they heard or tell about other things that make similar sounds. They might compile booklets of the sounds of home, school, cafeteria, or office.

Observation is a process that continues throughout the day. Teachers use every opportunity to help children locate information by observing. Look for ways to challenge children as they observe. Use questions such as "What else do you see? Is it larger than . . . ? Smaller than . . . ? How does it feel?" and statements such as "Look at this part," "Find another one just like it," "It's green just like. . . ." and "Look at the dots on it." These questions and statements help children collect information through close observation of the environment.

You can provide additional activities to check children's observing ability and foster their observation skills. The following suggestions make good transition experiences between activities:

1. Three or four children face the class in a line. Ask the other children to observe them closely and then close their eyes. When eyes are closed, rearrange the children in the line. Then ask the other children to open their eyes and describe what has changed. As children show an increased ability to observe and describe changes, have the children in the line change or remove something they are wearing—eyeglasses, a pin, a scarf, or a headband—and then ask the others to tell what is different.

2. Put a few objects on a tray. Ask the children to look closely and then close their eyes. While their eyes are closed, remove one of the objects or change the positions of the objects on the tray. Then ask children to tell what is missing or what has changed.

3. Make sounds behind a screen, using a piece of cardboard or a large box as the screen. Crumple some paper, whirl an egg beater, hit wood blocks, ring bells, and make other sounds, asking children to identify each: "What do you hear?" "What do you think made the sound?"

4. Cut up an apple, a turnip, a radish, a pear, a potato, or an other white fruit or vegetable. Cut the pieces into identical sizes and shapes, removing the outer skin or coloring. Ask children to taste the cubes and describe their observations: "What does it taste like?" "How does it feel?" Children can describe what they observe through taste, touch, and sight; then ask if they can guess what they are tasting and name the fruit or vegetable. With any tasting projects, children must be mature enough to be aware of the dangers of identifying unknown substances by tasting them. Without frightening them, caution children against ever trying to find out about some strange material by tasting it. Tell children always to ask an adult before tasting, smelling, or feeling something they do not know about.

Kindergarten and primary-age children will want to begin to locate information through references and resource materials. Locating information through the library and other media sources does not take the place of direct observation but is used in addition to it. When children ask, "Where does the garbage go after it's in the truck?" "Why did the orange tree die?" or "How does the telephone work?" you can reply, "I don't know, but let's find out." In this way, children can use prints, photographs, pamphlets, magazines, newspapers, maps, and other reference materials to collect information.

Organizing and Interpreting Information

Once children have collected information, they must organize it. The process of concept formation serves to organize information; children become aware of the need to classify, compare and contrast, summarize, and interpret the information, ideas, and questions that arise from their observations.

Classifying

Classification, the process of arranging information into categories, is basic to concept formation. It is used to impose order on a collection of objects or events, to identify objects or events, and to show similarities and differences, as well as interrelationships, among them. Children classify without direction from adults. They sort, group, and regroup buttons, sticks, acorns, rocks, and toys as they play with them. Given any group of objects, one of the first things children begin doing is to sort them by placing them into groups and categories.

Gelman (1998) documents that children have an impressive understanding of categories. They understand the distinction between appearance and reality, use names as a guide for making inferences, and realize that growth is an orderly, natural process. This understanding of categories is an important tool for thinking.

Children's ability to classify follows a set pattern of developmental stages:

- *Stage 1.*   Children sort objects according to a single property that is perceptually obvious, such as color, size, or shape. Or they may classify according to some category they cannot communicate or are not really aware of themselves. They change their categories frequently, beginning again. When asked why he put all the buttons in this pile, a child might shrug and say, "I don't know," or "All of those are like my mother's."

- *Stage 2.*   True classification refers to abstracting a common property in a group of objects and finding the same property in other objects in that group. All of the red buttons, and so forth, are grouped together, and children can identify how they have classified the objects.

- *Stage 3.*   Multiple classification refers to objects grouped on the basis of more than one common property. Multiple classification entails a recognition that any given object could belong to a number of different classes at the same time. For example, children will group all the large red buttons together.

- *Stage 4.*   All/some relationships appear at this level. All/some refers to children's being able to recognize a distinction among classes on the basis of a property that belongs to all members of the class and one that belongs only to some members of a class. For instance, in a display of red squares, red triangles, and red circles, understanding all/some relationships would enable a child to recognize that all the shapes are red but that only some of them are squares, circles, or triangles.

- *Stage 5.*   Class inclusion relationships refer to children's ability to form subclasses of objects or events while including all subclasses within a larger class. For instance, in a container of plastic chips, some red and some blue, there is a subclass of red chips and one of blue, both of which belong to the class of plastic chips.

By age 5, children can usually classify in terms of one characteristic, later by two. Classification by the function that is performed develops even later. Children's first experiences with classification should be completely exploratory in nature, without adult interference. Later you might ask them why they put all the objects together, if there are any other ways they could think of to group the objects, and how they would name the groups. Children can classify people at work or play, tools used by workers, or happy or sad faces.

Comparing and Contrasting

Comparing (the process of noting similarities between things) and contrasting (noting differences) are used as children classify and sort things into categories. Comparing and contrasting mean that children observe details and features of things and mentally sort them into categories of likenesses and differences. Comparing and contrasting are used to form concepts and are considered basic to thinking. You can use any experience to help children see likenesses and differences among objects or events. A kitten wandering onto the playground can lead children to wonder how the kitten is like them and different from them. Determining likenesses is difficult for young children; but with help, they can see that the kitten eats, sleeps, and has two eyes and two ears. Children can compare and contrast themselves, animals they raise, jobs their parents do, pictures they see, books they read, movies they watch, or stores they visit.

Critical thinking might be part of comparing and contrasting. As children see how things are alike and different, you can ask them to state their preferences for one or the other. When they make selections about the way they like to sing a song, hear a story, or play a game, you might ask why they made the selection: "What parts of it do you like?" "How does it make you feel?" "Why do you like it?" and "Why didn't you choose something else?"

Having collected, compared, classified, and contrasted information, children need to summarize it. In connection with unit topics, lessons, or something of interest they have experienced, children can summarize their findings:

- Report to the class, either by speaking, writing, or dictating to the teacher, who then reports to the others
- Draw, paint, or model something that describes their findings
- Act out a skit or a play or tell a story about the topic
- Make charts, tables, records, or graphs of their experiences

Graphing

Children can present information and convey ideas in many ways. Charts, graphs, sketches, cartoons, and pictures are useful for summarizing and presenting information in simplified form. Graphs can be used by young children, especially if the children construct them (Martin & Miller, 1999). They should be closely related to children's experiences and based on their interests.

"Amy has the most brothers in her family; see—she has more boys on our family graph than anybody else," pointed out Cannala, age 4, to the visitor, demonstrating that she could interpret pictures in the form of a graph and gather useful information. Graphing (portraying information in pictorial form) is usually introduced to children in the fourth grade. However, when children graph their own experiences, they appear to grasp readily the relationships and information the graphs illustrate (Polonsky, 2000).

The skill of interpreting graphs and being able to present information in the form of a graph is becoming increasingly important in our technological society. A graph condenses numerous facts and bits of information into an easy-to-see, easy-to-read pictorial form and is an efficient way of communicating information.

Several different types of graphs can be introduced to young children. The picture graph, which uses symbols or pictures instead of bars or lines, is usually introduced first. The bar graph is introduced after children have become familiar with the picture graph. Line graphs, made by drawing lines at right angles to each other, may be too abstract for the youngest children but can be introduced to primary children who have had many previous experiences with picture and bar graphs.

Children learn how to interpret graphs by making their own graphs to illustrate relationships they have experienced. You must introduce graphing with concrete materials and experiences, gradually progressing to abstractions.

For example, two pupils working together may each take a few handfuls of colored cubes, counters, or other suitable objects from a box. After counting up all of the yellow ones taken, you could say, "Jack has five such cubes, and Kim has two." These cubes are then placed vertically or horizontally so that the children can see how many yellow ones were collected.

Following discussion of this experience, the number of colored blocks each child collected can be represented using colored paper squares, the same color as the blocks, pasted to another paper. Later any kind of information—types of leaves, number of children with brown eyes, types of bottle caps, sizes of acorns found, or number of pets—can be collected and recorded. However, the teacher should not rush in moving children from graphing real objects to the use of paper.

Graphing experiences with kindergarten and primary children take them from the concrete to the abstract. Discussing family similarities and differences, children lined up in front of a mark on the board that represented their family type and composition. To make the children conscious of the need to record information, the teacher asked them if they could stay in their lines for a week or more so they could talk about family size. When the children protested that they would get sleepy, hungry, or tired, the teacher asked if they could use something else in the line instead of themselves. Having rejected the use of cats, who would run away, and pianos, which were too big and expensive, the children decided on blocks, and they replaced themselves in the line with blocks. The next problem was to find a substitute for the blocks, which had to be put away. A flannel board, with felt squares representing the children, was the final abstraction.

Once children have had experience in making graphs with concrete objects, they can illustrate other experiences. Some experiences that can be illustrated graphically might arise spontaneously; you can structure others.

One class, riding buses for the first time, became nervous and anxious as the time neared to return home. Several began asking the teacher what bus they rode on, worrying that they would get on the wrong bus. The teacher quickly drew a graph on the board showing which children rode which bus. As the principal announced each bus, the teacher pointed to the graph and read the names of the children riding that bus. The children readily saw the relationship illustrated by this graph and, the next day, constructed it on a bulletin board. They consulted it for several weeks, and the children were reassured that they would catch the right bus. Several of the children

On a field trip, children learned that a farmer measured her horse with her hands. Back in the classroom, children measured things with their hands and created a pictorial bar graph.

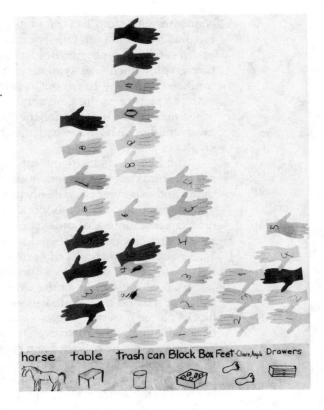

horse   table   Trash can Block Box Feet-Clare,Angela Drawers

pointed out that bus 70 was an empty set because none of the children in their room rode on that bus.

A kindergarten class visited a farm where the farmer told them that the pony they had ridden on was 13 hands high. Using her hand, she showed them how ponies are measured. Returning to the classroom, the teacher noted the children's interest in measuring objects in their room using their hands. As the children traveled around the room measuring everything in sight, the teacher began transferring their observations to a graph. Later, the entire class constructed the graph. Each child in the class, when asked, was able to point to the trash can, the tallest thing measured in the class, and feet, the shortest thing measured.

A graph illustrating how many states each child had visited was constructed in a first-grade classroom in a city in Florida, which is heavily populated with families from every state in the nation. The teacher suggested and structured this graph to initiate a discussion of where the children had lived and to acquaint them with the states of the nation.

You might suggest graphs showing the number of children who have a birthday during each month; the number of sunny, rainy, or cloudy days in a month; or the number of children with the same hair color. As the children play with sand or water, you could ask them to graph how many cups each of their containers holds. Children's weight and height also lend themselves to graphical representation.

Question children about the graph. Try to probe children's understanding of the relationship between variables. Ask, "What does this mean?" "How is this related to . . . ?" Or you might ask children to show which has the most, the least, more than, less than, or fewer than; and you can encourage them to discuss the representations of the graph.

Seeing Relationships and Beginning to Generalize

Generalizations are relationships between two ideas or two or more concepts usually expressed as declarative, highly abstract statements such as "The earth is constantly changing," or "We are all interdependent."

Because generalizations are highly abstract, educators once believed that teaching them in the preschool or primary classroom was inappropriate. Today educators recognize that generalizing (the process of connecting one idea with another) cannot be taught but can only be learned through experiences.

The child who said, "Mud and paint are the same—they both feel slippery," could not have done so without experiencing both paint and mud. The child who generalized that everyone has a home could not have done so without first observing the homes of rabbits, birds, and classmates. Both children could have collected information from various media and then reflected on, organized, and analyzed this information.

Skillful, reflective teachers can plan experiences that are presented as a continuous whole instead of isolated activities. A thread of meaning should run through them, with one experience building on another.

A group of 4-year-old children took a walking field trip around their school to collect fall leaves. After the trip, the teacher asked the children to look through the leaves they had collected and find three different types—maple, oak, and sweet gum. The children made a graph of the three types of leaves and placed the leaves on a chart board. The teacher then read a book about trees. On a windy day, the children again went outside to watch leaves fall from trees. They talked about how the leaves twirled and swirled as they fell. Back in the classroom, the children danced like falling leaves while the teacher played the piano, matching the music to their motions. Throughout the experiences, the teacher took photographs, which, when organized on a wall chart and in a photo album, helped children reflect on their experiences and reach generalizations about trees and leaves.

A first-grade group decided to study animals, beginning with cats. They first observed their own cats and wrote stories about them. The children sorted and classified pictures of cats roaming freely in the world and those in zoos and homes. Next, the class visited a veterinarian, who described how cats and dogs grow, showed pictures to the children, and let them see the skeleton of a cat. After this experience, one group of children decided to study bones, and another continued to expand its knowledge of cats by consulting books and other media. Both groups wrote stories, painted, and drew pictures. To culminate the experience, the groups presented their findings to each other. These experiences, presented as a continuous whole, gave the children the opportunity to develop conceptual relationships and generalizations between and among concepts from biology, mathematics, language, and science.

Planning continuity in field trips is another way in which teachers can foster children's ability to reach generalizations. First field trips for 3-, 4-, and 5-year-old children, who are just beginning to master relationships within their immediate environment, should be walking field trips in or around the school. Taking children away from their familiar environment may confuse them rather than clarify their thinking and enable them to make associations. By the primary grades, however, children have gained sufficient knowledge of their world, as well as the necessary cognitive maturity, to recall past experiences and relate them to new ones.

To be able to generalize, children must first have a solid understanding of the concepts to which the trips are related. Thus, some field trips and experiences should be repeated to give children the opportunity to grasp and understand the embedded concepts.

Teachers' thoughtful questions and comments help children see associations. For instance, the teacher who had the children classify leaves might have asked them, "What other leaves have points like this one?" or "How are these alike, and how are they different?" During the study of cats, the teacher asked, "Can you give another example of that?" "How is this cat like the one in the zoo?" "Where else did you see this?"

Interpreting, Reflecting, and Reaching Conclusions

When you ask children about the meaning of an experience, you are asking them to interpret. Children can discuss their experiences with others, sharing their ideas about and perceptions of some event. Following a field trip, a visit from a police officer, or the experience of sitting on a firetruck, children can tell each other how they felt, the part that frightened them, and generally give their interpretations of the event. When all children are encouraged to contribute, either formally or in spontaneous discussions, they begin to see how each person brings a different perspective to the same idea or experience. Through vicarious experiences, children can also use the skill of interpreting—telling about their impressions of a picture or photograph; dancing and moving to a record; drawing, painting, or illustrating in some other way their interpretation of a book or movie.

Real problems that need solving also require children's interpretations. Children must observe all the information present in the situation, understand the meaning of the events, and interpret those events to come up with a solution. In these kinds of situations, Dewey's (1933) requirement for thinking—seeing something ahead instead of something behind—is present.

You can use any problem that presents itself for children to interpret:

- Why were these blocks left out? How can we arrange things so it won't happen again?
- Why have the plants died? How can we find out, and what can we do about it?
- The bathroom toilet is always stopped up and overflows. The janitor said it's because of all of the paper towels in the toilet. What should we do?

- Too many children want to paint at the easel at the same time. How can we solve the problem?

- How many different ways can you use these materials?

You can focus children's attention on the problem to be solved by asking, "Why did it happen?" "How can we keep it from happening again?" "Where did it go?" "What should we do?" These questions might help children predict, suggest hypotheses, and evaluate their interpretations to solve the problem.

An experience is not complete unless children reflect on that experience and think about it. Young children are generally not as attuned to their own cognitive processes as older children are. Adults can help children think about their own thinking. During the preschool-primary grades, adults can introduce children to the idea that at times they will be confused and not have clear ideas. However, by thinking about things, they can reach a better sense of what to think and do.

The process of thinking about thinking might begin by helping children distinguish between understanding and not understanding things. Teachers help children to think about their thinking in other ways. By organizing their ideas through graphing, classifying, or sorting materials into categories, children will be thinking about their own thinking. Other opportunities to reflect and think about their own thinking are formally planned. Teachers can do the following:

- Ask children to stop working on a problem or project—to pull away and think again about what they want to accomplish, what they have done so far to achieve this goal, and what they still have to do.

- Help children organize their ideas. Either group or individual activities enable children to do so. They may dictate or write a story, create a book or a chart, or write a poem. Journal writing, keeping a diary, or writing "My History in First Grade" are other ways for children to organize their ideas.

- Have children present their ideas to others. They might describe and discuss how they completed their project, found a solution to some problem, or put on a play. One kindergarten class became intrigued with different bears in the stories they had enjoyed. Comparing the bears in *Winnie the Pooh* (Milne, 1991), *The Three Bears*, and *Little Bear* (Minarik, 1978), the children put on plays about the different bears. One group created a display for the room of stuffed bears and books about bears, and other children made a bulletin board and a mural illustrating what they had learned about bears.

CONCEPT FORMATION

Good teaching invariably concerns itself with conceptual understanding because concepts are the ingredients for thinking. In *Clan of the Cave Bear* (Auel, 1980), the members of the clan had no word or gesture to represent tree. With brains limited to memorization only, the clan members had to name and think about each kind of tree separately. They were unable to conceptualize or categorize trees into a singular concept or idea. Thus, they were limited in their ability to think and to solve problems.

With the ability to group things into categories or to think in terms of concepts, we are freed from focusing on each isolated fact. When children have an idea or a concept, they have knowledge about how facts and pieces of information are related and interrelated. They understand something; and because they've organized the information into a concept, it holds meaning to them.

Memorizing facts as isolated bits of data is meaningless. With enough drill and practice and perhaps a lot of reinforcement, children can memorize a great number of facts. Unfortunately, children who are taught social studies facts by rote are rather like parrots who have been taught to recite. Neither parrot nor child has any idea or concept of what has been memorized. "A teacher who tries to do this usually accomplishes nothing by empty verbalism, a parrot-like repetition of words by the child, simulating a knowledge of the corresponding concepts but actually covering up a vacuum" (Vygotsky, 1986, p. 74).

Teaching for concept formation leads to more learning because learning concepts is never complete. This incompleteness leads children and learners of any age to continue to want to learn still more in an attempt to complete their understanding. Hence, unlike a compilation of isolated facts, a store of concepts motivates a child to continue to learn more (Prawatt, 2001).

Not only do concepts foster learning; they make it easier. Concepts are like mental filing cabinets. Children can use concepts to organize and categorize their experiences into meaningful wholes. Even the youngest children begin to understand the world by sorting the things they see, smell, taste, and hear into categories. Infants learn broad categories first—things to suck on that produce food; things to suck on that give no food; things that are painful; those that are pleasurable; faces that are familiar; those that are not.

Toddlers build broader categories of concepts (Gelman, 1998). For example, they first construct the idea of things that are dogs and not dogs. As they experience dogs and have the names of different dogs labeled for them, they begin to construct an idea.

Thus, the social studies are organized around concepts key to each process and discipline content area. As Dewey (1916) advised, the National Council for Social Studies (1998) today advocates organizing social studies around teaching concepts, not isolated facts. By organizing social studies around key concepts or ideas, conceptual themes, and units, children will be able to make sense of abstract ideas and facts and begin the lifelong process of acquiring knowledge.

Key Concepts

Meaningful and conducive to future learning, the concepts considered key in each social science discipline organize children's learning experiences. In *The Process of Education*, Jerome Bruner (1960) pointed out that each subject, every discipline, has its own structure. This structure is identified through concepts that are key and that define the discipline. Teachers use these key concepts, or ideas, to organize and direct interactions with the children. When teachers think about and internalize concepts that are key to any social studies discipline, they then have a way to think about content, the way in which children understand content, and how to organize the children's experiences in the school setting.

The key concepts that relate and connect isolated facts into a unified whole also enable teachers to organize a whole, unified, and integrated curriculum. When the focus is on big ideas, teachers are not able to teach isolated facts but only the connection between facts. Thus, the wholeness of the child, and of knowledge, is honored.

Long before Bruner, Lucy Sprague Mitchell (1934) demonstrated how teachers bring children and social studies together by organizing their interactions with children around key ideas from geography. Before that time the social studies curriculum had been based on isolated facts that children memorized. Mitchell called this curriculum "Pops and Caps," an abbreviation for "populations and capitals of the 48 states," which children had been forced to memorize.

Decrying this sterile and meaningless curriculum, Mitchell (1934) designed a continual, meaningful curriculum in *Young Geographers* revolving around key concepts in geography. She matched the key ideas from the field of geography with the interest drives, orientation, and tools of children from infancy through adolescence. She observed how the infant, before walking and talking, attends to and experiences the qualities of things and how the understanding of the relationship of self to not-self develops. The tools of the infant are the use of the senses and muscles in direct exploration; the content of geography is the direct experience of the immediate environment. Mitchell specified a continuous geography curriculum for each stage of a child's life, ending with the 12-year-old who has adult interests and orientations to anything three-dimensional, the use of a wide variety of tools, and the capacity for abstract thought.

Continuing today, the social science disciplines of history, geography, economics, global education, and others are organized around key concepts. This text, for example, is organized around the concepts considered key in each of the social science disciplines; it describes what is known of how children understand them, and it offers suggestions for expanding children's embryonic concepts into fully developed, complete, and accurate ideas. Using key concepts of any given discipline, teachers can nurture children's concept formation.

Concept Development

The process of learning concepts takes place from the moment of birth. Entering the world without a store of knowledge, infants cannot think because they have nothing to think about. They have not yet constructed any ideas or knowledge. Infants, however, are very efficient learners and at birth immediately begin their lifelong pursuit of constructing concepts.

Hearing, smelling, tasting, and seeing, infants start to organize and categorize their experiences, continually seeking out and responding to their environment. The initial instincts with which infants were born—seeing, grasping, sucking—become more complex, more coordinated, and eventually more purposeful. This process is

Children begin the lifelong process of developing concepts.

called adaptation. Assimilation and accommodation are the processes that make adaptation possible (Franklin, 2000; Piaget, 1959).

Assimilation

Assimilation is the term Piaget used for "taking in." Assimilation is absorbing new material into an already-existing idea or schema. An infant sucks and has a sucking schema. Infants suck on nipples and get milk, but this same sucking gets no milk when used on finger, toes, or their mother's hair. They have to accommodate, or change their sucking schema, to make it fit things that are not nipples. A child was given a whole orange for the first time and bit into it as she would an apple. She had an idea or construct of apples—whole fruits that were bitten into—but no construct of fruit that needed peeling. She was assimilating the orange into an already-existing pattern, idea, or schema for fruit. The next time she was given an orange, she peeled it, changing her pattern of thought to accommodate the new information gained through experience.

Adaptation-Accommodation

Assimilation and accommodation are not separate or independent but take place at the same time. Piaget also calls this interaction adaptation. Through their interactions and experiences, children construct ways of thinking that are more effective in enabling them to deal with their environment. As they gain more experiences, they acquire more structures and thus can adapt to more and more complex situations.

Early Concepts

Every day, children spontaneously form and use concepts that they construct through the processes of assimilation and accommodation. These ideas, or ways of thinking about the world, develop without schooling, without any type of instruction. Piaget calls them spontaneous concepts.

These first concepts are embryonic in nature. Children's early concepts "stand in the same relationship to true concepts as the embryo to the fully formed organism" (Vygotsky, 1986, p. 58). Every day, spontaneous concepts are pseudoconcepts, often based on the way things look or seem to be rather than on scientific fact. Although inaccurate, incomplete, and vague, children's early concepts are sufficient to permit them to make simple classifications of things in their world. They recognize a man but frequently cannot distinguish among different individuals belonging to the same class.

Children's incomplete concepts are full of misconceptions, which sometimes get them into trouble. A 4-year-old has a concept of car as something that has life and intent. A car, alive with headlights that are eyes that can see, will obviously stop when seeing the child in the street. Children may see a toy or candy in the store that they desire and simply take it. They have no concept of purchasing, of exchanging money for goods.

As children mature, so do their concepts. Their ability to see, hear, and feel increases. They can attend to and perceive more and more of their environment and gradually recall and remember the things they have seen, heard, felt, and tasted.

NURTURING CONCEPT FORMATION

Concepts cannot be taught; they can only be constructed by each individual. Teachers can, however, nurture children's embryonic concepts by providing a rich environment and conditions that will foster the development of fully formed, accurate, and complete concepts of social studies. Such conditions of teaching must be matched to the readiness of each child.

The Problem of the Match

"The task of teaching a subject to a child at any particular age is one of representing the structure of that subject in terms of the child's way of viewing things" (Bruner, 1966, p. 33). This is the problem of the match—of matching what we want to teach the young child with the child's prior knowledge, ways of knowing, and abilities to learn (Figure 7.3).

In a way, matching teaching to the child is similar to the old concept of readiness, of waiting to instruct until the child is ready. Yet Bruner (1966) wrote that this concept of readiness isn't what he meant: "Readiness is a mischievous half-truth. It is a half-truth largely because it turns out that one teaches readiness or provides opportunities for its nurture, one does not simply wait for it" (p. 76).

Vygotsky (1986) refers to this as teaching to the zone of proximal development. The problem is for the teacher to understand the zone of proximal development,

---

The Problem of the Match

Chapter 2 offers a number of suggestions you can use to gain a better understanding of a child and his cultural background. Additionally, you might try these techniques to uncover the child's level of concept learning.

Try to get children to tell you all they know about something. Talk with a child or a small group of children and ask

❏ What can you tell us about . . . ?
❏ What can you draw or write about . . . ?
❏ What can you do to show us about . . . ?

Get children to dig into their past experiences by asking them to give an example of what they are saying, draw an illustration of what they mean, or act out a "for instance."

Then, too, you can observe children, asking yourself,

❏ What does the child do in this situation?
❏ How does she work with the materials confronting her?
❏ What does she choose to do and say in this instance?
❏ What did the child choose to do and say in a previous instance?

Ask children to think through their actions, guiding them with questions such as

❏ How did you get your answer?
❏ Why do you say that?
❏ Why do you suppose this is so?
❏ What do you think would happen if you did that?

Analyze the children's responses and your observations, asking yourself,

❏ Are the child's errors consistent?
❏ Is there a pattern to them?
❏ Are they logical?

Figure 7.3   Uncovering children's concepts.

which means to understand a child's current mental age and the level of understanding that the child reaches in solving problems with assistance. Vygotsky maintains that good teachers do not wait for this to develop but "march ahead of development and lead it." Instruction "must be aimed not so much at the ripe as at the ripening functions" (p. 104). Teachers must try to determine the lowest threshold at which instruction can begin, as well as the upper threshold, and then lead children to what they cannot yet do.

If this were easy to do, all children would be successful learners. Obviously, it is not. Even if teachers had all the time and assistance in the world to uncover each child's zone of proximal development and match instruction in every content area to it, they would have difficulties.

First, concepts are unique to each child, developed through personal experiences and constructed by each individual. No two people hold the same idea, or concept, of something. Ask a group of people to describe their concept of beauty, truth, or loyalty, and no two will have the same idea. Beauty is an abstract concept; but even concrete concepts, such as dog and cat, are individual to each child and influenced by experience, temperament, and environment.

Then, too, children may have fairly accurate concepts but be unable to verbalize them. Children probably do have fairly accurate concepts of cooperation, family, and neighborhood—after all, they do cooperate and live in a family and a neighborhood—but are unable to tell us about these concepts. On the other hand, children may tell us all about something, like space travel or gravity, and have no concept of it whatsoever.

Still, teachers must try to discern children's understanding of concepts. If they do not have this discernment, they cannot match their instruction or the experiences they plan to the maturation level of the child, and failure will result. Missing a child's level of understanding by offering some experience the child has already mastered, teachers can turn children away from schooling. Without some challenge, children are bored and find school a useless, meaningless activity. Conversely, the greatest failure results when teachers try to introduce children to some concept beyond their capabilities and understanding. Not only do children find this instruction meaningless, but they sense their failure to achieve and feel less able or willing to take the risks involved in learning something new. When the school reinforces this sense of failure through grouping or retention practices, children know they are failures and will try to distance themselves from the source of failure—the school—in the future.

By analyzing children's responses and behaviors, teachers will have a better understanding of children's existing concepts. This understanding permits them to better match content to children, bringing the social studies and young children together with meaning.

Guidelines for Concept Formation

Another aid to matching social studies content and children's understanding is for teachers to recall the universal characteristics of children at a given age or stage. "Research on the intellectual development of the child highlights the fact that at each stage of development the child has a characteristic way of viewing the world and explaining it to himself" (Bruner, 1960, p. 33).

This is the focus of the National Association for the Education of Young Children's *Developmentally Appropriate Practices: Serving Children from Birth through Age 8* (Bredekamp & Copple, 1997). By identifying the characteristics of children at a given age and describing the teaching practices that match them, this book ensures instruction appropriate for children of a given age.

Position Statement: Guidelines for Appropriate Curriculum Content and Assessment in Programs Serving Children Ages 3 through 8 (NAEYC, 1998) uses the broad parameters of stages in children's concept formation as a base for making decisions

Guidelines for Appropriate Curriculum Content and Assessment in Programs Serving Children Ages 3 Through 8

What children do	What teachers do
Awareness	
Experience	Create the environment
Acquire an interest	Provide opportunities by introducing new objects, events, people
Recognize broad parameters	Invite interest by posing problems or questions
Attend	Respond to child's interest or shared experience
Perceive	Show interest, enthusiasm
Exploration	
Observe	Facilitate
Explore materials	Support and enhance exploration
Collect information	Provide opportunities for active exploration
Discover	Extend play
Create	Ask open-ended questions, "What else could you do?"
Figure out components	Describe child's activities
Construct own understanding	Respect child's thinking and rule system
Create personal meaning	Allow for constructive error

Figure 7.4   Model of learning and teaching.

Source: From "Position Statement: Guidelines for Appropriate Curriculum Content and Assessment in Programs Serving Children Ages 3 through 8" by National Association for the Education of Young Children, 1991. *Young Children, 46*(3), p. 36. Adapted by permission.

about appropriate curriculum content (Figure 7.4). At first, children are only aware of events, objects, people, or concepts. Next they explore these ideas, beginning the process of figuring out the components or attributes of events, objects, people, or concepts. Inquiry is the next process of developing understanding of commonalities across events, objects, people, or concepts; and utilization is the functional level of learning, at which children can apply or make use of their understanding.

To learn something new, children must become aware, explore, inquire, use and apply. This process occurs over time and reflects movement from learning that is informal and inciden-

What children do	What teachers do
Inquiry	
Examine	Help children refine understanding
Investigate	Guide children, focus attention
Propose explanations	Ask more focused questions, "What else works like this? What happens if . . . ?"
Focus	Provide information when requested, "How do you spell . . . ?"
Compare own thinking with that of others	Help children make connections
Generalize	
Relate to prior learning	
Adjust to conventional rule systems	
Utilization	
Use the learning in many ways; learning becomes functional	Create vehicles for application
	Help children apply to new situations
Represent learning in various ways	Provide meaningful situations to use learning
Apply to new situations	
Formulate new hypotheses and repeat cycle	

tal, spontaneous, concrete-referenced, and governed by the child's own rules to learning that is more formal, refined, extended, enriched, more removed in time and space from concrete references and more reflective of conventional rule systems. (NAEYC, 1998, p. 36)

The process continues over and over throughout life and learning.

SUMMARY

Organizing the social studies around the skills of thinking and concept formation is essential. Thinking, a continuous process, begins when the curriculum is organized around children's experiences with the world and their play. Through play, children sense problems and begin to question. Teachers then use these questions and problems to encourage children to locate information, organize data, interpret data, and reach conclusions.

Teaching for thinking is also teaching for concept formation. Teachers identifying key ideas or concepts from each of the social science disciplines then use these to organize children's learning experiences. Knowledge of each child's level of understanding of the concepts is necessary to plan experiences that will foster children's thinking and concept formation.

Extend Your Knowledge

1. Observe children at play. Note and record their questions, the problems they sense, and how they solve the problems. Which of the other processes involved in thinking—locating information, organizing data, inferring, generalizing, and reaching conclusions—are observed?

2. What ideas do children have about social studies concepts? Ask children to tell you what a family is or to give a definition for brother or sister. Are children's concepts everyday, spontaneous concepts or adult-like? Report your findings to the class.

3. Take a concept, such as family, and design a lesson plan that takes children from awareness to complete utilization of the concept.

Resources

Every early childhood teacher should read the original writings of both Piaget and Vygotsky:

Piaget, J. (1959). *The language and thought of the child*. London: Routledge & Kegan Paul.

Vygotsky, L. (1986). *Thought and language* (Rev. ed.). Cambridge, MA: MIT Press.

The following book offers a myriad of suggestions for fostering children's thinking in a variety of situations:

Sure, M. R. (2000). *Raising a thinking child workbook*. Champaign, IL: Research Press.

References

Auel, J. (1980). *The clan of the cave bear*. New York: Bantam.

Bredekamp, S., & Copple, C. (1997). *Developmentally appropriate practices: Serving children from birth through age 8* (Rev. ed.) Washington, DC: National Association for the Education of Young Children.

Brodrova, E., & Leong, D. J. (2003). Chopsticks and counting chips: Do play and foundational skills need to compete for the teacher's attention in an early childhood classroom? *Young Children, 58*, 10–17.

Bronson, M. B. (2003). NAEYC resources in focus: Choosing play materials for primary school children. *Young Children, 58*(3), 24–25.

Brown, A. (1997). Transfoming schools into communities of thinking and learning about serious matters. *American Psychologist, 52*, issue 4.

Bruner, J. (1960). *The process of education*. Cambridge, MA: Harvard University Press.

Bruner, J. (1966). *Toward a theory of instruction.* Cambridge, MA: Harvard University Press.

Dewey, J. (1916). *The school and society.* Chicago: University of Chicago Press.

Dewey, J. (1933). *How we think.* Boston: Heath.

Dewey, J. (1944). *Democracy and education.* New York: Free Press.

Dyson, A. H. (1988). The value of time off tasks: Young children's spontaneous talk and deliberate text. *Harvard Educational Review, 57,* 534–564.

Franklin, M. B. (2000). Meanings of play in the developmental interaction tradition. In N. Nager & E. K. Shapiro (Ed.), *Revisiting a progressive pedagogy* (pp. 11–47). Albany: State University of New York Press.

Gelman, S. (1998). Categories in young children's thinking. *Young Children, 53*(1), 20–27.

Langer, S. (1942). *Philosophy in a new key.* Cambridge, MA: Harvard University Press.

Martin, L., & Miller, M. (1999). *Great graphing.* New York: Scholastic.

Milne, A. A. (1991). *Winnie the Pooh.* New York: Dutton.

Minarik, E. H. (1978). *Little Bear.* New York: HarperTrophy.

Mitchell, L. S. (1934). *Young geographers.* New York: Bank Street College.

National Association for the Education of Young Children (NAEYC). (1998). *Position statement: Guidelines for appropriate curriculum content and assessment in programs serving children ages 3 through 8.* Washington, DC: Author.

National Council for the Social Studies (NCSS). (1998). *Social studies for early childhood and elementary school children: Preparing for the 21st century.* Washington, DC: Author.

National Research Council & Institute of Medicine (NRC & IM). (2000). *From neurons to neighborhoods: The science of early childhood development.* Washington, DC: National Academy Press.

Piaget, J. (1959). *The language and thought of the child.* London: Routledge & Kegan Paul.

Polonsky, L. (2000). *Math for the very young: A handbook of activities for parents and teachers.* Chicago: University of Chicago Press.

Prawatt, R. W. (2000). The two faces of Deweyan pragmatism: Induction versus social construction. *Teachers College Record, 102,* 805–840.

Prawatt, R. W. (2001). Dewey and Pierce, the philosopher's philosopher. *Teachers College Record, 103,* 667–721.

Robison, H., & Spodek, B. (1965). *New directions in the kindergarten.* New York: Teachers College Press.

Seefeldt, C., & Galper, A. (2000). *Active experiences for active children: Social studies.* Upper Saddle River, NJ: Merrill/Prentice Hall.

Sousa, F. (2000). Reconstructing children's experience when teaching and assessing them: Lessons from Dewey. *Journal of Early Childhood Teacher Education, 21,* 313–320.

Vygotsky, L. (1986). *Thought and language* (Rev. ed.). Cambridge, MA: MIT Press.

Whitehurst, G. J., & Lonigan, C. J. (1998). Child development and emergent literacy. *Child Development, 69,* 848–872.

PART THREE

THE CONTENT OF THE SOCIAL STUDIES

CHAPTER 8

Children's Study of Time, Continuity, and Change: History

Knowledge of history is a pre-condition of political intelligence.

National Center for History in the Schools, 1994, p. 1

After you read this chapter, you should be prepared to respond to the following questions:

- What concepts are key to the study of history?
- What concepts of time do young children have? How can time concepts be taught?
- How are concepts of change introduced to young children?
- How can holiday celebrations introduce children to the concept that there is continuity to human life? What other ways are children introduced to the idea that life has continuity?
- How are children introduced to the past?
- What are the methods of the historian, and how do children use them?

"Tell me again about when I was just a little baby," 5-year-old Kristie Marie asked her grandmother, "and you took me to the beach, and I picked up a seashell and tried to eat it!"

Who hasn't heard a child appeal for "just one more story about the olden days, when I was really, really little"? Young children are highly interested in their past. The stories of what they did yesterday appeal as nothing else does. Dewey (1966) recognized children's interest in the study of history: "Teaching history is not difficult because the child's interest in the way people lived, and how and why they lived as they did, what kinds of houses they had, what kinds of clothing they wore, and how they did business, that interest is endless and ceaseless" (p. 12).

Children's interest alone is sufficient rationale for including history in the early childhood curriculum (Barton, 2002). But history is important for other reasons as well. Human beings seek to understand themselves by understanding their past. To be able to know the past helps us develop a historical perspective and to answer "Who am I?" "What happened in the past?" "How am I connected to the past?" (NCSS, 1998). Dewey (1966) saw other values in the study of history, which he believed was "essential to gain in power to recognize human connections, and to enrich and liberate more direct and personal contacts of life by furnishing that context background and outlook" (p. 258).

Today, the study of history is considered even more critical. Theoreticians believe that, without knowledge of the past transmitted through a common national memory of the study of history, children would be unable to identify with their na-

The study of history is time-oriented.

tion and assume their civic responsibility as adults (NCHS, 1994; NCSS, 1998). "Without history, a society shares no common memory of where it has been, of what its core values are, or what decisions of the past account for present circumstances. Without history, one cannot undertake any sensible inquiry into the political, social, or moral issues in society" (NCHS, 1994, p. 1).

KEY CONCEPTS

The study of history has been defined as a time-oriented study that refers to what we do know about the past. A theme of the National Council of Social Studies is *time, continuity, and change*. Its study should enable children to seek to understand their historical roots and to locate themselves in time. Knowing how to read and reconstruct the past allows us to develop a historical perspective and to answer questions such as "Who am I?" "What happened in the past?" "How am I connected to those in the past?" "How has the world changed and how might it change in the future?" "Why does our personal sense of relatedness to the past change?" (NCSS, 1998).

Using this definition, teachers can introduce the following key concepts to young children:

- *Time.* The study of history is time-oriented (Jantz & Seefeldt, 1999; NAEP, 2002). As children use sequencing to establish a sense of order and time in their daily routines, they are introduced to, and become aware of, concepts of time.

- *Change.* History helps children accept the inevitability of change. Through actual experiences as well as by listening to stories of the recent past and long ago, children can learn that change is constant and should not be feared (NCSS, 1998).

- *The continuity of human life.* The human connections that Dewey (1966) writes about might be thought of as the continuity in human life, which children can discover through their own experiences.

- *The past.* Children have experienced the immediate past. They can discuss and record it. Children can also handle objects and records from the more distant past and listen to stories and poetry about the past to gain an understanding of life before their time.

- *The methods of the historian.* The goal of the study of history is not to make children into historians. Nevertheless, it can help children to use the methods of the historian to make their lives more meaningful, richer, and fuller. Using the processes of inquiry, children are taught to recognize problems and ask questions; to observe, analyze, and infer as they collect and examine evidence; and finally to reach conclusions.

The national history standards, *History for Grades K–4* (NCHS, 1994), recognize the complexity and abstractness of the concepts considered key to the study of history. Still, the authors of the standards believe that children, even in the earliest grades, can begin to build historical understandings and perspectives and to think historically. When history is presented to them in ways that are appropriate to their development, young children can do the following (NCHS, 1994):

- Gain concepts key to the study of history
- Learn to differentiate time present, time past, and time long, long ago
- Find history to be interesting and meaningful when it is centered around their own lives, families, and communities
- Appreciate history when its study is embedded in myths, stories, legends, and biographies
- Get a firsthand glimpse into the lives of people who lived long ago, using records of the past, artifacts, letters, diaries, family records, and photograph albums
- Begin to use the methods of the historian, learning to question, study, and reach conclusions

TIME

Mark, a 6-year-old, was asked, "How long is a day?"
He replied, "It's today until you get to tomorrow!"
He was then asked, "How long is that?"
Mark replied, "Today is when you get up, and you play, and you eat lunch, and you play some more, and you go to school, and you come home, and it's nice outside, and then it's night, and you go to sleep, and when you wake up it's tomorrow!" (Jantz & Seefeldt, 1999).

Like Mark, young children do have a sense of time, but it is more intuitive than conventional (see Table 8.1). During early childhood, children can distinguish past from present and begin to describe daily events in a sequential pattern. Like Mark, young children associate chronological time with personal time, as reflected by the cyclical nature of daily events (Barton, 2002; Levstik & Barton, 1997).

Development of Time Concepts

Limited to their perception of the succession and duration of time, and to their ability to sequence and organize daily experiences, children's intuitive ideas of time are subjective. This subjectivity leads to errors. Five-year-olds know that waiting for 10 minutes will be harder than waiting for 5, but they also conclude that it takes less time for a fast-turning wheel to spin for 5 minutes than it does for a faucet to drip for the same amount of time (Vukelich & Thornton, 1990).

Intuitive time is distinct from operational time. Operational time involves the understanding of relations of succession and duration and is based on analogous operations in logic, which may be either qualitative or quantitative (Piaget, 1946). Not

Table 8.1 Time Concepts Develop

Sensorimotor Age 0–2	Preoperational Age 2–6/7	Concrete Age 6/7–10
Observes, follows routines by 2, aware of day/night, attends to environment	Ideas of time are personal and subjective	Uses clocks, watches to tell time
	Measures time with arbitrary units	Ready for instruction in time concepts
	By 5, some understanding of time units such as day	Conventional concepts will not develop until formal operational period at age 12+
	Recalls past, plans for future	
	By 5, can sequence events of a day and use time words	

until children enter formal operations, near the beginning of adolescence, are they able to master operational time.

Perhaps because temporal sequencing requires only qualitative comparisons, such as little versus large, children as young as age 4 or 5 can demonstrate some understanding of the ability to sequence events. Four- to 6-year-olds can order actions in sequence to achieve a goal; they know that events happen in order and can sequence their day around cyclically organizing daily occurrences (Vukelich & Thornton, 1990). Four-year-olds can accurately judge temporal order at above-chance level; by age 5, children can judge the backward order of daily activities and the forward order from multiple reference points within the day and can evaluate the lengths of intervals separating daily activities. By about age 7, children can also judge the backward order of events from multiple reference points.

Children learn temporal sequencing concepts—such as before and after, tomorrow and yesterday, or those that require only that children position two points in time—more readily than quantitative temporal relations. To understand quantitative temporal relations, a child must realize that the interval between, say, 1:00 and 2:00 is the same as that between 2:00 and 3:00. Children who understand only the sequence may not fully appreciate that the intervals are equal. Parenthetically, this same problem with equal intervals characterizes a child's initial mistakes in using linear distance.

By the time children reach kindergarten, they use terms involved in telling time with a clock. Although they have not internalized the concept of duration of an interval, such as hour and minute, they understand that these terms do have meaning. Children first begin to associate activities with the regular daily class schedule; then they associate this schedule with time by the clock. Next, concepts of hour, half-hour, and quarter-hour develop.

Five-year-olds begin to understand temporal units of time—such as day, date, and calendar time, formulated on the temporal or sequential order of events—and

Children will not be able to measure time conventionally until after age 8 or 9.

can orient themselves in time, associating time with an external event: "It is day; the sun is shining," or "It is night; the stars are out." Understanding calendar time includes the ability to identify time concepts such as first, last, next, later, sooner, before, and after. By age 5, children can tell what day it is and will use general terms such as *wintertime* before they will use the general terms *today*, *before*, or *in a few days* (Ames, 1946). Children can first respond to a time word; next, they can use the word themselves; finally, they can use the time word to answer a question correctly. At ages 6, 7, and 8, children can begin to use conventional methods to orient themselves in time. Then clocks, watches, and calendars start to have some meaning.

Knowledge of children's developing concepts of time leads to the idea that young children are receptive to planned instruction in time—that is, when this teaching is based on the cyclical, recurring, and sequential events of a child's day and life. Although it is inappropriate to ask children to memorize the names of the days or months, to tell time, or to learn operational time concepts, it is appropriate for adults to give children labels for these things and to make certain their life has a routine. By experiencing routines, measuring time and its passage with arbitrary measures, children will gain initial concepts of time.

Routines That Teach Time

"I don't know what time it is, but my daddy always comes to take me home after my nap," states a 3-year-old in a child-care center. As Piaget believed, it seems desirable to help children develop time concepts based on daily routines. In a school for young children, routines and predictable procedures can help develop understandings of time as well as feelings of security.

Even though schedules in the preschool and primary classroom are flexible, there are regular routines: "After breakfast, we play outside." "Before our snack, we wash." "Recess follows lunch, and outdoor play follows your nap." Children in the primary grades can chart their own routines and take more responsibility for scheduling their day according to their own desires. Those in the third grade have even found written day planners useful in helping them organize and use their time wisely.

Literature supplements children's firsthand experiences with routines. *Bunny Day: Telling Time from Breakfast to Bedtime* (Walton, 2002), *Get Up and Go!* (Murphy & Greenseid, 1996), *Night-Time* (Pettigrew & Kimber, 1992) and *My Grandmother's Clock* (McCaughrean, 2002) are examples of the many available books that might help young children understand the regular, timed routines of the day.

In addition to structuring regular routines and reading stories to children that deal with concepts of time, teachers should take every opportunity to convey ideas about time to children. They should give children the correct time words and phrases to connect their experiences, such as "today," "this morning," "next," "a little later," "this afternoon," "yesterday," and "last week."

Measuring Time

Children will not be able to measure time conventionally until after age 8 or 9. Rather than asking them to measure time with a clock in the preschool or primary classroom, you can structure experiences using arbitrary measures. This gives children meaningful experiences with concepts of duration, sequence of events, and temporal order, which will prepare them to tell time in the traditional way later. Give the children some of the following equipment:

• A stopwatch is fun for children to use independently or during activities structured by the teacher. The children can use the stopwatch to see how long it takes them to put away the blocks, hang up their coats, put five pegs in a pegboard, or hop across the room. You might help them record how long they can bounce a ball, hop on one foot, or jump or run in place. Four-year-olds and younger children enjoy playing with the watch and using watches as props for their play. The accuracy of the watch is immaterial; you only want children to experience measuring time.

• Children can use an hourglass to see if they can wash the tables, pick up all the art scraps, put the doll clothes away, or get ready to go home—all before the sand empties into the other half of the glass.

• A cooking timer buzzes when the set time has ended. Children enjoy keeping track of time this way. They might use the timer to determine when the bread should be taken from the oven, when the cookies will be finished, or when the vegetables have simmered for 5 minutes. Or they might see if they can complete some task before the buzzer sounds.

• An old alarm clock is a good prop for play. Children can turn the hands, take it apart, or set the alarm. These clocks, purchased at a local thrift shop or donated to the classroom, can give the children another opportunity to take an active part in measuring time.

The Passage of Time

Learning about history requires that children develop a sense of the passage of time (Figure 8.1). "What did you do today?" you can ask the 2-year-old, as you help him into his coat before going home. The teacher of primary children asks, "Do you remember what we did for the Halloween party?" "What things should we include in our Valentine's party?" Using the children's actual experiences, these questions can help them to develop a sense of the passage of time.

Questions that might help children recall the immediate past and foster an understanding of the passage of time include the following:

• For the very young: "What did you like best about today?" "What did we have for lunch today?" "What did you like best about our walk in the rain?"

• For the kindergarten child: "How many days has it been since Karl's birthday?" "What did we have for lunch yesterday?" "What did we do last week?" "What did you like best about kindergarten this week?"

			Observation—Time Words		
				Time Words Used	
Date	Center/Area	Children	Not at all	Some	Accurate

Figure 8.1 Assessing children's time concepts.

- For the primary child: "How many sunny, rainy, and snowy days did we have last month?" "How many days has it been since our Thanksgiving party?" "What can you do this year that you could not do last year?"

Nothing is more interesting to the young child than his own life. Help the child to understand the passage of time by capitalizing on this egocentrism. In the beginning of the year, you might start a history booklet for each child. Snapshots taken throughout the year, pieces of work the child has completed, paintings or stories dictated or written, records of weight and height, and some of the interesting things said can all be recorded in a history book. At the end of the year, the children will have individual life booklets that will give them a meaningful understanding of the passage of time (Figure 8.2).

CHANGE

In many respects, the study of history is the study of change. Some changes represent progress; others do not. Nevertheless, change is universal. No matter where we live or how, change will be part of our lives (Brophy & Alleman, 2002). Being able to accept and adapt to change is crucial to living fully. Rather than fearing change, children can be taught to accept the inevitability of change and learn ways to adapt to the changes they experience.

Surrounding children with opportunities to experience change, the immediate environment offers many learning tools. From the school, neighborhood, nature study, and themselves, children can learn that (1) change is continuous and always present; (2) change affects their lives in different ways; and (3) change can be recorded, and these records can help others to understand the things that have changed.

Observation—Measuring Time		
Date Center/Area	Children	Measuring Time (record how, why)

Figure 8.2 Evaluating children's abilities to measure time.

In School

Whether in a child-care center, a kindergarten, or a primary classroom, things are constantly changing. The children may help rearrange the furniture for some special activity or for more efficient use of space. Painting or other redecorating of the school classrooms is a change that occurs often. Animals or plants in the classroom offer opportunities for the children to observe changes.

Changes also occur in the school building. Rooms are decorated for holidays; the building is readied for the demands of the changing seasons. Older primary children can study the changes that have occurred in the school building. They might be able to find pictures of the building before it was remodeled or discover records of what once stood where the school is located. How the school got its name, who it was named for and why, how many people have been principals, and the backgrounds of the teachers in the school are all possible topics for study.

Second or third graders might make a time line for their school that can help make history come alive. A good time line might begin with the date the school was built, include its naming and dedication and any renovations or changes, and end with the present.

In the Neighborhood

Leaving the school building and yard helps the children recognize the many changes in their immediate neighborhood: new neighbors move in, a house goes up, a building is torn down, the street is repaired, or a park is built. You can use the changes around the school to foster children's awareness of the continuous nature of change (Figure 8.3).

The National Center for History in the Schools believes that these observations permit children to identify and compare changes in their community over time. They suggest that children should look at current photographs of the community and ask, "What things could have been here long ago?" "Why?" "What things look newer?" "Why?"

Primary children can make a record of the changes that have occurred in the neighborhood by (1) interviewing the residents to find out what changes have taken place, (2) finding records of the past in the city clerk's or newspaper office, or (3) reconstructing the past with models.

In Nature

Watching an apple tree change outside the window can provide a class with a year's activities involving the concept of change. In the fall, the children can collect and count the leaves and sort them according to size, color, and shape. They can gather apples, cut them open, eat them for a snack, and make applesauce. The class could make a booklet of the changes that occurred to the tree during the winter. The chil-

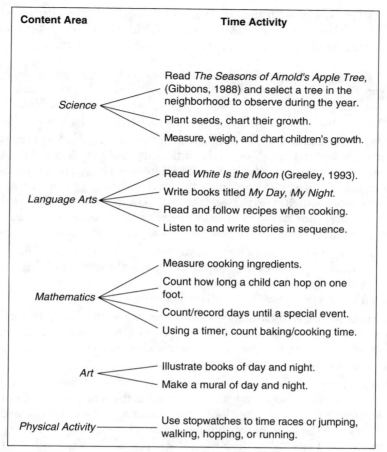

Figure 8.3 Incorporating time concepts in different content areas.

dren might pose questions about the life of the tree during the winter: "Is it dead?" "Will it ever have leaves again?" "What will happen to it?" When the first buds appear in the spring, the class will conclude that the tree did not die.

This activity, although not an everyday one, can continue throughout the year as the teacher asks questions and focuses the children's attention on the tree. The outdoors yields still other changes; it may be possible for children to observe changes in caterpillars, tadpoles, or other living things.

In Children

We know that, to be effective, every learning experience we present to young children must have deep personal meaning. Accordingly, the study of time and change, of history, begins with the children themselves. Children change—they grow, learn new skills, lose teeth, get their hair cut. Children's study of history can begin with the study of children themselves. Focus on how they change:

• Celebrate their birthdays. You can make a badge or a sign for the birthday child to wear. Put a large age numeral on the badge. Let children decorate cookies or cupcakes using cream cheese frosting, raisins, nuts, or pieces of fruit. Suggest they use the same numbers of candles, fruit, or decorations as their years of age.

• Have the children find out how much they weighed when they were born. Fill a bag with sand so that it weighs about the same as their birth weight. Let the children weigh the sandbag on a bathroom scale. Holding a bag of 6 or 8 pounds of sand, children gain a concept of how small they were when they were born. Weigh the children, record their current weight, and compare it to the birth weight. This experience is not intended to measure exactly sand and birth weight but to give children a concrete example of how they have changed since they were born.

• Let the children taste a bit of strained baby food, perhaps some green beans; then let them taste whole cooked green beans. Ask the children: "Why did you need the strained food when you were babies?" "What can you eat now that you couldn't eat when you were babies?" "How have you changed?"

• Examine items of clothing children wore when they were smaller. Some children may be able to bring diapers, baby shoes, sweaters, hats, or other items of clothing they wore in the past. Encourage the children to compare these items with similar articles of clothing they are wearing now.

• Ask them to bring in snapshots that were taken of them in the past, when they were infants, first began to walk, or learned to dress themselves. Comparing the photographs with the way they look now, children can develop the understanding that they are still the same people but have changed. Ask them: "What could you do when you were babies?" "What things couldn't you do?" "What will you be able to do in the future when you get bigger?" "How will you change?"

• Make a picture time line of children's lives. Using photos from home and drawing pictures to fill in gaps, arrange children's pictures of their lives chronologically on long sheets of paper. Discuss how they have changed since they were babies.

Reading books to children can stimulate discussions about change. For example, *The Growing Story* (Kraus, 1947) motivates thinking. After reading the book, you can ask children how they are like the boy in the story: "Have you ever outgrown clothes?" "What did you do with them?"

The poem "The End" (Milne, 1955) begins, "When I was one, I was just begun; when I was two, I was barely new." Teachers can use this poem as a lead into making a mural on the theme of growing. On a large sheet of wrapping paper, print the numerals 1, 2, 3, 4, and 5. Have the children draw pictures of something they could do at each age, and paste the pictures on the chart. Ask the children how they have

First graders illustrate A. A.
Milne's poem "The End."

changed. Remind them that they are the same people, even though they, and the world around them, has changed.

Children will continue to change. First and second graders may think about the future. You can initiate a discussion of how they will change in the future and what they will want, need, and be like when they are teenagers or adults. They could draw pictures of what they will look like when they are 14, 45, and 75. Or ask them to write or dictate a story about their life in the first, second, or third grade, with a parallel story that projects what their life will be like when they are in the fifth grade, high school, or college. Ask them, "What will you be learning?" "How will you learn it?" "What will you be like?"

You might take a field trip to another playground or school and let the children observe older children at work and play. Ask them to identify skills the older children are demonstrating that the younger children cannot do. Ask them how they think they will learn the skill and what other skills they will learn in the future.

Children experience change as they adapt to modifications in daily routine. Routines always remain stable points in the day; yet they are often changed by necessity, and these variations help children accept the inevitability of change. "Today our picnic is canceled because of the rain. What can we do instead?" "Sabrina's grandmother was coming today, but she couldn't make it, so she will come tomorrow." "Let's watch the custodian; we can have our juice later."

THE CONTINUITY OF HUMAN LIFE

Although life is constantly changing, there is a continuity to human experience (Figure 8.4). Exploring their family histories, children can gain a sense of this continuity. Celebrating holidays, as people have always done, also gives children the feeling of connection among human experiences (Seefeldt, 1993).

The Family

"To bring history alive, an important part of children's historical studies should be centered in people—the history of families and of people" (NCHS, 1994). Each family has something unique from the past to give to its children. You can help parents see the value of talking to their children about the parents' own past. You may need to prepare the parents for the questions their children might ask them about their past. Otherwise, some parents, faced with the struggles and problems of day-to-day living, might find such questions rude or prying.

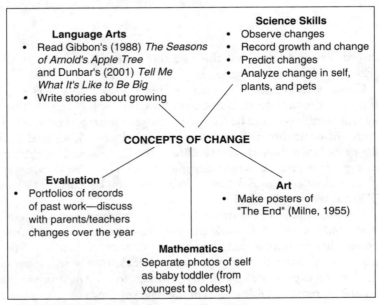

Language Arts
- Read Gibbon's (1988) *The Seasons of Arnold's Apple Tree* and Dunbar's (2001) *Tell Me What It's Like to Be Big*
- Write stories about growing

Science Skills
- Observe changes
- Record growth and change
- Predict changes
- Analyze change in self, plants, and pets

CONCEPTS OF CHANGE

Evaluation
- Portfolios of records of past work—discuss with parents/teachers changes over the year

Art
- Make posters of "The End" (Milne, 1955)

Mathematics
- Separate photos of self as baby toddler (from youngest to oldest)

Figure 8.4   Change in the integrated curriculum.

Second and third graders can create a history of their family. Each family has its own history. By filling in the blanks of this book you can create a history book of your family.

My Family History

My name is _____

I am _____ years old. I live at _____

My mother's name is _____

   My mother's maiden name is _____

      She was born on _____

      in _____

      Her mother's name is _____

      Her father's name is _____

   My father's name is _____

      He was born on _____

      in _____

      His mother's name is _____

      His father's name is _____

You may have a nontraditional family. If so, write about the family you live with.

This is a story of our family.

Here are our family traditions.

Figure 8.5 Family history book.

Primary children could investigate and analyze their family. They could ask parents about their past—where they lived and what they did. Parents could share family artifacts, historical documents, sites, and other records of their past with children (NCHS, 1994). In class, children could compare and contrast likenesses and differences between families' lives, activities, beliefs, traditions, family structures, institutions, and so on at various times in the past and present (Figure 8.5).

Stories and narratives of family life long ago put primary-age children in touch with the continuity of life. Reading this type of historical fiction and nonfiction can give children an understanding that, even though life changes, humans continue to share many of the same emotions and feelings. You might read children *The 18 Penny Goose* (Walker & Beier, 1998), the story of Letty, who wants to save her beloved goose, Solomon, during the Revolutionary War. *Grandma Susan Remembers* (Morris, 2001), *On the Trail of Sacagawea* (Peter, 2001), and *Full Steam Ahead* (Gibbons, 2001) tell stories of eras when life was hard and special events were communicated by word of mouth.

Intergenerational Contacts

"The continuity of all cultures depends on the living presence of at least three generations" (Mead, 1970, p. 3). In our culture, it is not easy for three generations to share one another's living presence. Older people are often separated from the young by physical and social distance. Rather than developing informal relations in the family, at church, or in the neighborhood, the ages may remain separate from one another. Thus, the connections between the young and the old are broken, and their natural ways of interacting and relating are no longer available.

Recognizing this problem, many educators are promoting intergenerational programs in school and nonschool settings to provide a space for the living presence of at least three generations. In these intergenerational programs, children, adults, and elders interact with one another, reestablishing the relationships of caring and continuity of life.

Today an estimated 100,000 older persons are involved as volunteers in schools and are working with young children. Programs exist in child-care centers, preschools, elementary and high schools, as well as Head Start and Follow Through programs, libraries, parks, recreation centers, museums, 4-H clubs, and many other community agencies. Sponsored by private organizations and federal agencies, these programs often have the primary goal of reestablishing links between young and old.

The programs build on the love and affection the young and old in our country have for one another. Researchers have found that children do have a feeling of affection for older persons, calling elders "friendly, good, rich, and wonderful" (Seefeldt & Warman, 1990). Children believed it would be fun to play checkers, cards, and other games with older persons. But at the same time, the children saw old people as sick, tired, sad, bossy, wrinkled, crippled, and ugly. Further, they indicated that they themselves would never grow old. They feared and dreaded their own eventual aging and death. It is important to note that the children in this study reported few contacts with older people either inside or outside the family unit.

Perhaps if these children had contact with older people who were healthy, happy, active, and fulfilled, they would not classify the old as tired and sick, nor would they dread their own aging. If children could share the love of an older person and do things with elders that were of interest in their own schools, it might be more difficult for them to accept the stereotypical ideas of age and aging (Seefeldt & Galper, 2000).

Older people also report enjoying the company of children. In one study, they said that children would be fun to do things with and would make good friends for older people. They thought children were very interested in learning new things and were "the hope of the future" (Seefeldt & Warman, 1990).

Intergenerational programs in the school can provide a way for children and elders to enjoy one another's company, to learn from one another, to share feelings of affection, and function as a concrete example of life's continuity. You can invite older neighbors, people on the school staff, or children's grandparents or older relatives to visit the class frequently. Just letting your community—churches, civic organizations, senior-citizens organizations, and other groups—know you would like elders to work with children in your school puts you into contact with volunteers.

Once the children and the older volunteers are comfortable with one another, the older persons might do the following:

- Read stories to one or two of the children at a time, holding them close.
- Take part in a birthday party for a child. The volunteers can tell the children how many candles their own cakes need or recall some of their early birthdays.
- Play with the children, helping them informally with their activities.
- Help the children prepare a special treat—making peanut butter or baking cookies.
- Talk with the children about the olden days and the things they like to do with their own grandchildren.
- Sing, listen to music, or learn to play musical instruments.

For the children, the benefits of intergenerational contact are great. They sense the continuity of life, learn about the past, and have the attention of one more adult. But the rewards are just as important for elders (Glanz, 1991).

Holiday Celebrations

Celebrating holidays helps children see the rich cultural heritage of their past and the continuity of life (Vygotsky, 1986). Holiday celebrations with young children can be pure fun and relaxation; at the same time, they can impart historical knowledge in an accurate and authentic manner. Holidays can serve as occasions for projects that will acquaint pupils with social studies concepts and information. They are occasions for teaching students about important ideas and customs that coexist with one another in our country and in the world (NCSS, 1998).

On the other hand, when poorly planned or thought out, holiday celebrations are disasters, serving only to indoctrinate children and perpetuate myths and stereotypes. When the social studies curriculum revolves around the celebration of holidays or when the focus is on a "tourist curriculum" (Derman-Sparks, 2003), children visit a culture by participating in a few activities and then go home to their regular classroom life, which leads to cultural stereotypes and trivialization—all those people do is dance, wear special clothes, and eat.

Holiday celebrations planned around the children's activities and experiences can be meaningful and enjoyable when they do the following:

- The routines of the regular school day are preserved. Any dramatic change in routine is upsetting to young children. Missing a nap or changing lunchtime might be disastrous for preschoolers. Eliminating work time for primary children is unnecessary; instead of reading from a basal text or doing the usual work, primary children might research library books about the holidays or solve puzzles with holiday words. Work time might include special materials associated with the holiday—orange and black paper and paint for Halloween or scrap papers in pink, red, and white, plus glitter, for Valentine's Day.

- Parents or other members of the community are involved to ensure sensitivity to the culture of the children. Involving parents or members of the community in planning the holiday celebration ensures, at least in part, that the culture and ethnic diversity of the children, their families, and the community will be respected. Some celebrations, such as Halloween, Valentine's Day, or others, may be offensive to parents from differing ethnic groups or religious backgrounds. Parents can also add meaning to the celebrations by telling stories of their celebrations in another country or the history and meaning of specific holidays.

- The children are fully involved in planning the celebration. Children grow as they assume responsibility for their own lives. Planning holiday celebrations is an ideal opportunity for them to assume this responsibility. Young children have simple wants and are pleased when they can plan their own activities. They usually plan for very simple, manageable celebrations. "Let's play Simon Says and make cupcakes," and "We'll sing 'Flag of America' and listen to the story of Daniel Boone again," were suggested as party activities in one first-grade class.

- The activities are kept simple and low-key. Celebration of major holidays such as Christmas, Halloween, and Valentine's Day may result in tears of frustration and fatigue if children are overexcited and stimulated. A simple snack, perhaps something the children have planned and prepared themselves, can be added to the usual milk or juice break. Games familiar to the children can be played, with some variation added. Rather than playing Simon Says at Halloween, the children can play Witch Says. Doggie, Doggie, Who Has Your Bone? might become Steven, Steven, Who Has Your Valentine?

- A few key concepts are selected for development. Focusing on only one or two of the main ideas of the holiday, you can plan relevant activities. A discussion of some of the key concepts inherent in major holidays follows.

Columbus Day

By concentrating on the ideas of courage, vision, discovery, and inquiry that characterize Columbus and other explorers, young children can commemorate Columbus Day with integrity. Kindergarten children could explore their school, neighborhood, or community with the goal of finding something that is new to them. First and second graders might make a dream for their own lives or draw or write about a vision they have for their own future. They could also define the word *courage* and read about others who have used courage to make discoveries or do things for people.

Some teachers have celebrated the day by focusing on sailing ships, on different forms of water travel, or on floating and sinking. One teacher, who wanted to make the point that Columbus didn't discover America because one can't discover a place already inhabited by many peoples, brought items to the class that Native Americans gave to Columbus. Over a number of weeks, the children tasted chocolate, peeled and cooked potatoes, and shelled ears of popcorn, which were later popped and eaten. Another teacher focused the day around spices, asking children to find out where spices grow and why Columbus was searching for new spices. They then cooked apple slices with and without spices and determined which they liked the best.

Halloween

Halloween is truly a children's holiday because it gives children a number of opportunities to be in control. First, by dressing up as a witch, a monster, or some other scary character, children become in charge, bigger than life. Just the fact of seeing other children dressed as monsters and being able to control their own fears gives children a great deal of satisfaction. The best part of Halloween is being in control of adults, who, "fearful" of a trick, will on demand give children a treat.

Regardless, very young children may find the holiday frightening. They may be unable to understand that they and others who dress up stay the same person, even though their appearance has changed. For children younger than age 4, activities should be low-key; depending on the group of children, you may not want to include masks. Since this is a time of pretending to be frightened, one teacher used Halloween to discuss fears. In this kindergarten, the children listed their fears, found stories that included the theme of being frightened, interviewed adults to find out what they were afraid of, and dictated a class report about the nature of fear.

Halloween can also foster a sense of community in young children. One second grade went to the school parade as "101 Dalmations." The teacher showed the children how to make construction-paper ears. Then each child painted spots on a large white t-shirt. In another class in the same school, children dressed in orange, jack-o-lantern, plastic trash bags. Stuffing the bags and attaching them at the neck and legs required partners to work together. Dressed as pumpkins, the class went to the school parade as "The Pumpkin Patch."

Thanksgiving

Thanksgiving is a time for people to be together and share their thankfulness. Children can thank all of the people in the school or in their homes and community who help them. Thank-you notes or booklets might be appropriate. The children might prepare cookies, roast some nuts, or make applesauce or some other gift to share with another class in the school or to give to others as a symbol of their thankfulness.

The typical celebration of Thanksgiving often includes a great many stereotypes about Native Americans. Derman-Sparks (2003) proposes that, rather than perpetuating the myths about native peoples, Thanksgiving be a time for appreciating Native American peoples as they were and as they are, not as either the Pilgrims or their descendants might wish them to be:

- Start by asking children what they know about Native Americans.
- Teach something about the daily contemporary life of specific Native American groups.
- For children in kindergarten and the primary grades, compare the differences between daily life and ceremonial activities, compare the past with the present, and compare folktales of different Native American peoples.

Hanukkah

A happy holiday in the Jewish religion, Hanukkah is also a time to gather with friends and family. Meaningful observances of the holiday can be planned by parents or experts. Children enjoy hearing the story of the Maccabees, lighting the menorah candles, playing with a dreidel, and eating potato pancakes as they relive the traditions of Jewish families. Because Hanukkah falls close to Christmas, teachers must be cautious about distorting its meaning. Hanukkah does not have the same significance to Judaism that Christmas has to Christianity. Other more important Jewish holidays might be observed—Rosh Hashanah and Yom Kippur in the fall and Passover in the spring.

Christmas

Christmas is often overdone and loses any real significance. Celebrations in preschools or the primary grades often reinforce the commercialism that has become deeply connected with North American observance of the holiday. The celebration of Christmas in non-religiously affiliated schools and centers can also contribute to the development of ethnocentrism in majority children and isolate those of minority faiths.

Celebrations of Christmas could be associated with charity and compassion and with peace on earth and good will toward others. Try the following:

- Limit Christmas activities to 2 or 3 days.
- Emphasize the giving aspects of the holiday rather than getting presents.
- Ask parents to communicate their beliefs to children.
- Become aware of the important celebrations of other religions.
- Maintain professional judgment in the face of pressures of the holiday season.

Other Winter Holidays

Incorporate celebrations of Christmas with December holidays from several cultural groups. Depending on the culture of the children, you might celebrate Kwanzaa (an African American holiday) or the winter solstice (a Native American tradition) as well as Hanukkah.

Patriotic Days

Lincoln's and Washington's birthdays might stimulate concern for our nation. You can focus on ecological concepts and the things we must all do to protect our land. Try to find factual narratives about Lincoln and Washington to read to the children. You can use patriotic days to encourage children's interest in the flag or the Pledge of Allegiance, or you might take the class to visit some historical spot in their city dedicated to great people of the past.

The historic struggle for freedom, self-determination, justice, and peace is an appropriate theme for patriotic days. To explore our nation's quest for freedom, children in kindergarten and the primary grades might listen to historically accurate stories about the American Revolution and the Civil War or even something about the two world wars. They could also explore the ideas of freedom and justice within their own group, school, and neighborhood.

Valentine's Day

Today, Valentine's Day is a day of love. In one school, Valentine's Day was just one of the days observed during the school's Month of Love celebration, which took place throughout February. Children discussed the concept of love. Groups wrote stories about love and read what others had written about the subject. One class of second graders collected all the U.S. LOVE stamps they could find. Then in small groups, they designed their own LOVE stamps and forwarded these designs to the post office for consideration.

Best of all, however, were the songs of love the children learned. Each group within the school selected their favorite song of love to present to the entire student body. During lunchtime, individual tables of children selected a favorite song of love and then stood and sang it.

Valentine's Day also lends itself to a study of the mail system. Pictures drawn by younger children and placed in envelopes addressed to themselves are received with wonder and great joy and stimulate a great deal of discussion among the children, their parents, and teachers.

Children can send letters through the mail to a friend, their parents, other relatives, or neighbors. Teachers in the kindergarten or primary grades can read books about Benjamin Franklin's life before and during the study of the post office. Second graders can easily trace the history of the post office and speculate on how we would communicate without it.

Other forms of mail might be explored as well. Perhaps children can find a greeting-card web site and send free cards to one another, or they could e-mail each other Valentine's greetings.

Other Holidays

Lesser known holidays can also receive attention in preschool and primary classrooms. Earth Day, a time to care for the earth, to clean the classroom, plant something on the playground, or do something for the community, can be a meaningful day for young children. United Nations Day, with its focus on what the United Nations is, how it functions, and what it represents, can be informative as well as enjoyable. Martin Luther King, Jr.'s birthday provides an excellent opportunity for children to become acquainted with the life of an important black leader and his contribution to our nation.

THE PAST

Children are intensely interested in both the immediate and the distant past. And although dates have little or no meaning, children as young as 5 years old are able to recognize the difference between past and present and have demonstrated the ability to order events chronologically, using photographs and pictures, with broad distinctions such as "long ago" and "close to now" (Barton, 2002; Barton & Levstik, 1996).

Helping children understand and explore the past does not mean you must teach them a true historic sense of time. In helping children to gain a concept of the past, adults must shuttle back and forth with children from the present to the past as they react to the ever-present urge to understand what has gone before. This dipping into the past without concern for a logical development of chronology from the past to the present does not violate basic principles of learning. To wait until they can handle true chronology is to deprive children of one of the most important learnings of early childhood.

Even though the past is untouchable and far away, vicarious experiences with the past are possible for young children. Many resources are available to help young children understand the past, and some are discussed in this section.

People

Parents, grandparents, the school staff, and neighbors are all resources for helping children understand the past. You can invite these people to the school to tell the children about the olden days. The grandmother who tells children how her grandmother taught her to crochet and then shows the children how to crochet a simple chain or the grandfather who tells his story of marching out of northern Korea at the end of the Korean War both give children a vicarious sense of the past.

Primary-age children can make a family tree or a time line of their families' history for the past two generations. Or they can portray their family and its history in the form of a narrative.

Children's own lives lead to the study of the immediate past. The drama recorded in time lines of children's own history is also enjoyed. One teacher posted large calendars in a hallway on which the events of each day, week, and month were recorded. The children frequently referred to these calendars, recalling their immediate past and telling one another their interpretation of the days, weeks, and months that had passed. In the process of telling their own narrative of the past, these children developed the realization that history is the story of people, recorded by people like themselves, and that they were "right now making the future" (NCSSS, 1989, p. xi).

Primary-age children can create a narrative of their own lives. Choosing a genre, they can write the story of their own lives, providing a beginning, a middle, and an end.

Objects

"What is it?" "What is it made of?" "How does it feel?" No picture, movie, or computer program can compare to real objects, to things that children can see, hear, touch, smell, or even taste for themselves. Real objects help children understand the past and life far from them and help them see significant relationships within their own neighborhood. Objects might be obtained from families, local museums, or historical societies. Any object you can use to foster social studies knowledge is appropriate. Some examples follow:

- *Plants.* "How is this plant like the ones we know? How is it different? Where does it grow? What does it need to live?"
- *Foods.* "Taste them. Where were they grown? Who grew them? How did they get here?"
- *Old tools.* "Who used them? How were they used? For what purpose? What tools do we use today?"
- *Clothing.* "Who wore this? Why? Who made it? What is it like?"
- *Models.* "How is this car (train, boat) like a real one? How is it different?"
- *Furniture.* "How was it made? When was it used? Who made it?"
- *Old photographs.* With old photographs of their school, neighborhood, or community, or of the children's families, their parents, and even themselves, children can compare and contrast past and present. You might ask, "What is the same? Do you wear the same kind of clothing? What is different today?"

Objects alone stimulate children's language and thinking without adult questioning or interference. A spinning wheel, a model ship, an old-fashioned coffee mill, or a photograph from the past provides sufficient motivation for children to begin asking questions and seeking information.

Children can compare hand eggbeaters, wooden cookie cutters, rolling pins, and kettles from the past with the newer versions. Children are fascinated by the differences when beating an egg with an old-fashioned hand eggbeater compared with an electric mixer.

Objects from the past stimulate thinking and language.

Children are interested in toys and models that depict things from the past. Cars, boats, and planes, modeled after those no longer in use, give children an opportunity to make comparisons between the things they know and use today and things from the past. Scrapbooks of old-fashioned cars, trains, or toys might interest children of kindergarten age; primary children might classify models according to use or age and could make charts sequencing the models from the oldest to the newest.

Even though objects stimulate play and discussion, you could help extend and clarify children's ideas: "Why do you think the train was made like this?" "Who do you think used this?" "How do you know it was used a long time ago?" "How is it just like the one we use today?"

Some objects from the past, like quilts, can lead to a unit or project. Primary-age children could make their own quilts. You could read *Sewing Quilts* (Turner & Allen, 1994) and teach children how to design a block, put the blocks together, and then to quilt. You could also read *The Name Quilt* (Root, 2003). *The Quilt-Block History of Pioneer Days: With Projects Kids Can Make* (Cobb & Ellis, 1997) is another valuable resource. Other antiques that cannot be handled by the children can still be shared in the classroom. Parents and friends often have interesting and valuable items from the past that they are willing to demonstrate to the class.

Almost every community has some type of museum to preserve the traces of the past. The local library, fire station, or church may house relics that children can observe. If only large museums are available in the community, you might select one room or section for the children to visit. Children also enjoy visiting older homes and buildings that have been renovated and restored.

Narratives

History becomes especially accessible and interesting to children when approached through stories, myths, legends, and biographies that capture children's imaginations and immerse them in times and cultures of the recent and long-ago past (NCHS, 1994). Well-chosen biographies and engaging accounts of the past—such as *When I Was Young in the Mountains* (Rylant, 1992) or *Tell Me a Story Mama* (Johnson, 1989)—can bring a meaningful awareness of the past to even the youngest of children.

Some educators believe that books used to promote awareness of the historic past should be factual and truthful (Brophy, 1990). These educators claim that, if myths or fictionalized accounts of the past are used to teach historic time, then children might learn to distrust teachers, who, after all, are supposed to be truthful (Brophy, 1990). Others disagree and recommend the use of all kinds of narratives to teach children history (Egan, 1997; Levstik, 2002). Narratives are inherently causal and explanatory in nature, familiar to young children—who have experienced them in daily interactions as well as in stories, which make up the bulk of their early contact with text—and appeal to them not only because of the story structure but because children can follow the sequence of events.

Focusing on the human aspect of narratives—feelings, emotions, ambition—teachers can foster primary children's understanding of the past. One primary teacher led children through an inquiry project on why Christopher Columbus was famous. Children were asked to consider two questions: how does the past influence the present, and how does the present influence our understanding of the past? These ideas were brought together through the concept of fame (Levstik, 1991).

METHODS OF THE HISTORIAN

Right from the start, children can begin developing the skills of the historian. To do so, they must be engaged in developing inquiry skills. Children learn to question and find out about their current and more distant past. Real historical understanding requires that students engage in historical reasoning, think about cause-effect relationships, analyze records of the past, and reach conclusions (VanSledright, 2002).

Throughout their early educational experiences, children can be encouraged to do the following (Figure 8.6):

• *Identify the problem.*   Children must be able to identify their own problems; at the least, they must perceive the problem as their own. When you determine the problem and present it to the children for solving, it becomes an exercise for them

Interview and record children's responses to the following questions:

1. Tell about something you like or remember that happened a long time ago, something that happened to you this week, and something you think will happen when you are older.

2. What has changed since you first came to school? What have you learned? What can you do now that you could not do then? What will you learn?

Analyze children's responses for

• Completeness

• Accuracy

• Number of details

Figure 8.6   Evaluate children's understanding of history.

rather than a problem. Problems that arise spontaneously in the classroom, school, home, or immediate community are real to the children. Learning to question, to ask, "What's happening here?" "Why?" "Who said so?" fosters children's sense of inquiry.

• *Gather information.*   To solve a problem, children must gather information. They might examine traces of the past to solve historical problems. Children as young as 3 can conduct surveys. Primary-age children might interview older people, their parents, or those who work in their school to find out what and how those people felt about a current or historical event. Kindergarten and primary children can also examine library books, watch videos, visit museums, or locate relics from the past.

• *Observe the data.*   Having gathered the necessary information, children need to observe carefully. You can foster children's skills in learning to observe by asking them to describe what they see, feel, taste, touch, and hear throughout the day.

• *Analyze the information.*   Once children have gathered and observed the information, they can analyze it and make inferences from it. What did most of the people interviewed think about invading Iraq? What do authors say about how people lived or what school was like long ago? Having gathered data from the past, historians consider them and make inferences about life—what it was like, how people lived, what they did, and what they believed in.

• *Draw conclusions.*   Just as historians do, children reach conclusions about the past based on the available data. They may reach conclusions that are incomplete because (1) the traces of the past may be incomplete, (2) there is no one to interpret their discoveries of the past, or (3) their inferences are less than accurate. A group of children, after a visit to George Washington's home at Mount Vernon, might conclude that people in those days were very short because the beds were so small. When encouraging problem-solving skills in children, you need not be as concerned about their reaching the correct conclusion as about their ability to use the historian's method of solving problems.

SUMMARY

Children do have a sense of the past and are interested in studying their personal history. From these beginnings, you can foster concepts of history through the regular activities of the preschool-primary classroom. Focusing on the key concepts of time, change, the continuity of life, the past, and the methods of the historian, children can begin to develop an understanding of history.

It is true, however, that children's experiences in history must be as concrete as possible and vitally relevant to the child. Learning about their own pasts, experiencing the passage of time, interacting with older volunteers, studying the immediate past (what did we do today), and using the methods of the historian must all be based on children's activities and experiences.

Extend Your Knowledge

1. Start personal history books for children in the class. You might ask the children to bring baby pictures to include in their books and compare them with current photographs. Other items you could include are a graph of each child's height and weight and a discussion of the things each likes or does not like to do. Leave several blank pages in the book to fill with the same information at the end of the year. Children can then discuss the changes that have occurred in themselves during the school year.

2. Invite older persons to the class to discuss the things they remember about life when they were young boys or girls. Ask each one to bring a childhood photograph or an object that they used as a child.

3. Begin your own family history book by starting a family tree tracing your heritage.

4. Have the class make a history book of their school. They can find out when the school was built, what was on the land before it was built, who the school was named for, and how many people have been principals of the school.

Resources

To initiate an intergenerational program in your school, you might first locate organizations that sponsor intergenerational programs. Contact the following:

Administration on Aging
E-mail: esec@ban-gate.aoa.dhhs.gov
Website: *http://www.aoa.gov*

American Association of Retired Persons
601 East Street, NW
Washington, DC 20019
Website: *http://www.aarp.org*

Contact the National Council for History Education for information about teaching history to young children:

National Council for History Education
26915 Westwood Road, Suite B-2
Westlake, OH 44145
E-mail: NCHE19@mail.idt.net
Website: *http://206.183.13.178/nche/main.html*

To obtain information about the national standards for teaching history in kindergarten through grade 4, contact the following organization:

National Center for History in the Schools
University of California, Los Angeles
405 Hilgard Avenue
Los Angeles, CA 90014-1473
Website: *http://www.sscnet.ucla.edu/nchs/usk4-toc.htm*

References

Ames, L. (1946). The development of the sense of time in the young child. *Journal of Genetic Psychology, 18,* 97–125.

Barton, K. C. (2002). "Oh, that's a tricky piece !" Children, mediated action, and the tools of historical time. *Elementary School Journal, 103,* 161–186.

Barton, K., & Levstik, L. (1996). "Back when God was around and everything": Elementary children's understanding of historical time. *American Educational Research Journal, 33,* 419–454.

Brophy, J. (1990). Teaching social studies for understanding and higher-order applications. *Elementary School Journal, 90,* 351–419.

Brophy, J., & Alleman, J. (2002). Learning and teaching about cultural universals in primary school social studies. *Elementary School Journal, 103*(2), 99–14.

Cobb, M., & Ellis, D. (1997). *The quilt-block history of pioneer days: With projects kids can make.* New York: Millbrook.

Derman-Sparks, L. (2003). Holiday activities in an antibias curriculum. In C. Copple (Ed.), *A world of difference* (pp. 149–156). Washington, DC: National Association for the Education of Young Children.

Dewey, J. (1966). *Lectures on the philosophy of education.* New York: Archambault/Random House.

Dunbar, J. (2001). *Tell me what it's like to be big.* New York: Harcourt Brace.

Egan, K. (1997). The arts as the basics of education. *Childhood Education, 73,* 346–349.

Gibbons, F. (2002). *Full steam ahead.* Honesdale, PA: Boyds Mills.

Gibbons, G. (1988). *The seasons of Arnold's apple tree.* New York: Voyager.

Glanz, D. (1991). Intergenerational proximity, propinquity, and social contact: An analysis of two Israeli university-based programs. *Educational Gerontology, 17,* 465–476.

Greeley, V. (1993). *White is the moon: Kindergarten level.* New York: Macmillan.

Jantz, R. K., & Seefeldt, C. (1999). Early childhood social studies. In C. Seefeldt (Ed.), *The early childhood curriculum: Current findings in theory and practice* (pp. 159–179). New York: Teachers College Press.

Johnson, A. (1989). *Tell me a story Mama*. New York: Orchard Books.

Kraus, R. (1947). *The growing story*. New York: Harper.

Levstik, L. (1991). Narrative constructions: Cultural frames for history. *Social Studies, 86*, 848–853.

Levstik, L. (2002). Introduction. *Elementary School Journal, 103*, 93.

Levstik, L., & Barton, K. (1997). "Any history is someone's history": Listening to multiple voices from the past. *Social Education, 61*, 48–51.

McCaughrean, G. (2002). *My grandmother's clock*. New York: Clarion.

Mead, M. (1970). *Culture and commitment: A study of the generation gap*. New York: American Museum of Natural History.

Milne, A. A. (1955). The end. In *Now we are six* (p. 104). London: Dutton.

Morris, A. (2002). *Grandma Susan remembers: A British-American family story*. Brookfield, CT: Millbrook.

Murphy, S. J., & Greenseid, D. (1996). *Get up and go!* New York: HarperCollins.

National Assessment of Educational Progress (NAEP). (2002). *NAEP in U.S. history*. Washington, DC: U.S. Department of Education.

National Center for History in the Schools (NCHS). (1994). *National standards: History for grades K–4*. Los Angeles: Author.

National Commission on Social Studies in the Schools. (1989). *Charting a course: Social studies for the 21st century*. New York: Author.

National Council for the Social Studies (NCSS). (1998). *Curriculum standards for social studies: Expectations of excellence*. Washington, DC: Author.

Peter, L. (2001). *On the trail of Sacagawea*. Honesdale, PA: Caroline House/Boyds Mills.

Pettigrew, E., & Kimber, W. (1992). *Night-time*. New York: Annick.

Piaget, J. (1946). The child's concept of space. In H. E. Gruber & J. J. Voneche (Eds.), *The essential Piaget* (pp. 576–645). London: Routledge & Kegan Paul.

Root, P. (2003). *The name quilt*. New York: Farrar, Straus, & Giroux.

Rylant, C. (1992). *When I was young in the mountains*. New York: Dutton.

Seefeldt, C. (1993). Learning for freedom! *Young Children, 48*(3), 4–10.

Seefeldt, C., & Galper, A. (2000). *Active experiences for active children: Social studies*. Upper Saddle River, NJ: Merrill/Prentice Hall.

Seefeldt, C., & Warman, B. (1990). *Young and old together*. Washington, DC: National Association for the Education of Young Children.

Turner, A., & Allen, T. B. (1994). *Sewing quilts*. New York: Simon & Schuster.

VanSledright, B. A. (2002). Fifth graders investigating history in the classroom: Results from a researcher-practioner design experiment. *Elementary School Journal, 103*(2), 131–160.

Vukelich, R., & Thornton, S. J. (1990). Children's understanding of historical time: Implications for instruction. *Childhood Education, 66*, 22–25.

Vygotsky, L. (1986). *Thought and language*. Cambridge, MA: MIT Press.

Walker, S. M., & Beier, E. (1998). *The 18 penny goose*. New York: HarperCrest.

Walton, R. (2002). *Bunny day: Telling time from breakfast to bedtime*. New York: HarperCollins.

CHAPTER 9

People, Places, and Environments: Geography

The field of geography, unlike the world it studies, has no boundaries.

Bucknell Geography, 2003, n. p.

After you read this chapter, you should be prepared to respond to the following questions:

- What is the definition of geography?
- What are the skills of the geographer that children can develop in the preschool-primary grades?
- What concepts are considered key to the study of geography?
- How do children develop concepts of direction and location, and how do teachers foster these concepts?
- What mapping skills can young children develop?
- How would you best introduce children to concepts of relationships within places, spatial interactions, and regions?

Taking a walk to mail letters, a group of first graders stops to watch a squirrel hiding acorns under a tree stump. Two children spot a nest of leaves high in a tree and wonder if this is the squirrel's home. Cars pass by and stop at the intersection. Some children see a picture of a blue heron on the license plate of one of the cars and talk about the blue heron they saw at the beach. After crossing the street when the light turns green, each child places a letter in the mailbox.

Although they did not know it, these first graders were experiencing and learning geography. But this learning did not involve memorizing countries and their capitals or locating them on a map. Like geographers everywhere, children learn as they observe, experience, and develop beginning understandings of the nature of their world and their place in it (Schoenfeldt, 2001). Through these early explorations of their world, children, like geographers, begin to answer the two major questions of geography: where are things, and how did they get there? (Geography Education Standards Project, 1994). And like geographers everywhere and at every age, children, as they explore the earth they live on, develop and use the four skills that "will allow the student to better understand the world around him or her, and will couple social studies to the continual process of the student's trying to determine just where he or she is in the world" (NCSSS, 1989, p. 44).

The national geography standards, *Geography for Life* (Geography Education Standards Project, 1994), list five skills that children begin developing during their preschool and primary years:

1. *Asking geographic questions.* Questioning comes naturally to young children. Toddlers, driven by their innate curiosity about the world, ask, "What's dis?" "What's dat?" By 2 years of age the why questions begin. Why questions extend beyond just asking, "Why?" to asking, "Why is it this way?" Three- and 4-year-olds want to know "Why is the sky blue?" "Why did you do that?" "Why do I have to do this?" By the time children are in the primary grades, they ask actual geographic questions: "What caused the lake?" "What made this hill?" Later, they ask speculation questions: "Does corn always grow in this field?"

2. *Acquiring geographic information.* Locating, collecting, and processing information from a variety of primary and secondary sources, including maps, forms another set of skills. Lucy Sprague Mitchell (1934) said these skills begin right from the start, unofficially at birth. Watch as an infant flails his arms in space as if attempting to determine where self begins and ends. Watch as she stares at a mobile with a questioning frown as if trying to make sense of its movement. By the time children are toddlers, they can collect information, process it, and make differentiations—for example, "This is a chair; this is a sofa." In the preschool and primary grades, children consult secondary sources, books, authorities, pictures, and maps as they build their geographic skills.

3. *Organizing geographic information.* Although humans begin to organize and process information through their senses from the moment of birth or even before, not until children are in the preschool and primary grades do they begin to develop the skills of organizing geographic information by preparing maps and displays, telling and writing stories, or constructing graphs.

Like geographers, children learn as they observe and experience.

4. *Analyzing geographic information.* In the preschool and primary grades, children learn to use maps to locate themselves in space and learn to interpret graphs. Preschool-primary students use many kinds of textbooks, encyclopedias, and literature to study geographic relationships.

5. *Answering geographic questions.* Reaching conclusions, the final stage in the thinking/problem-solving process, completes the geographic skills to be developed in the preschool and primary grades. Children can present their findings to the group, write a story, paint a mural, or construct a replica of a place to demonstrate how they draw conclusions and make generalizations.

KEY CONCEPTS

Planning to teach geography begins with a study of children's immediate physical environment and their ability and opportunity to observe, speculate about, analyze, and evaluate that environment. Both the environment and children's explorations within it are complex and complicated. To help teachers organize the possibilities for children's geographic learning within an environment, the national geography standards, *Geography for Life* (Geography Education Standards Project, 1994), and the National Council for the Social Studies (1998) have identified major themes and concepts key to the study of geography. Believing that the study of geography is more than just place geography, the project designers call for integrating place geography with the study of human-environmental relationships by structuring geographical studies around five main themes:

1. *The earth is the place where we live.*   It is covered with land and water and is a part of the solar system. The physical characteristics—landforms, water bodies, climate, soils, natural vegetation, and animal life—and the human ideas and actions that have shaped their character are included in the concept of place. As children develop concepts of the earth as the place they live in, they can also be introduced to the concepts, attitudes, and values inherent in learning to care for their earth.

2. *Direction and location.*   From birth, children start orienting themselves in space. By age 4 children have an intuitive sense of space and are able to construct representations of space (Barry-Davis, 1999). Although they do not develop a complete sense of direction until after the age of 11 or 12, they experience concepts of direction through their own movement early in life. Being able to orient oneself in space also means being able to locate oneself in space. The ideas of distance and measurement are included in these concepts. Maps are vital tools for locating oneself in space. Children begin developing mapping skills by making and using maps rather than by reading them.

3. *Relationships within places.*   Humans interact on the earth. People adapt and modify the natural environment in ways that reveal their cultural values. Human population density is spread unevenly across the earth. People live in different communities and interact with others by means of travel, communication, and the use of products and ideas that come from beyond their immediate environment.

4. *Spatial interactions.*   There are patterns of movement of people, products, and information. People are scattered unevenly over the earth. How do they get from one place to another? What are the patterns of movement of people, products, and information?

5. *Regions.*   Regions are convenient and manageable units on which to build knowledge of the world and study current events. Children live in a region; its geographic description dictates how they live.

THE EARTH IS THE PLACE WHERE WE LIVE

"All stones have been made by builders out of the earth and the earth is broken stone." "Mountains made themselves so we can ski." These explanations of the nature of the earth were given in reply to questions posed by Piaget (1965, p. 207), and they aptly demonstrate young children's thinking about the nature of the earth. Piaget has labeled this stage of thinking *artificialism*, the idea that children view things on the earth as for their own use, made for purposes (usually theirs), and also either made by themselves or by others—the mountains made themselves, the builders made the stones. (Table 9. 1).

In attempting to determine where children obtained this line of thought, Piaget ruled out religious education or educational experiences of any nature: "Artificialis-

Table 9.1   Geography Skills

Sensorimotor Ages 0–2	Preoperational Ages 2–6/7	Concrete Ages 6/7–10
Attends to qualities of things: self, earth, sky	Moves on earth	8+, still having difficulty with left and right
Moves in space	Orients self in a given space (e.g., in a room)	Still confused about relating directions
	Represents world in buildings and drawings	12+, understands cardinal directions
	Draws rough maps, can find treasures with rough map	
	Begins orientation to distance	

tic thought may simply be a matter of never having considered the question before. Or it could arise from the powers parents, who appear to be godlike to children, have over them, leading children to believe that powerful people, like their parents, could crush stone to make the earth" (p. 207).

Keeping in mind young children's thinking, you can help children build more accurate concepts of the earth by providing them with concrete, direct experiences structured around their immediate environment. In planning earth-study experiences, you need to ask yourself: "What have these children learned through their own experiences about the way the world functions?" "What have they learned about the natural phenomena—the action of earth forces, how water runs down a hill, the effects of the growth of plants and animals?" You can use the answers to plan experiences for children based on an identified key concept of geography: knowledge of the earth.

Our Environment

We are alive, and we live on the earth. What a simple idea—unless you are a child under 6 or 7 years of age who believes that everything that moves is alive and that even some things that do not move, like poison, which could intend to kill you, are also alive (Piaget, 1965). To young children, cars, boats, clouds, rivers, and all sorts of things that move have life and consciousness.

As children are experiencing their environment, you can ask questions to help them sort living things from nonliving things. Ask them whether the objects or materials they are playing with are living or not living. Based on their answers, you can ask other questions or offer suggestions. Try to extend children's thinking by asking, "Do you think it's alive?" "Why do you think it's living?" "How can you tell?" "Are you living?" "What other things do you know that are alive?" "What things are not alive?"

After a walk outside, you could set up a table, a bulletin board, or a chart sectioned into living things and nonliving things. Children could place objects or pictures representing things they have seen on their walk into the appropriate sections. Rocks, sand, and pictures of houses might be placed in the nonliving section and pictures or pieces of plants and trees and pictures of animals and birds in the living section. You might also help children make booklets or scrapbooks of living and nonliving things.

Other experiences can foster the concept that we live on the surface of the earth. When playing outdoors, children can classify things that live on the earth. You could use this activity to initiate a discussion of living and nonliving things.

The purpose of these experiences with living and nonliving things is not to change children's thinking but to increase their awareness of the world around them. Thus, teachers are not concerned with trying to move children to the next stage of thought; rather, they want to provide children with experiences that will be useful when they reach the next stage of thinking. Talking with children about living and nonliving things, you can gain an understanding of their thought processes, which is necessary for planning and evaluating the teaching-learning process(Figure 9.1).

Land and Water

By experiencing their immediate environment, children can begin to make distinctions between the different surfaces covering their earth and the relationships between these surfaces and how they live. Children need time to play with, experiment

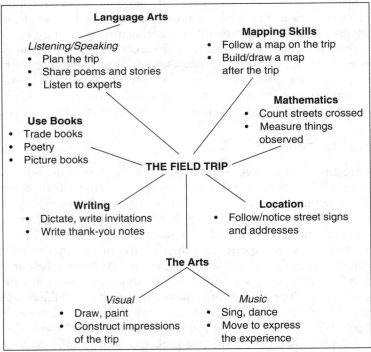

Figure 9.1 Geography—the integrative power of a field trip.

with, and explore the nature of sand, water, and dirt—inside and outside—to learn the nature of the surfaces covering the earth. All this messing around with sand and dirt and playing with mud and water helps children construct the physical knowledge of the earth on which they live that is so necessary for later formal thinking about the earth (NRC & IM, 2000).

Children's exploration with water, sand, and mud can help them to discover that these substances take on the shape of the container they are in and practice the idea that the amount of material remains the same, even when poured into containers of different shapes. On a graph or in some other form, primary-age children can count and record the number of cups of sand, water, or dirt it takes to fill a large container. Ask them to pour a filled cup into another container and to predict whether or not the amount of water has stayed the same. They can test their hypothesis by pouring the material back into the first container.

Remember, too, that these experiences are only exploratory. Even though children through the primary grades will explore the nature of water and land, it is inappropriate to attempt to teach children about evaporation, the water cycle, or other abstract concepts of the nature of land and water. Research suggests that even after instruction involving firsthand experiences, 7- and 8-year-old children believe that water that has evaporated from a dish has somehow soaked into the dish. After all, sponges and towels soak up water, so why not a dish? (Landry & Forman, 1999).

Within the school and or immediate neighborhood, children can find different land surfaces. The playground may be grassy, paved with concrete or blacktop, or contain sand areas. Children can feel the different surfaces and classify them as hard, soft, rough, or smooth and discuss the purpose and use of each. Ask, "Why is the street hard? What would happen if you fell on it?" "Have you ever fallen on the sidewalk? What happened?" "Ride your bike on the blacktop, on the grass, and then on the sand. Where is it easier to ride? Why?" Some of the surfaces may have been made by humans; others occur naturally. Kindergarten and primary-age children may be able to classify the surfaces.

Trips taken in the wider community allow children to observe that the earth is covered with water as well as land. One second-grade class in Boston took an overnight trip with their parents and their teacher, who had been with them since they entered school as 4- and 5-year-olds, to a lake resort to see Deep Creek Lake, swim in the lake, climb the mountains surrounding it, and actually experience different landforms for themselves.

Even with field trips, children will not be able to actually experience all the earth's surfaces: "The schools' task is to furnish source materials." (Mitchell, 1934, p. 31). Vicarious experiences with photographs, pictures, and reference or audiovisual materials may be used to help children develop an awareness of the different types of earth surfaces.

Choose both factual reference books as well as children's literature to extend children's knowledge of the surfaces that cover the earth. Begin by selecting books about children's own neighborhood and community. Depending on where you are located, you might find these books useful: *It Could Still be a Tree* (Fowler, 2001),

Field trips give children experiences with different land forms.

Rivers and Streams (Vaughan, 1998), and *Mountains and Volcanoes* (Taylor, 2002). Use other books to take children to places they may not have experienced. *One Morning in Maine* (McCloskey, 1952) and *Blueberries for Sal* (McCloskey, 1976) give children a feel for the earth and water of Maine. Older primary children enjoy reading or listening to *Black Cowboy, Wild Horses: A True Story* (Lester & Pinkney, 1998), a story of the Wild West that depicts its sweeping plains. *Seven Brave Women* (Hearne, 1997) tells the story of how women came to and then created America, showing farms, forests, oceans, and plains. *Beneath the Stone: A Mexican Zapotec Tale* (Wolf, 1994) follows a 6-year-old and his family through their life in a mountain valley village.

Depending on children's firsthand experiences with land and water and the books they have read, they could do some of the following activities:

- Make a two-part mural labeled "On Land, On Water" and include pictures of things that live on land or in the water, placed appropriately.

- Classify a group of pictures of land surfaces—hills, mountains, valleys, deserts— as land and another group of pictures of water surfaces—streams, waterfalls, lakes, oceans—as water. Children can then sort the two groups of pictures into appropriately labeled box lids.

- Discuss and draw pictures of the kinds of activities that take place on land and in water, making a booklet or a chart for the classroom. Swimming, fishing, and boating are classified as water activities; camping, playing ball, and gardening are classified as land activities.

Caring for Our Earth

It is particularly worrisome that many children are disconnected from what we call nature. We ourselves are part of nature, having evolved along with the other plants and animals. We ought to take more heed of our habitats, knowing that their loss is a primary cause of species extinction (Rivkin, 1995).

Every individual, beginning with children, must learn to care for the place we live in—our earth. Each individual must be concerned about the chain of life; the welfare of birds, insects, grass, and trees; and the conditions of the air, water, and land.

As with any area of study, learning to care for the earth (1) is an ongoing process; (2) involves multiple disciplines; (3) must be age-appropriate; (4) must be related to children's firsthand, everyday experiences; and (5) must include concepts as well as attitudes and values. You can begin by encouraging children to learn to observe their environment, providing experiences that enable them to develop an understanding of interdependency, aesthetic awareness, and social consciousness—all parts of environmental education.

Observation Skills

We need to concentrate on allowing children to explore, to experience the marvels of nature themselves (Mitchell, 2000). Encouraging children to become totally familiar with their environment is accomplished, in part, by teaching them to observe. As children observe and experience their environment, conceptual learning follows. Teach children that they can really observe by looking. Preschool children can examine their eyes. Ask, "How many eyes do you have?" "What color are they?" "What parts of your eye can you see when you look in the mirror?" Give children the names for eyebrows, eyelashes, pupils, and eyelids.

You can relate children's learning about their eyes to the environment, discussing the nature of the eyes of fish, mammals, birds, and reptiles that may live in the classroom. Primary children can conduct an entire study of eyes, observing the eyes of insects, reptiles, and mammals and conducting library research.

Next, ask children to use their eyes to identify the things they can see inside and outside their classroom. Encourage them to note colors, shapes, and sizes. Ask them to look again, focusing on a specific detail in the environment. Primary-age children can also explore what happens when they look through things, such as windows, magnifying lenses, and prisms, and what happens when they look into things, such as mirrors.

As they observe, children use other senses. Observation experiences lead children to use the senses of hearing, smell, and touch as they explore their environment. They might discuss and chart the meanings of different sounds and smells.

Field trips within the school building, on the playground, and in the immediate neighborhood focus children's attention on the natural environment. In a field trip around an inner-city block, first graders noted more than 40 different types of plants growing between cracks in the sidewalks, in the street, and even between bricks of the row houses. It seemed impossible to imagine, when first looking at the cement and brick city, that so many plants could survive. The children not only observed their immediate environment but went on to classify the plants, noting their likenesses and differences and identifying the conditions that supported this life. To help them focus their observations, the teacher gave the children cardboard paper-towel tubes to look through.

Another teacher asked second graders to look up and observe the sky. A flock of birds happened to catch the children's attention. Back in the classroom, the children identified the birds they had seen and planned ways they could provide for birds in their school. One group made birdhouses from empty milk cartons and hung them on trees around the schoolyard, and another located a large discarded plastic garbage-can lid and made a birdbath. All the children took part in spreading peanut butter on pinecones and rolling them in birdseed to make feeders for their school and homes.

Next, the children observed and recorded the birds that were attracted to their school and homes. The children found that some of the birds they observed had migrated miles to nest in the area. They marked the birds' migration paths on a map.

After interest in birds subsided, the teacher again took the children outside to observe, but this time she asked them to observe life on the ground. Turning over rocks, the children observed a variety of worm and insect life. Their observations led to their discovery of a number of different insects, worms, and grubs. The children consulted books and found that worms are necessary to human life because they enrich the soil and that other insects are useful in cleaning up the environment. Leaving an apple core in a corner of the playground, the class observed which insects ate the core and how many days it took before the core was completely gone.

Observations logically lead to other thinking processes. You can ask children to make inferences, predict outcomes, and suggest hypotheses: "Why do you think it's like this?" "What made the trees die?" "What would happen if . . . ?" "How can we find out?" Such questions can help children see connections between their observations and protection of the environment. During field trips, you can point out the interrelatedness of land, water, air, plants, and animals.

Still, questions should be used cautiously. Judith Dighe (1993) reminds us that some children can quickly be turned off by the "what's-its-name?" approach: "Surprising to me, the what-do-you-think . . . ? questions that teachers have been taught to ask can fall flat too" (p. 59). Asking, "What do you think made that hole in the acorn?" has "the effect of stopping a child's investigation when my intent was just the opposite" (p. 59). Dighe suggests that when children are observing and exploring their environment, it's best to take your cues from them—listen, watch, share interest and delight first; then ask questions that will help children further their own investigations.

Interdependency

The concept that one form of life is dependent on another is basic to learning to care for our earth and stems from the biological and physical sciences. Through observations, children become aware of the chain of life around them and of their influence on that life. You can instill a reverence for life by being cautious about picking wildflowers, tearing branches from trees, or removing a toad to place in a jar in the classroom. Your caution lets children know that the environment deserves respect.

Keeping a variety of living things in the classroom helps foster the concept of interdependency. The care of living things demonstrates to the children the precarious balance found in nature. Reptiles cannot live without insects; insects without plants; plants without sun, water, or soil. The reptiles themselves may become food for other living things. Keeping an aquarium in balance is sometimes difficult in a classroom, yet it teaches the importance of balance in maintaining life in one type of environment. You can stress children's interdependence with other living things. To live, children depend on and need to protect plants, animals, land, air, and water.

Aesthetic Awareness

Interwoven with the skills and concepts of environmental education is an aesthetic appreciation of the natural environment. As children learn to appreciate the beauty surrounding them, they become more aware of the chain of life and thus more concerned about protecting their environment.

Aesthetic education is subtle: a classroom that is ordered; contains prints of famous paintings, growing plants, and other living things; and is decorated with the work of the children leads them to appreciate the beauty of the environment. Dewey (1900) wrote, "If the eye is constantly greeted by harmonious objects, having elegance of form and color, a standard of taste naturally grows" (p. 307). You can point out the delicate beauty in the construction of a spiderweb; the strong veins of a maple leaf; the smooth, shiny, purple elegance of an eggplant; or the intricate parts and patterns of a wildflower. At times you may want to display a single perfect flower, a sculpture, a wood carving, or another object of beauty. In observing the beauty of the environment, encourage children to use all their senses: to look at the object from different perspectives; to notice shapes, sizes, smells, textures, and colors; and to share with one another the interesting things they find in their environment.

Social Consciousness

Living in a democracy calls for the development of a strong social consciousness, which is basic to learning to care for our earth. It requires each individual to assume responsibility for environmental protection. If children have developed an awareness of the beauty of the natural environment and understand the concept of interdependence, then the development of a social consciousness—assuming individual responsibility for the common good—is the next step in environmental education.

The development of children's social consciousness, especially for the protection of the environment, may be a highly controversial goal. Parents and the community must be involved in formulating the objectives of an environmental education program. You will want their input into the kinds of activities you will provide to foster these goals. Many people believe that protecting the environment without concern for progress will destroy society; others, with vested interests in industry or production, might object for reasons specific to their interests.

Developing respect for the dignity and worth of life and sharing responsibility for the care of private and public property are part of developing social consciousness. Caring for their immediate environment leads children to concern for the wider environment.

To foster social consciousness, introduce the three *R*'s of being a good environmentalist into the classroom: (1) recycle, (2) reduce, and (3) reuse.

Recycle.   Young children do not understand how goods get to a store and will not understand concepts of manufacturing until nearly their adolescence. Thus, they will have difficulty understanding the concepts involved in recycling. Regardless, even the youngest children can be taught the habit of recycling. They can learn to recycle glass bottles, jars, paper, and aluminum foil used in pie plates, TV dinner trays, and cans. Set up boxes to enable children to sort their trash and arrange for them to take the containers to a recycling center. Parents can be involved and asked to purchase recycled notebook paper, stationery, and greeting cards.

Reduce.   All of us, even the youngest, can begin to learn to reduce our use of materials—to cut down on what we consume. Children can do these things:

• They can learn to reduce their use of water. They can be taught to brush their teeth by first wetting their brush and then turning off the water and to use water cooled in the refrigerator instead of letting the water run from the faucet to cool off. Teach children to remember to conserve water by saying, "Presto on! Presto off!"

• They can ask themselves if they really need a paper bag to carry a book home and if presents need fancy wrapping paper.

• They can conduct a waste audit. First and second graders can conduct an inventory of the amount of waste in their school. They might focus on the cafeteria and observe the food placed in trashcans after lunch or focus on their room alone, counting how much paper, electricity, water, or paint is being wasted. Or they might conduct a waste audit in their own homes. After the audits, they can report their findings to the class.

• They can get into the habit of using string bags or canvas totes to carry things.

• They can look for things to buy that are not wrapped in elaborate, unnecessary packaging. Even though they love individual pudding snacks or fruit juice containers, they might find other ways to have individual snacks that conserve packaging.

• They can use a lunchbox instead of brown paper bags.

• They can learn to reduce the amount of art materials used.

Reuse.   Children can be taught to reuse whatever possible.

• They can learn how broken toys and other items can be fixed.

• They can save plastic bags to use again. If the bags are dirty, turn them inside out, rinse them, and hang them up to dry. A caution: do not reuse plastic bags with printing or pictures on them, such as bread bags, in this way. The dye in the printing contains lead and can contaminate food.

- They can wash off aluminum foil, let it dry, and put it away.
- They can think of ways to use empty containers or other trash.
- They can cut up brown paper bags to use for wrapping packages, for mailing, or for drawing or painting.
- They can use computer paper for other projects.
- They can give books, toys, and materials they no longer use to someone else who can use them.
- They can use old greeting cards, catalogs, and magazines in their collages and other artwork.
- They can reuse empty milk cartons as plant containers.

One second-grade teacher initiated a unit on recycling. She first asked the children to predict the amount of material they would find in the trashcans from the school's office, their own room, and the duplicating room, where the copying machines and art and classroom supplies were kept. After the children charted their predictions, they collected the trashcans and sorted the trash into materials that really were trash and needed to be discarded, those that could be recycled, and those that could be reused. The final activity was following the trash collected in their own room on its path to the landfill. The group met with representatives from the sanitation department, mapped and followed the route of their trash, and observed a landfill. They speculated about what would happen to the trash when this specific landfill was full.

The children then formed groups to find out where and how materials could be recycled or reused. After identifying how materials could be recycled, one group canvassed the entire school and gained the cooperation of all to institute a recycling program. Another group made toys from recycled materials, including rhythm instruments, a kaleidoscope, and milk-carton dollhouse furniture.

Following the interest of the children, the teacher broadened the unit to include concern for the wider environment. The children picked up trash around their school and learned how it was disposed. Awareness of waste processing can also be followed by making or decorating trashcans for the playground and posters for the school about recycling, reducing, and reusing.

A Nearly Round Sphere in a Solar System

How can young children, or any of us (except perhaps the astronauts), discover through personal experiences that the earth is round and is part of the solar system? These two concepts can only be taught through vicarious experiences. Children do, however, appear to have the concept of a spherical earth (Takahashi, 2000). Perhaps children, as we all do, learn about the roundness of the earth through photographs and books and by using globes.

One useful book to inform children about the spherical nature of the earth is *Looking Down* (Jenkins, 1995), a wordless picture book that illustrates the perspective of astronauts viewing the earth from space. *Earth from Above for Young Readers* (Arthus-Bertrand & Burleigh, 2002), for older children, could be read to younger children, who will enjoy the photographs and illustrations of the earth.

Most classrooms for young children have at least one globe. Recognizing that children under 7 or 8 years of age are cognitively unable to study the globe, teachers use it instead to enable children to become aware of the fact that the earth is round and can be represented as a sphere. Most teachers of young children find that the single value of using globes in primary classrooms is to provoke curiosity and a basic awareness of the shape of the earth.

Our Sun Is a Star (Martin, 1969) presents a simple yet accurate account of the earth as part of the solar system. Primary children can read the book themselves, and 4- and 5-year-olds enjoy the beauty of the illustrations and the text when it is read to them.

Movement in Space

A complete and accurate understanding of the rotation of the earth on its axis and its revolution around the sun is not possible for young children. Yet beginning experiences with the consequences of the earth's movement are possible and can form the foundation for later, more advanced understandings.

One effect of the earth's rotation is the appearance of night and day. Talk with the children about their day and night experiences. Ask if they can remember what they did at night after they went to sleep. Just as children believe all moving things are alive, they believe that dreams really happened. They will not believe an adult who tells them, "It was just a dream." Nevertheless, discussing night and day dreams and constructing murals or booklets of "Our Dreams" let children express their feelings about dreams.

You can encourage children to talk about what night looks like, how it feels, and how it differs from day. Ask, "How is the sky at night different from the sky during the day?" Children can draw two different pictures—"My Room at Night" and "My Room by Day"—or they can make night and day collages. Using two different pieces of construction paper, one black and one white, they can cut pictures from magazines and paste them onto the appropriate piece of paper.

Day and night can also be represented in a circular format. Prepare construction paper circles by cutting a large half-circle out of black construction paper and another half-circle the same size out of white paper. Tape the two together to represent the two halves of our 24-hour day. Children can use white tempera to paint nighttime phenomena on the dark side and colored tempera to draw daytime phenomena on the light side.

Playing with shadows can help children understand the earth's daily rotation. Some children may be able to figure out for themselves that the changes in a shadow's position, size, and shape are related to the time of day the shadow is made; other children are content to play. Some may want to know why there is no shadow at all at a particular time of day or why the shadow is directly in front of the school building at one time of day and is off in another direction at another time. Other children may not relate the position of a shadow to the position of the sun at all. Children will absorb different depths of understanding from their experiences, and they need to be able to set their own pace with shadow play. You will want to respect children's individuality, for they are engaging in research as they explore and experiment with their shadows.

You cannot plan just when children will be able to experiment with shadows but will have to take advantage of the weather conditions as they occur. You might want to explore shadows on sunny, cloudy, and windy days as well as at different times of the day and year. Children can do the following:

- Find out what kinds of shadows they can make with their bodies.
- Make shadows with different objects—umbrellas, boxes, or different kinds of toys.
- Mark the shadows of a landmark—the school building, a tree, or a fence—at different times of the day. Discuss how the shadows differ and talk about the effects of the earth's rotation around the sun. Draw around shadows at different times of the day and compare the drawings.
- Play shadow tag.
- Play Simon Says with shadows: "Simon says: touch your shadow; stand with your shadow in front of you; hide in your shadow; step on someone's shadow." Take turns being leader.

In a child-care center in Reggio Emilia, Italy, children's spontaneous play with shadows on a sunny day turned into an extensive exploration of the properties and magic of *l'ombra* (the shadow). Teachers used this natural response to the environment as the building block for a long-term investigation of shadows.

As children played with shadows, the teacher captured the event through photographs. The sharing of the photographs stimulated many more days of play with shadows. Children used a variety of objects to create shadow images, and the teacher followed their lead, providing other props, asking some questions, and suggesting experiments: "How many ways can you make a shadow of a pear?"

After each experience, the teacher asked the children to draw their understanding of the experience or answer the question, "How are shadows created?" with a drawing. Finally, the teacher added a provocation, placing a sticker "sun" on each child's paper and asking them to draw themselves and their shadow in relation to this sun.

Climate Conditions

Observing and recording climate conditions is the first step in understanding the revolution of the earth around the sun and the effects of this revolution on people. Many of these experiences will occur incidentally as children work or play; you can structure others.

You can use seasonal changes in weather to focus children's attention on the climate. Whether it is sunny and warm, cool and rainy, or cold and snowy, children can observe how weather changes throughout the year and draw conclusions about its effects on people's lives. Children can do the following:

1. Stand in the sun and then in the shade. What is different?
2. Stand in the wind and in a protected spot on the playground. What is different?
3. Discuss and examine different clothing worn in different weather conditions. Why are boots, hats, wool clothing, sun hats, snowsuits, or shorts worn?
4. Explore the nature of the wind. Go outside and blow soap bubbles: give each child a paper cup half filled with soapy water, a straw to blow into the cup, or a pipe cleaner to swish through and make bubbles with.
5. Fly a kite.
6. Make pinwheels and take them outside to play with in the wind.
7. Take a walk in the wind. Walk with your back against it. How did it feel? Walk facing the wind; walk with the direction of the wind. Which way was it easiest to walk?
8. Watch cloud formations and play "Do you see what I see?" Then go inside, make cloud pictures, and read a poem about clouds.
9. Wash some doll clothes or dress-up clothing. Dry them in the shade, the sun, or the wind. Where do they dry the quickest? Why?
10. Take a walk in a light rain. What happens to the surfaces of the playground in the rain? Write your own class book of rain, as did students in a first-grade class in Nevada, who wrote *Rain Song* (Evans, 1995).
11. Catch snowflakes on a piece of dark construction paper.
12. Read Tomie dePaola's (1975) *The Cloud Book*, the story of the 10 most common clouds identified in myth and story. Go outside, identify the clouds in the sky, and predict what the weather will be like. Then ask children to write their own myths or stories.

Kindergarten and primary children can begin long-term recording of weather conditions in the form of a time line with symbols for sunny, cloudy, cold, or warm days and other seasonal weather conditions. Children can also make charts or booklets of "Things We Do in Winter," "Clothes We Wear in Summer," or "Food for Summer" to focus attention on how the seasons affect people and their activities.

DIRECTION AND LOCATION

Directionality is a projection of a sense of body-sidedness (laterality) into objective space. As the child projects her body-sidedness into space, she is constructing for herself the coordinates of left-right, up-down, and front-back. Thus, through body movement, the child builds directional orientation.

Human development takes place in space. By the time infants are a month or two old, they are exploring space around them by visual and tactile means. When

Through moving in space children gain concepts of directionality.

children begin to walk, their investigations become more active and widespread. By 2 years of age, a child constructs what Piaget (1965) terms *sensorimotor space*—not the abstract representation of space an adult creates but something bound up with the individual's sense of self and with motor activities.

The initial concepts of space that develop from children's actions and direct experience of moving in space provide the basis for the subsequent formation of representational space. The child's discovery of space and of directionality within space will not be completed until the beginning of adolescence (Marzoff & DeLoache, 1994).

Children with physical disabilities that limit their mobility have a special need to experience space. Children who cannot move for themselves still need to experience space, direction, and location. One teacher took the time to position children with physical disabilities on tables in a circle to play games that other children experience. She believed that these children, even though restricted to a table, needed to experience playing Looby Loo, Farmer in the Dell, and the other games that help children orient themselves in space. She also planned field trips into the community so the children could use maps, follow directions, and experience themselves in a larger space. Using two vans and a volunteer for each child, the group visited fast-food restaurants, doughnut shops, supermarkets, and the gas station—places visited by most children daily but rarely available to children with severe physical disabilities.

Movement Exploration

A geography curriculum designed to help children orient themselves in space is a program of movement exploration. Movement exploration begins with the children becoming aware of their bodies and the things their bodies can do in space (Sanders, 2002). Children are made aware of the following:

1. Body awareness—the shape of the body in space, where the different body parts are, how the body moves and rests, the body's behavior when combined with other bodies, how the voice is a part of the body
2. Force and time—being limp, energetic, light, fluid, staccato, slow, or quick
3. Space—where the body is in a room; the body's level: high (erect posture or in the air), middle (crawling or stooping), or low (on the floor); the body's direction (forward, backward, or sideways); body size (bigness or smallness); the body's path through space; and extensions of the body parts into space
4. Locomotion—movement through space at various levels: lowest (wriggling, rolling, or scooting); middle (crawling, crouching, or using four limbs—ape walk); or highest (walking, running, skipping, galloping, sliding, leaping, hopping, and jumping)
5. Weight—relationship of body to the ground, ways to manage body weight in motion and in relation to others, body collapse, body momentum
6. Working with others—collaborating with others to solve problems, develop trust, explore strength and sensitivity, and feel a sense of belonging
7. Isolations—how individual body parts (head, shoulders, arms, hands, elbows, wrists, neck, back, upper torso, ribs, hips, legs, knees, ankles, feet) can move (swinging, jerking, twisting, shaking, lifting, tensing, relaxing, becoming fluid, pressing, gliding, floating, flicking, slashing, punching, dabbing)
8. Repetitions—getting to know a movement and how it feels when repeated often; being able to repeat a shape or action

The teacher acts as a guide and offers children a challenge or a problem to solve. You might say, "Show how many different ways you can walk," "Make your body very tall; very small," or "How many different ways can you move across the room?" Children select their own level of participation and creativity as they respond. You can comment to help them analyze their movements and become aware of (1) their relationship to the physical environment; (2) their bodies and what they can do; and (3) the components of movement—speed, direction, and force.

To increase and clarify the concepts of directionality stemming from movement exploration, have children write booklets or construct charts. These can be called "I Can Move" and can illustrate in writing and pictures the way in which children move: fast or slow; high, low, or sideways; with their hands touching the floor; on one or two feet; hop, skip, or slide; move with someone else; and so forth.

Directional Terms

You can introduce games to help children develop concepts of up and down and other terms suggesting directionality. Ask a child to stand by any object in the room. Now ask another child to name a different object in the room. The first child must identify body position in relation to the named object: for example, in back of the desk, on the side of the workbench, in front of the window. Some kindergarten children can begin this game, but it is more appropriate for primary-age children. The more experienced children may be able to respond by saying, "The teacher's desk is on my right side," using directional terms.

Up and Down

To learn concepts of up and down, children can sing "The Noble Duke of York," acting it out as they sing and pretending to be mountain climbers, rain, snow, falling leaves, airplanes, kites, or floating dandelion seeds. Teachers can play other games to check children's growth in understanding directions by having individuals place a truck, a doll, or a block in positions that the teacher or another child suggests. You can say to a child: "Place Raggedy Ann on top, over, under, to the side of, behind, next to, or to the right of the sand table," using terms the children need to learn.

Left and Right

Concepts of left and right develop very gradually. A study in England revealed that even 8- and 9-year-old children could not accurately identify left and right in many cases. Learning the concept of left and right occurs as children move in space, grow, and mature. There is no place for a directed, highly structured program of teaching left and right. These concepts will develop with time and with many experiences of moving and exploring space (Roberts & Aman, 1993).

You can use the terms *left* and *right* incidentally but always in connection with a real situation. You could ask the children to put the double blocks to the left of the cars when picking up blocks, to hold the bike with the left foot while reaching for something else, to park the wagon on the right, or to walk on the left side of the street on a field trip. Children can experience other left and right situations while playing Simon Says, Hokey Pokey, Looby Loo, or Follow the Leader.

There is no need to correct children when playing these games and learning left and right. The concept of left and right develops over time, and it is inappropriate to attempt to teach it directly. Nevertheless, you will want to introduce children to the concept and allow them opportunities to experience it.

Cardinal Directions

Children as old as 12 years of age do not appear to have an adequate grasp of cardinal directions. Frank Lord (1941) demonstrated that many children are not aware of cardinal directions until they have nearly reached adulthood. Children in our culture, with its abundant signs and guideposts, appear to have no pressing practical need to become direction-conscious; many of them, indeed, do not develop this awareness. Yet the ability to orient oneself and to acquire a sense of direction is essential. To foster this ability, activities with cardinal directions should be informal and used only as they apply to the actual experiences of young children.

One study, however, has demonstrated that direct teaching of cardinal directions to children in grades 1, 2, and 3 can be successful. Howe's (1969) study consisted of taking children outdoors around 8:45 A.M. to observe the position of the sun and telling them that this was the eastern part of the sky. The same process, conducted from a new location, was repeated as weather conditions permitted. After the children mastered the concept that the sun was in the part of the sky called the east, Howe proceeded to the second step, asking children in what part of the sky the sun appeared in the morning.

Steps 3 and 4 helped children acquire an association between the noon sun and the southern part of the sky. Leaving the school in advance of the usual 11:30 A.M. dismissal time, Howe established an association between south and east by asking the children where the sun had been in the morning. The fifth and sixth steps associated the later afternoon sun with the western part of the sky; this direction, in turn, was associated with the others by reviewing where the sun was at noon and in the morning.

Howe next introduced a shadow stick, and the children developed more complex skills. This apparatus was constructed of a square foot of board, with a 30-inch stick, not more than an inch wide, rising from the center of the board and perpendicular to it. The children took the shadow stick on field trips when they left the playground and used it to find the cardinal directions wherever they were.

At the end of 10 weeks, Howe tested the children. More than 50% of the first graders could answer correctly all the questions pertaining to cardinal directions; 75% of the second and third graders were successful in answering all the questions. Howe concluded that young children, if taken outdoors, can be taught cardinal directions in relation to the sun and that this teaching would later lead to the elimination of confusion over cardinal directions that many of us still have.

Relative Position

For developing concepts of relative position, second- or third-grade children can play a game called Who Is at My Side. Ask one child to stand before the group, facing away from the children. Ask another child to stand to the left or right of the first child. Give directions to the child standing on the side: "Stand in front of the child who is It; stand in back; stand facing; stand to the left." All the children can take turns with this game. This game is for second or third graders, not for kindergarten or younger children.

After children are familiar with the game, ask a group of three to stand in front of the class with their backs to the others. Ask the middle child to tell who is standing on the left or right. Then the other two children can each tell where the middle child is in relation to them.

Location

Concepts of location begin to develop as infants explore and attend to the qualities of things in their environment, including their own bodies and visual and tactile senses. From age 14 months to 3 years, children can distinguish between objects that are near and can be grasped and those farther away and begin to distinguish the space boundaries of their immediate environment, such as the bedroom or the yard.

Initially, infants work out their own location and then go on to discern the whereabouts of other objects in their environment. With increasing visual skills and mobility, children expand their space boundaries. The greater the children's opportunities to roam about, the greater their ability to keep track of position and location.

By the early preschool years, children have an understanding of the spatial relationships between objects. Children express these concepts as they build with blocks, play with sand and water, and construct with other materials. Throughout the preschool and primary grades, their concepts of location continue to develop and are refined through children's direct exploration of their immediate neighborhood and community.

Many concepts of location can be developed through children's experiences in the school and community. Activities that foster concepts of location include the following:

• Ask the children to locate their classroom while on the playground or in front of the school building. Can they locate the office and the lunchroom? After walking around the building to another place, can they locate their room again?

• Take the children for a walk inside the school to find the signs that indicate location. Some schools may even have a map by the office door showing the school's floor plan. Other signs might include the exit and entrance and signs over the stairs.

• Take the children outside to find street signs that indicate location: the sign that names the street where the school is located or the address of the school. Walk around the school with the children and ask them to tell how they would locate it if there were no street signs or addresses.

• Use the children's addresses to teach concepts of location. Ask them to draw a picture for, or write a letter to, their parents. Then either dictate or write the children's addresses on their envelopes and mail them. Make a bulletin board of "Our Neighborhood"; the children can exhibit drawings of their houses and label them with their addresses.

• Make a class address book listing children's names, addresses, and phone numbers.

• Role-play a visitor game. Have a child pretend to be new to the area. The other children will help the visitor locate a street or a specific point in the neighborhood.

Concepts of location are, in part, concepts of direction because being able to orient oneself in space means locating oneself in space. Concepts of location also include understanding distance.

Distance and Measurement

Watching children at play, you can see them use their hands, feet, or sticks to measure off boundaries and distances. The concept of distance is important to the study of geography as well as for day-to-day living. It seems crucial, however, that experiences with the measurement of distance be informal, arbitrary, incidental, and based on actual experiences; children who cannot conserve quantities cannot understand measurement. Piaget (1952) concluded that "there could be no more striking evidence that measurement is impossible without conservation of the quantities to be measured, for the very good reason that quantities that are not conserved cannot be composed" (p. 225).

The Nuffield Mathematics Project (1969) suggested that teachers begin to introduce concepts of distance as children play by "considering the vocabulary which children use in their natural play. They all use the word big. In this context, our aim must be to refine the use of the word big so that high, low, far, near, deep, wide, tall, up, down, long are meaningful to them" (p. 68). Recognizing the importance of play, the Nuffield Project recommended that teachers use all the play situations they can to refine children's vocabulary. In addition, it is helpful to ask children to think of the largest, the deepest, the nearest, and the farthest thing they know. You can play a riddle game with the class: "I am thinking of something nearer than . . . ; I am thinking of something farther than . . . but not as far as. . . . "

Children can use arbitrary measures—hands, feet, lengths of string or ribbon— as well as standard measures to measure from one side of the room to the other, all the way around the desk, or to the top of the bookshelf. Preschool children play with rulers, tape measures, and yardsticks at the woodworking bench to simulate carpenter play but do not use them as actual measuring tools.

Here are some other materials children might use for measuring:

- They can use trundle wheels to measure around the playground or the length of the hall, the room, or the school building. At least two children can use the wheel: one to push it and the other, or several others, to record the clicks.
- Bamboo sticks or broom handles are useful measuring sticks.
- Although preschool children will not use odometers as measuring tools, they can use one on a field trip to see that distance is measured in this way, too.

Maps and Globes

Maps are used to help people position themselves on the earth. Because maps are abstractions of reality, the skills needed to read and use them do not develop until children reach the age of 11 or 12. The ability to use maps requires an understanding of the following:

- The map is a representation. It is a small picture of a much larger place from a bird's-eye view.
- Symbols have meaning.
- The map is a way to orient oneself in space, which requires an understanding of location and direction.

For children to conceptualize the total relationship of a map to the objects it represents or to infer information based on those relationships, they need a cognitive

MAPPING OF THE	GRADE	MATERIAL	
Classroom	* 2–3	Blocks	
School	K–3	Boxes	
Playground	K–3	Dollhouses	
House	K–3	Sticks	From the concrete to the abstract
Route to school	K–3	Paper	
Immediate neighborhood	1–3		
Wider community	1–3	Drawing materials	
* Years of age (child care or preschool)			

Figure 9.2   Continuum of mapping experiences.

maturity not possible until early adolescence. But maturity is not enough. Without a foundation of spontaneous, playful and exploratory experiences with maps, children, no matter how mature cognitively, will not be successful map readers or users (Figure 9.2).

Introducing Maps

When planning to introduce maps and map-reading concepts to young children, you might want to (1) survey the children to find out what their concepts are, (2) remember that all mapping must be done in connection with the children's own experiences, and (3) identify a few key concepts from the numerous skills involved in map reading.

Survey the Children.   Showing the children a map of their city or town, you ask, "What is this used for?" "Have you ever seen one before?" "What do maps tell you?" "What do you know about maps?" "What are these lines for?" "What does this blue part stand for?" Other clues for questions arise as the children discuss their experiences with maps. Answers such as "It shows you where you live," or "There's the ocean," give you an idea of the children's knowledge of maps and can direct lesson plans for extending this knowledge.

Young children seem to have a personal understanding of maps. Researchers have found that, without any hesitation or need for prompting, children as young as age 3 interpreted aerial photographs and maps in geographical terms. They identified roads and decoded other environmental features. Although the children could not explain perspective, scale, or how the photos and maps were constructed, they did understand the concept of map.

Research has not yet demonstrated the exact developmental sequence of children's understanding of maps; however, all experiences with maps in the preschool-primary classroom are simple, based on children's actual experiences and used to acquaint children with maps and map reading in order to build a foundation they can use later, when they have the maturity to think abstractly through the use of symbols (Gouteux, 2001; Miller, 1985; Mosenthal & Kirsch, 1991).

Use Firsthand Experiences.   Mitchell (1934) wrote: "Here again, I'm afraid of words with no images" (p. 18). Already an abstraction, maps must be introduced to children in relation to their actual experiences. Many concrete opportunities present themselves for introducing maps. A field trip to visit a neighbor or buy a flower at the local nursery finds children consulting a map, while the arrival of a new student has children locating the newcomer's neighborhood on a large map.

Three and 4-year-olds play with small picture maps in the housekeeping/ dramatic play area and with wheel toys, cars, and trucks. Board games such as Candy Land, Cherry Tree, Chutes and Ladders, and others are played.

Five-year-olds begin to use maps in connection with their experiences. Using personal knowledge, they can follow a map as they walk on a field trip or find a hidden treasure on the playground. They enjoy a map showing the school, where the children live, and the routes they follow to school.

Over the age of 5, children use maps as they build with blocks and will make maps of their school and room. By the primary grades, maps are a regular part of classroom activities, with children locating their homes and places far away from them on either maps or globes.

One third-grade classroom mapped e-mail friends. Using their families' e-mail addresses, children sent out e-mails requesting e-mail responses. They wanted to see how many different places e-mails came from and would place a pin on the location of each e-mail they received in return. They found that their families had friends all around the world.

In one study, children in the primary grades said they liked maps, but when questioned, did not really grasp the concept of maps. Using constructivist theories, cooperative learning, and other cognitive strategies, however, these second graders were able to develop an understanding of maps and the ability to use them in their everyday lives (Whiteside, 2000).

Children of all ages need to draw and write about their observations with maps. Researchers find that children who are encouraged to represent their experiences through drawing and writing gain a better understanding of mapping concepts. By creating their own journal pages and drawings, children are able to depict their ways of seeing and understanding, constructing or reconstructing the phenomena through their own lens of experiences (Shepardson & Britsch, 2000).

Develop Concepts.   Key concepts can help you plan for teaching map reading to young children. Before children can comprehend maps, they must understand representation, symbolization, perspective, and scale.

The concept that one object can represent another is not new to young children. They have looked at pictures representing cars, trucks, or animals and have seen photographs representing themselves. To fully understand maps, children must be able to understand that a map represents something else—a place.

The idea that a map represents a place can be taught to children as they make their own maps. "Young children make maps before they read them" (Mitchell, 1934, p. 91). It may be that the children have already begun making maps as they work with blocks—laying out streets, shopping centers, and airports.

Blocks, which give children a semiconcrete experience, are useful in map construction and in fostering the understanding that maps do represent some other thing.

Using blocks, you and the children can work together to make a map of their room or playground. When using blocks to map the playground, classroom, or nearby neighborhood, you can help the children orient their building in the correct direction.

After children have become familiar with the idea of using blocks to represent a place that is familiar to them, they can transfer their map-making activities to paper. A walk around the block is an excellent time to draw a simple map of the area to consult during future walks.

Rearranging furniture in a classroom provides additional opportunities for making maps. During informal work time, one teacher began to arrange different pieces of construction paper on a larger sheet. Curious children were asked to help "find a way to arrange the furniture." Telling them that this was a floor plan of their room and that the red paper represented the piano, the blue paper the bookshelf, and the yellow paper the tables, the teacher and children moved the pieces around until they were satisfied with the arrangement. Later, the teacher and the children used this room map to place the furniture. Stimulated by this activity, the children made similar maps of their bedrooms, their houses, and their routes to school.

After traveling to someplace in the city or community, children often represent their trip by building the visited places with their blocks. To foster mapping concepts, Mitchell (1934) often added strips of blue oilcloth and long brown paper to the supplies of blocks. The children used these to lay out streets and to represent water as they constructed with the blocks, further extending their concept of representation.

One teacher in New York City created a floor map of Manhattan for children to use with their blocks. This map, about 10 by 20 feet, was constructed using brown wrapping paper and colored construction paper and was covered with clear plastic. Using their personal experiences and ideas as a guide, the children erected buildings representing the Empire State Building and Wall Street.

Children can also make maps from large pieces of linoleum, varnished wrapping paper, or canvas. When such maps are placed on the floor, 3- to 8-year-olds build small-scale buildings, bridges, and lighthouses on them, working out their own ideas of scale, direction, location, perspective, and orientation.

Mitchell (1934) called this type of map a *tool-map*. Tool-maps are not accurate maps. They are "rough maps which are not an end in themselves, but a means to better play and better thinking" (p. 28). Tool-maps, which can be made by the teacher or the children themselves, force children to actively work out relationships and organize their thinking.

All map play and map making designed to foster the development of the idea of representation should stem from children's own experiences and be on a continuum from the concrete to the abstract.

Using incidental experiences and the children's interests, expand children's understandings of the concept of representation with maps. Children who are moving to another city or state or who have entered the class from another state can be shown on a map where they have come from or where they will be moving. You can help children route visits to grandparents, vacations, and other trips, showing them on a road map where they will travel. News stories of interest to the children are also occasions for you to use a map or a globe to show the children where the event has taken place.

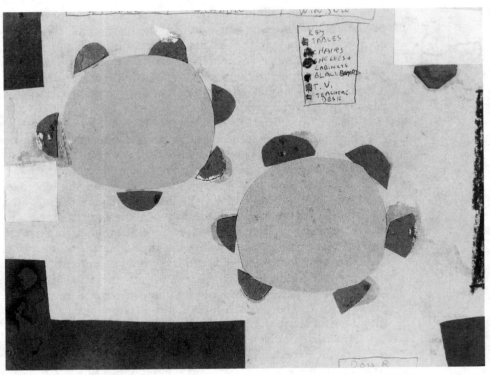

Children map their room.

Play with maps may also foster children's understanding that maps represent places. You can put road maps near the bikes, in the housekeeping area, or near the wheel toys and blocks, encouraging children to use a map to "take a trip." Some commercial table-block games come equipped with maps for arranging trees, houses, buildings, and cars, giving children another experience in the representational nature of maps.

A map, itself a symbol for a place, uses other symbols. Colors symbolize land and water, lines symbolize roads and railroad tracks, and other symbols are used for houses, churches, or schools. Children are already familiar with some symbols—letters for the sounds in their names, traffic signs—and can learn how other symbols are used in maps.

While constructing their own maps, children will often want to portray trees, playground equipment, cars, and other things in the environment. You can present these symbols in pictorial form during their initial experiences. As their understanding of symbolization increases, you can introduce more abstract symbols.

To help children see the use of symbolization in maps, you might pin a small picture or cutout figure of each child to a map of the country to show each child's birthplace. Later you can substitute a thumbtack or a pin in place of the picture.

Color is used in a variety of ways on maps to symbolize different types of data. Young children can understand that the blue areas on the map generally represent water and other areas—brown, green, or some other color—symbolize land.

You might introduce primary children to the use of a map's key and teach them how to use a map's legend. They might make their own maps, using colors to represent land and water and lines to represent railroad tracks, highways, or boundaries (Figure 9.3).

The concept that a map pictures a place as if you were looking at it from above is often difficult for young children to grasp. You must foster their understanding of a bird's-eye view.

Perspective is a most difficult concept for young children, but you can introduce it. Children may not develop a complete understanding of looking down on the top of an object, yet you can expose them to the idea of a bird's-eye view. Living in New York City gave Mitchell (1934) the opportunity to take her kindergartners to the top of a tall building to look down on the city. Following this trip, children's drawings indicated that they had gained the idea of perspective.

You can provide other experiences, such as taking the children to various elevations to view the neighborhood. Photos depicting the same area from different points

---

Assessing children's map skills is a continuous activity done on an individual and group basis using observations and structured interviews with individual children.

Map Skills

How often, and where, do children play with maps?	Date	Date	Date
• Housekeeping area			
• Blocks			
• With wheeled toys			
• Other			

How often do children	Dates
• Refer to maps as if they were taking a trip?	
• Talk about something on a map?	
• Consult a map as they are building/painting?	
• Try to locate a place?	
• Refer to scale (e.g., "This is much smaller.")?	
• Talk about perspective (e.g., "It's like a bird looking down.")?	
• Draw, paint, or build maps?	

Which children use maps?	Names

Which children do not use maps?	Names

Figure 9.3 Assessing children's mapping skills.

of view can help children gain experience with this concept. Some computer programs for children give them the opportunity to manipulate graphical perspective of objects and areas.

A block activity you might introduce in the primary grades involves asking children to select one block and trace around it on a piece of paper. Next, ask the children to see how many blocks of the same size and shape they can fit onto the form on the paper, piling one block on top of the other. This activity demonstrates to them that, no matter how high they build, the shape of the block on top remains the same as the shape drawn on their paper. This shape, which shows only the top of the block, represents the way that maps show only the tops of areas. Experiences such as these may not fully develop the concept of perspective in young children, yet they will form a foundation on which you can build future learning (Figure 9.4).

Maps reduce the size of an actual place. Children can be introduced to the idea that a map is like the original place, except it is much smaller. Making maps small makes it easier for people to think about the place and to hold the map.

You can plan simple experiences with scale for young children. It will be years before they can interpret the scale of distance on a map, yet they can understand the

---

Name _____   Date _____

You will need a small map to show the child and paper and markers or crayons.

Show the child the map and ask: <u>Correct</u>   <u>Incorrect</u>

   What is this?

   What do we use it for?

   Point to various symbols and ask:
   • What do these lines (street, highway) mean?
   • What does this blue (river, lake, ocean) mean?
   • What does this bell (school) mean?

   Why is the map so small?

Give the child a piece of paper and markers and ask the child to draw a map of how he would go from the school to his home.

Judge the map:

   The child's map demonstrated: <u>Yes</u>   <u>No</u>
   • Understanding of scale
   • Perspective
   • Use of symbols
   • Knowledge of place

Figure 9.4   Individual evaluation of children's mapping skills.

concept of scale—a map shows a real area made smaller (Liben & Downs, 1993). Comparing the children's floor plans, block maps, or maps they use to find where they were born, you can continually point out that each is a map, just like the thing it represents, only smaller.

Photos of the children and pictures of familiar things are useful in demonstrating the concept of scale: "This is a picture of you. It's just like you, only you're much bigger, and this picture is very small." You can use model cars, boats, doll furniture, and dolls in the same manner, pointing out that there is a difference between the real object and the toy: "The toy is smaller; it's not real; it's a scale model." When Karl rushed into the classroom with a map of his bedroom, he told the other children, "It shows my bedroom just like it is, only this is much smaller." The teacher realized that Karl was beginning to grasp the concept of scale.

RELATIONSHIPS WITHIN PLACES

Geographers study how humans and environments are related, what advantages and disadvantages are present for human settlement, and how people modify and adapt to the environment. They try to find out why people live where they do, what the potentials are of this place or that, and how much of what is where.

Young children can be introduced to the ideas that humans have taken control of their environment but, at the same time, are also controlled by their environment. For example, to introduce children to the idea that they can control the nature of their world, they might do the following:

• They can look at the way in which they control their own environment. Children in kindergarten and the primary grades could work with you to arrange and rearrange their room or the playground. Where should the new shelf be placed? If it's placed against the wall, how will children be able to reach it? Will placing it at an angle disrupt the flow of traffic to and from the bathrooms?

• They can take trips into the neighborhood to observe others changing the nature of their physical world. Children can observe people creating hills, ponds, and flat surfaces to build roads or make room for new buildings.

• They can control the environment around their school, perhaps planting a garden, flowers, or shrubs or taking part in building a sand area.

• They can visit a private farm or a farm maintained by the city parks to acquaint children with farm life. At the farm, children can be introduced to the idea that people use soil, water, and sun to grow crops. They build fences to keep animals secured and use ponds or streams for their water (Fromboluti & Seefeldt, 1999).

• They can observe how others have shaped their environment. Children in the primary grades might visit a bonsai garden or a reservoir, take a trip through a tunnel that goes under water or through a mountain, or observe a house being built on a hillside.

Humans respond to the environment. Although they will not explore why people settled where they did or how they used the resources of the land until they are in the middle grades, preschool and primary children can do other activities:

• They can take a trip over a river and talk about why people built bridges over the water.

• They can go for a walk in the woods or go camping. It is easy to understand why we wear long pants and shoes where there are rocks and brambles on the ground and to realize the importance to early settlers of being near water when you no longer have the convenience of a faucet (Fromboluti & Seefeldt, 1999).

• They can take a nature walk through a park or a wildlife reserve to learn about local plants and wildlife and how natural features change over time.

• They can find out the name of the city they live in or the name of the city nearest to them. Third graders can take a trip to a nearby city and speculate on why people settled in an area.

SPATIAL INTERACTIONS

Regardless of where we live, we interact with others far from us. A part of the study of geography is understanding that people interact with others far from them. We depend on other places for food, clothes, and even items like pencils and paper. We also share information with each other using telephones, newspapers, radio, and television to bridge the distances. Children can do the following:

• They can take a trip to the local supermarket to observe the food delivery system. Children can chart the types of trucks used to deliver the goods and find out where the goods came from, who grew the produce, and how many different types of preparation were required—picking, packing, canning—before the food got to the supermarket.

• They can make a graph of the transportation systems they have traveled on. They might graph the boats, buses, trains, or cars they have been in.

• They can find out how many different ways they can move on the surface of the earth. They might walk, run, hop, skip, jump, crawl; use a bike, a wagon, roller skates; and so forth.

• They can explore how animals move on, through, or above the earth or in the water.

• They can study the school's communication system, noting all of the machines used in the school for this purpose.

• They can use the mail system, writing and sending letters to one another or to their parents.

The booklet *Early Childhood: Where Learning Begins, Geography* (Fromboluti & Seefeldt, 1999) lists other ways of fostering the idea of spatial interaction:

• Give children opportunities to travel by car, bus, bicycle, or on foot. Whenever possible, take other forms of transportation such as airplanes, trains, subways, ferries, barges, and horses and carriages.

• Use a map to look at various routes you can take when you try different methods of transportation.

• Watch travel videos and movies.

• Third graders can play a license plate game, seeing as many different states' plates as they can and noting what each plate tells about the specific state. Children might look at the plates of parked cars.

• Let third graders walk around the school building and identify where things come from. They might even look at labels in their own clothing to determine where their clothes came from. At lunch, talk about where the foods were grown. Where is the nearest dairy? Where did the bananas and oranges come from? How did they get to the school?

• Have primary children chart their family history by asking relatives where they came from. They could find these places on a map and make a chart of them or make their own chart, mapping their own birthplace. They could discuss how and why they or their ancestors left this place or stayed.

• Interview older people to find out what the neighborhood was like when they were young. Specifically, ask about how they traveled, what they used for refrigeration, the foods they ate, the clothes they wore, and the schools they attended. How have things changed since the older people were children?

REGIONS

A region is an area that includes a number of places—all of which have something in common. Geographers categorize regions in a number of basic ways, two of which are physical and cultural. Physical regions are defined by a particular type of climate, landform, or vegetation. A cultural region has a cultural and historical continuity that separates it from other adjacent or distinct regions. In these areas, people speak the same language, observe the same holidays, practice similar religions, and share political identity.

Physical Regions

All children live in a community of some kind. You can take the class on trips into a neighboring community to acquaint them with its characteristics. As children walk through the community, you can ask: "Why do people live near one another?" and "What do you think makes a neighborhood?" Back in the classroom, they could list all the things they found in the neighborhood.

Trips acquaint children with the concept of regions.

Third graders might be asked to differentiate how geographic areas in their community are alike and different. The students might take a trip to a park, a shopping center, or an industrial area and chart changes within these areas over the year. Students can interview people living or working in the regions to find out how the changes affect their lives.

Cultural Regions

Culture is transmitted through language, art, music, and games. Children of all ages can be introduced to the songs, rhymes, arts, and oral traditions of their culture and the culture of others. Preschoolers enjoy learning nursery rhymes, role playing them, and even creating new endings for the rhymes. Involve parents in learning rhymes by asking them what rhymes, folktales, and sayings they were taught as children. They could visit the class and teach them to the entire group to expose children to a variety of cultural traditions.

Primary-age children, who glory in learning new words, enjoy learning a few words of another language as well as songs and simple poems in other languages. They can learn how other cultures play familiar games and compare them to the games they play themselves. For example, hopscotch is played in nearly every culture in the world. Teach children how to play hopscotch. Then teach them how to play Vietnamese hopscotch. For this hopscotch, two children wrap arms around each other's backs and hop together from square to square. If either touches a line, both are out of the game, and another couple takes a turn. Ask children to interview their grandparents, parents, and other relatives to find out how they played hopscotch. As a group, review the many ways to play hopscotch, make a chart of similarities and differences, speculate why hopscotch differs among cultures, and vote on your favorite way to play hopscotch.

Cultural regions are defined by art, music, literature, and social organization. Primary children can do the following:

- Visit museums to see the art of many cultures.
- Listen to stories and folktales from other nations and compare them to the folktales and poetry of our nation. For example, the common theme of the physically weak triumphing over a bully, found in the Norwegian folktale *The Three Billy Goats Gruff* and the Mexican tale *Borrequita and the Coyote* (Aardema, 1991), illustrates that people, regardless of where they live or what culture they come from, share many of the same feelings.

SUMMARY

Keeping in mind that children learn by doing, you can help preschool-primary children develop basic geography concepts. They can experience the earth on which they live, learning the names and qualities of its land and water surfaces. They can experience the rhythms of day and night and of changing seasons.

Through movement exploration and other physical activities, children begin to understand the concept of direction. Learning their addresses, taking field trips, and locating themselves and objects in space, children learn the concept of location. They can explore the nature of geographical regions through field trips and vicarious experiences, such as movies and other audiovisual aids.

Knowing how people interact, even though they are separated in space, helps children develop the concept of spatial interactions. And children are introduced to the idea of mapping their world as they draw and build their own maps.

When you teach young children geography concepts, it is important to keep in mind the directives of Mitchell (1934): children learn by doing, through action, and with concrete experiences; we need not hurry them into the realm of the abstract.

Extend Your Knowledge

1. Interview a group of 5-, 6-, and 7-year-old children to determine their concepts of land and water. You might ask them to observe a dish with a small amount of water placed in the sun early in the day and again at the end of the day. Ask them what happened to the water. You might do the same with things that float and sink, dissolve, or change form.

2. Working with a small group of children, ask them to construct a map of their classroom with blocks. How do the children indicate understandings of the basic concepts of mapping: representation, symbolization, perspective, and scale?

3. Strengthen your own concepts of geography by reviewing the national geography standards. Which of these standards do you understand; which could you learn more about?

4. Take a walk around a school's neighborhood. What land forms do you observe? What are the physical characteristics of the area that make it unique? Design a learning experience for primary children based on your findings.

Resources

The National Geographic Society offers many free and inexpensive materials that can be used by teachers to plan social studies experiences as well as materials that children can use. The National Geographic Research and Exploration office of the National Geographic Society can be contacted for copies of *Geography for Life: National Geography Standards* (1994).

National Geographic Society
1145 17th Street, NW
Washington, DC 20037-4688
Website: *http://www.ngsstore.nationalgeographicsociety.com*

The U.S. Department of Education publishes *Early Childhood: Where Learning Begins, Geography* (1999) by Carol Sue Fromboluti and Carol Seefeldt. For a copy, write to U.S. Department of Education, Washington, DC 20208-5520.

Other types of resources and literature on social studies education can be found at:

Social Studies Development Center
2805 East 10th Street, Suite 120
Bloomington, IN 47408-2698
Phone: (800) 266-3815
Fax: (812) 855-0455
Website: *http://www.indiana.edu/~ssdc/ssdc.htm*

References

Aardema, V. (1991). *Borrequita and the coyote.* New York: Dragonfly.

Arthus-Bertrand, Y., & Burleigh, R. (2002). *Earth from above for young readers.* New York: Abrams.

Barry-Davis, J. (1999). Intuitive understanding of time and space at the age of four. *Dissertation Abstracts International, 60*(6-A), 0419–4209.

Bucknell Geography. (2003). Why geography? Available at *http://www.departments.bucknell.edu/geography.html.*

dePaola, T. (1975). *The cloud book.* New York: Holiday House.

Dewey, J. (1900). *Art as experience.* New York: Minton Barth.

Dighe, J. (1993). Children and the earth. *Young Children, 48*(3), 58–63.

Evans, L. (1995). *Rain song.* New York: Houghton Mifflin.

Fowler, A. (2001). *It could still be a tree.* New York: Dial.

Fromboluti, C. S., & Seefeldt, C. (1999). *Early childhood: Where learning begins, geography.* Washington, DC: U.S. Department of Education.

Geography Education Standards Project. (1994). *Geography for life.* Washington, D.C.: Author.

Gouteux, S. (2001). Reorientation in a small-scale environment by 3-, 4-, and 5-year children. *Cognitive Development, 16*(3), 853–869.

Hearne, B. (1977). *Seven brave women.* New York: Greenwillow.

Howe, G. (1969). The teaching of directions in space. In W. Herman (Ed.), *Current research in elementary school social studies* (pp. 31–43). Upper Saddle River, NJ: Merrill/Prentice Hall.

Jenkins, S. (1995). *Looking down.* New York: Houghton Mifflin.

Landry, C. E., & Forman, G. E. (1999). Research on early science education. In C. Seefeldt (Ed.), *The early childhood curriculum: Current findings in theory and practice* (pp. 133–178). New York: Teachers College Press.

Lester, J., & Pinkney, J. (1998). *Black cowboy, wild horses: A true story.* New York: Dial.

Liben, L. S., & Downs, R. M. (1993). Understanding person-space-map relations: Cartographic and developmental perspective. *Child Development, 29,* 739–752.

Lord, F. (1941). A study of spatial orientation of children. *Journal of Educational Research, 34,* 481–505.

Martin, B. (1969). *Our sun is a star.* New York: Holt, Rinehart, & Winston.

Marzoff, D. P., & DeLoache, J. S. (1994). Transfer in young children's understanding of spatial representations. *Child Development, 65,* 1–16.

McCloskey, R. (1952). *One morning in Maine.* New York: Viking.

McCloskey, R. (1976). *Blueberries for Sal.* New York: Viking.

Miller, J. (1985). Teaching map skills: Theory, research, and practice. *Social Education, 49,* 30–33.

Mitchell, L. S. (1934). *Young geographers.* New York: Bank Street College.

Mitchell, L. S. (2000). Social studies for future teachers. In E. K. Shapiro (Ed.), *Revisiting a progressive pedagogy: The developmental-interaction approach: Early childhood education* (pp. 125–137). Albany: State University of New York Press.

Mosenthal, P. B., & Kirsch, S. (1991). Understanding general reference maps. *Journal of Reading, 34*(1), 60–63.

National Commission on Social Studies in the Schools (NCSSS). (1989). *Charting a course: Social studies for the 21st century.* New York: Author.

National Council for the Social Studies (NCSS). (1998). *Curriculum standards for social studies: Expectations of excellence.* Washington, DC: Author.

National Research Council & Institute of Medicine (NRC & IM). (2000). *From neurons to neighborhoods: The science of early childhood development.* Committee on Integrating the Science of Early Childhood Development. Washington, DC: National Academy Press.

Nuffield Mathematics Project. (1969). *Early experiences.* London: Macdonald Education.

Piaget, J. (1952). *The child's conception of number.* New York: Humanities Press.

Piaget, J. (1965). *The child's conception of the world.* Totowa, NJ: Littlefield Adams.

Rivkin, M. S. (1995). *The great outdoors: Restoring children's right to play outside.* Washington, DC: National Association for the Education of Young Children.

Roberts, R., & Aman, C. J. (1993). Developmental differences in giving directions: Spatial frames of reference and mental rotation. *Child Development, 64,* 1258–1270.

Sanders, S. W. (2002). *Active for life.* Washington, DC: National Association for the Education of Young Children.

Schoenfeldt, M. (2001). Geographic literacy and young learners. *Educational Forum,* 66(1), 26–31.

Shepardson, D. P., & Britsch, S. J. (2000). Young children's representations of earth materials on the science journal page. Paper presented at the annual meeting of the National Association for Research in Science Teaching, New Orleans.

Takahashi, I. (2000). Children's understanding of their own vs. scientific views of the earth's shape. *Japanese Journal of Developmental Psychology,11*(2), 89–99.

Taylor, B. (2002). *Mountains and volcanoes: Geography facts and experiments.* New York: Houghton Mifflin.

Vaughan, J. (1998). *Rivers and streams.* New York: Raintree.

Whiteside, K. (2000). *Building geography skills and community understanding with constructivist teaching methods.* Report No. SO031905. Urbana, IL: ECEE.

Wolf, B. (1994). *Beneath the stone: A Mexican Zapotec tale.* New York: Orchard.

CHAPTER 10

Production, Distribution, and Consumption: Economics

Since adult economic illiteracy is so widespread, teachers will want to introduce economics to children early, so they can make wise personal economic decisions as consumers, workers, and citizens.

Carol Seefeldt and Alice Galper, 2002, p. 124.

After you read this chapter, you should be prepared to respond to the following questions:

- How do children's economic concepts develop?
- What concepts are key to the study of economics?
- Why is introducing children to the concept of scarcity important, even in the preschool-primary grades?
- What economic decisions can young children make?
- How can you introduce young children to concepts of consumer and producer?
- How do you prepare children today for careers tomorrow?

"I'll clean your car for 4 dollars," 6-year-old Sabrina told her grandmother, adding, "When I get 20 more dollars, then I'll have enough dollars to buy a Game Boy."

"Here," said 4-year-old Paul to the clerk, placing a handful of change on the counter, "I'm buying this book for Mark's birthday party."

Young children are aware of economic concepts because they experience them daily. While children are not ready to reason abstractly about economic issues until they reach the age of 10 or 11, they encounter economic concepts daily and express a high level of interest in them (Seefeldt & Galper, 2002).

Children enter the preschool-primary classroom knowing, at some level, that their wants often exceed their resources; that it takes money to make purchases; and that they can offer some service or product to get money. In preschool and primary classrooms, teachers plan to build and extend children's informal knowledge of economics. They do so not only because children are interested in money and what it can buy for them but because teachers know that economic literacy is essential for citizens of a democracy (Seefeldt & Galper, 2002).

According to the National Council on Economic Education (1998) and the National Council for the Social Studies (1998), it is critical that all children be economically literate in order to function in today's and tomorrow's global economy. "When students understand economic concepts they're better able to make sense of their world and better prepared for their adult roles as consumers, producers, and voters" (Meszaros & Engstrom, 1998, p. 7). *Economics America* recommends that, by age 12, children should have developed several kinds of economic knowledge in order to become competent citizens (NCEE, 2003). The associations suggest that all children need to be able to do the following:

- Maintain sound personal finances
- Understand and appreciate the contribution of the many groups of workers who produce goods and services
- Interest themselves in the economic system and understand how it operates
- Think critically about economic problems, assume responsibility for them, understand basic economics concepts, and reason logically about key issues that affect their lives
- Be ready to participate in economic production by preparing for future careers

If all people had everything they wanted, then knowledge of economic concepts would not be critical. But today there are major differences between what people need and what they can have. Thus, an accurate and workable image of the social system in general, and the economic system in particular, is increasingly essential to human survival. The concept of scarcity—the difference between the unlimited wants of people and the limited goods, services, and materials available—is a major concern of economic education.

DEVELOPMENT OF ECONOMIC CONCEPTS

Economics is the study of how goods and services are produced and distributed and the activities of people who produce, save, spend, pay taxes, and perform personal services to satisfy their wants for food and shelter, their desire for new conveniences

Children reveal economic concepts through play.

and comforts, and their collective wants for things such as education and national defense.

Children experience economic concepts daily. They observe parents exchanging money for goods, and they themselves participate in paying for some purchases. They receive money as gifts, sometimes saving it in a bank, or they may even participate in opening bank accounts. Advertising convinces children early in life that they need more than they can have. And children make decisions between the things they really need and those they only want.

In their play, children reveal some understanding of economic concepts. They use economic scripts as they play store, pretending to see and purchase goods; they pretend to use money to obtain services. Nevertheless, like geography and history concepts, children's economic concepts are far from fully developed. Not until after age 9 do children understand the value of money, become able to compare coins, and comprehend the idea of credit or profit.

Following Piagetian theory, children's stages of economic understandings have been identified as (1) the unreflective and preoperational level, exemplified by a highly literal reasoning based on the physical characteristics of objects or processes; (2) the transitional or emerging reasoning level, exemplified by higher-order reasoning and similar to Piaget's concrete operational stage; and (3) the reflective level of economic reasoning.

Researchers have found that 3-year-olds can distinguish between money and other objects but are unable to differentiate between types of coins. Until around 4½ years of age, children are generally unaware that money is needed to purchase things. Three-year-olds may take candy or toys from a store, totally unaware of the fact that money is exchanged for goods (Berti & Bombi, 1988). However, children under age 4 often "know that you can buy things in stores and recognize money and pretend to pay for things. They know the difference between 'yours' and 'mine' and identify adult activities as 'work'" (Berti & Bombi, 1988, p. 175).

Three-year-olds can distinguish between money and other objects but cannot tell the difference between types of money. Many arguments among 3-year-olds revolve around whether a nickel is worth more than a dime because it is physically larger.

Between ages 4 and 5, children still cannot distinguish between and name coins and believe that the larger the coin is physically, the more it is worth. However, they are aware that you need money to buy things. Children who are 4 to 5 years old develop play scripts of pretending to ask for and get goods, give and receive money, and go to work, suggesting that children of this age do have concepts of economic exchanges. They still do not understand the function of money in buying and selling but believe that shopkeepers give money to customers and that any type of coin is suitable for any type of purchase. No concept of production is present. At age 4 or 5, children believe that shopkeepers get their goods from some other shop, which gives them away without asking for money. These children do not understand that shopkeepers are customers as well (Berti & Bombi, 1988). When asked where milk came from, Josh, a student in Head Start, said, "From the store."

Even though they understand that people go to work to get money, children do not understand the relationship between work and pay. To them, a person works and also gets money rather than gets money *because* she works. When 5-year-old Danny's mother told him she didn't have enough money to buy the toy he wanted, he suggested they go to the "money store" to "buy" some more money.

By age 6, children are progressing into concrete operations and have a clearer understanding of money; they can distinguish between and name the various denominations of coins and know which coins will buy more things. They still cling to the idea that the larger and perhaps more elaborate the coin, the more it is worth. First-grader David's father, who traveled a great deal, brought David coins and bills from other countries. David was fascinated with the size, shapes, and colors of the money and was convinced that the coins of other countries were worth "much, much more" than American nickels, dimes, quarters, and bills because "they're so large and so much prettier."

Children also continue to believe that the shopkeeper gives customers money but are moving toward the idea that there is a manufacturer who produces goods for which the shopkeeper has to pay. Economic experts suggest that a best practice in economics education involves engaging children in literature, factual and fictional (VanFossen, 2003). Because children are in the concrete stage of thinking, reading

Table 10.1 Economics Concept Development

Sensorimotor, Age 0–2	Preoperational, Age 2–6/7	Concrete, Age 6/7–10
Observes and attends to shape and size of coins	Plays store, demonstrating initial concepts of consuming and purchasing	After 9, can compare coins, knows relative value of coins
Observes shopping, consuming, and purchasing	Counts more or less	Understands that people work to make money
	Recognizes coins/money	Some clarity in understanding employer-employee relationship
	Knows money is necessary to make purchases	

books about money, such as *Bunny Money* (Wells, 2001), *The Story of Money* (Maestro & Maestro, 1995), *My Rows and Piles of Coins* (Mollet & Lewis, 1999), and *Follow the Money* (Leedy, 2002), can give primary-aged children additional insights into the function of money.

Around 6 or 7 years of age, children know that, although you do not have to have the exact money to pay for a purchase, you do need enough. They are also moving toward some clarity of employer-employee relationships but are far from any clear understanding of customer and producer concepts (Table 10.1).

Seven-year-olds can compare coins and understand the value of money. They know that manufacturers are paid, as are employees, and that numerous persons and activities are necessary for the production and exchange of goods and money. Children no longer consider work as going someplace to get money but begin to make a connection between the activity and the benefits (Berti & Bombi, 1988). They now have some idea of production and selling and can describe a few paid occupations that they can actually observe and with which they have direct experience, such as a police officer or a bus driver. They also now seem to understand that people are paid differently for different jobs, but they say that police officers make much more money than doctors or shopkeepers do.

Between ages 7 and 10, pre-economic ideas are replaced by more accurate and conventional ideas. Nevertheless, not until the period of formal operations, ages 12 and older, are children able to understand that the price of goods is based on the costs of production, which include the cost of labor. They do not understand that the materials necessary for production are not old or broken things, and they still confuse making something with mending something. Raw materials are not recognized as natural products.

KEY CONCEPTS

Using knowledge of children's awareness of economic concepts and their direct experiences, teachers can introduce preschool-primary children to essential economic principles. By organizing children's experiences around economic key concepts recommended by *Economics America* (NCEE, 2003), teachers can introduce children to these main ideas:

- Scarcity: the wants of people everywhere are unlimited, but resources are limited
- The necessity of decisions regarding the use of resources
- The function of production and consumption, the concept of barter, and the idea that money is exchanged for goods and services
- Careers: educating children for future career choices and roles

Scarcity

Basic to all economic understanding is the concept of scarcity. In every society—classroom, family, neighborhood, state, nation—people have a wide variety of wants and desires. Everyone always seems to need more food, clothing, things, and services than are available. The concept that everyone wants more goods and services than they can have can be introduced through experiences at school. Later, these experiences can be related to the children's families and neighborhoods.

Wants and Needs

"Daddy, I wanna. . . ." Every young child has wants and needs. Learning how to distinguish between wants and needs and how to conserve time, goods, and services may help children develop concepts of scarcity.

1. Ask the children to pretend they can have anything they wish. Ask them to draw, tell, or dictate three wishes. Which of the things they've wished for do they think they will get? Which do they think they will not get? Why can't they have everything they wish for?

2. Make a booklet or folder called "I Wanted, I Want, I Will Want." Encourage children to discuss the things they have wanted in the past, whether they got them or not, why they wanted them, and if they want them now. Draw or write about these things under the title "I Wanted." Ask them about things they want now and the things they think they will want in the future. Do the children think they will be able to have all of these things?

3. Make dream cloud pictures, and have children illustrate things they want in the clouds as their dreams. Again, encourage discussion of the things the children say they want and those things they believe are realistic to have.

4. Tell folktales and stories about wanting things, such as "Cinderella," "King Midas," and "The Rabbit Who Wanted Wings," and discuss the stories. Were the people or animals wise to want the things they did? Why? What things did they really need?

5. Make bulletin boards titled "Things I Want for Summer," "Things I Want for Winter," and "When I Grow Up."

To make these activities meaningful for 4- and 5-year-old children, you might cut collections of pictures from catalogs or magazines so that the children can select pictures of the things that illustrate their ideas and paste them into scrapbooks or on a wall chart for the room. Older kindergarten children can draw their own pictures, and children in the primary grades can be encouraged to both illustrate and write their responses.

Many classroom experiences can be used to introduce the concept of scarcity. What things does the class as a group want? Which things do they need? Supplies and materials may be limited by shrinking budgets so that conservation is an absolute necessity. Scraps can be saved for later use, brushes no longer useful at the easel may be washed and used outdoors for water paint, or junk can be collected for sculpture projects.

The class might obtain some funding from the PTA or the petty cash fund. Deciding how to spend this cash can be a group project. Make a list of pictures of all the things the children suggest. After the list is made, instruct each child to place a check by the things she thinks the class should try to get. Then purchase the item with the most checks. You can then discuss use of the item, how long it will last, how many ways it can be used, and how many children can use it at the same time.

The needs and wants of the school give the children other experiences with the concept of scarcity. First, materialism and commercialism can be eliminated in the classroom. In "Buying More Can Give Children Less," Carol Holst (1999) suggests that teachers can make their classrooms places where children can experience the joy of their own imaginations. By reducing commercial materials and consumerism in classrooms, teachers model the need to use raw and available materials instead of commercial ones. By living with the idea that our wants are more than our needs, children are more likely to develop concepts of scarcity and needs.

Kindergarten and primary children can take a walk though the school to identify the things the school needs, or they can interview the principal to find out what she considers important for the school to have. What things do the children think are possible for the school to obtain? What things are just dreams?

The playground can be explored, with the children naming all of the play equipment they would like to have. Later, in class, the list can be narrowed down to items that the children think are realistic additions, and efforts can be made to obtain them.

Involve children's families. Families also have many needs, wants, and limited resources to obtain them. Ask the children to name all of the things their families need to live. The basic needs are shelter, food, and clothing. Since these needs are human universals (Brophy & Alleman, 2002), they can be used to extend children's knowledge and understanding of others, both close to them and far away in space and time.

Experiences studying universal human needs include the following:

• Ask children to draw a picture of the home they are living in. Classify these pictures according to type of home. Discuss the need for homes. Children who are age 5 and younger can make scrapbooks using precut pictures.

• Read carefully selected stories about the homes of others. For example, reading selections of *Buffalo Hunt* (Freedman, 1995) could lead to a discussion of why the Plains Indians required portable housing (Brophy & Alleman, 2002).

• Third graders could study other forms of shelter. They could branch out to study why some people live in homes built on stilts or in tropical huts.

• *Uncle Willie and the Soup Kitchen* (DiSalvo-Ryan, 1997) is about an uncle who volunteers in a soup kitchen. Third graders could use this book to develop consciousness of the problem of homelessness (Brophy & Alleman, 2002).

• Make booklets called "Things My Family Needs" and "Things My Family Would Like to Have." Primary children can write as well as draw their ideas.

• Have children discuss the foods they like to eat, why people eat food, what foods they would like to try, and what foods they eat only on special occasions.

Families also need clothing. Children can discuss the types of clothing they need for the different seasons in contrast to the clothing they would like to have. A lost-and-found box reinforces the idea of the importance of not having to replace clothing. What does it mean to the children if they lose an item of clothing?

Families also want things. Some want different kinds of recreational activities; other families want better housing and clothing or pets. Charts and booklets of "Things My Family Wants" and "Things My Family Needs" help children clarify and distinguish needs from wants.

Time is another commodity that must be used wisely. Incidental experiences help children realize that they must make choices about the way they use their time. "If we clean up now, we can have time to. . . ." Children should make plans for how they want to use their time. Even 4-year-olds can identify how they would like to begin their day and can list the things they think they will try to accomplish during the morning. When children make plans, they should be able to experience not having enough time to do all of the things they have planned. Recognizing the consequences of decisions is a true learning experience.

Experiences with the concept of scarcity can also arise from the subject of energy conservation. The following suggested activities may help children become more aware of energy waste and to think of alternatives to waste:

• Make a list of energy-saving habits, such as turning off lights and appliances not in use, riding a bike or walking instead of using a car, and limiting water use.

• Find something at home or in the classroom to recycle or repair, such as a toy or a shelf.

• Work on a recycling project, such as collecting aluminum or newspapers from parents or others in the community.

• Using the book *Allowance Kit, Junior!: A Money System for Little Kids* (Searls, 1997), primary children can create budgets for themselves.

Decision Making

The ability to make wise decisions is an integral part of the study of scarcity. People cannot have everything they want—sometimes not everything they need. People must make decisions about which things they need and which they want. Children can find many opportunities for making choices within the classroom. Primary children, who have had little opportunity to make decisions about their lives—which families they will have, the school or church they will go to, the neighborhood they will live in, or the clothes or food they use—need classrooms that are replete with opportunities to make choices and to experience the consequences of their choices. Teachers of young children seek to give them the widest possible freedom to choose what to play with, how to play, and how to make things, with a minimum of restrictive control.

It is also important for young children to be able to make decisions and experience their results in a secure classroom environment. According to Dewey (1944), there is no way to learn other than to experience the consequences of an action, yet children must have the right to make mistakes without the loss of self-esteem. As children experience the initial frustration of having made a wrong decision, they can learn how to live with the consequences of that decision and ways to decide more wisely next time.

Children can make decisions about which materials to use and how to use them; what to sing, play, or dance; where to plant the seeds; which group of children they want to work with; and even what things they want to learn. Other experiences with decision making include the following:

1. Read the poem "The Animal Store" by Rachel Field. The children can act out the roles of pet-store owner, the children purchasing pets, and all of the pets that might be found in the store. Discuss what they would buy if they had a hundred dollars to spend. Let the children make murals or pictures of the things they would buy.

2. Have children circle items that they would like to have in toy or other catalogs. Question the children: "Pick out the one toy you want. How did you decide on that toy?" Or for older children: "You each have 5 dollars to spend. Shopping in this catalog, decide on a purchase. Why did you choose that instead of something else?"

3. Let the children decide what items to buy for a class project or party. Discuss what they want versus what they need, both in relation to what is available and to how much money they have to buy it.

4. Read *Alexander, Who Used to Be Rich Last Sunday* (Viorst, 1978). Discuss why Alexander had nothing left in his pockets but bus tokens at the end of a week when he started out with a dollar. Primary children could make a pretend budget for Alexander.

Children in second or third grade may be ready to participate in discussions about decisions that affect the community. Perhaps a new highway is being built or the school system must eliminate jobs. Your students may be interested enough in some of these issues to speculate on how they would respond if they were adults. Ask, "Would you suggest that school-board members cut music, art, or other special areas?" "Do you think they should combine classes and eliminate teachers' jobs?" "Should money be spent on the new highway or a new school building?"

Even though resources are scarce and choices must be made to provide for ever-expanding human needs, you can help children understand that most decisions do not involve a choice between all or nothing. They do, however, require trade-offs among desirable alternatives or goals—that is, providing a little less of one thing in order to provide a little more of another.

Economic Production

Closely related to the concept of scarcity is the concept of production. The function of production, to some extent, is to try to meet the unlimited wants of consumers. In a democratic society, people choose the goods and services they consume and produce, although advertising and consumer demand influence both. The concept of exchange of money is related to economic production: consumers use money to purchase goods and services. Children can develop concepts of (1) being a consumer, (2) the function of money, (3) the differences between goods and services, and (4) production.

Consumers

Even before children can walk or talk, they consume goods, use services, and express their wants and needs. As they mature, they begin to choose what they buy. Their values influence the decisions they make; they will evaluate alternatives and select

Children are producers.

the best buy for their money and needs as well as act on their rights and responsibilities as consumers.

Throughout the school year, you can help children clarify their likes and dislikes. They might discuss and identify the stories they like or dislike, decide on materials they like, and explain why they did not select the alternative materials. Making lists, booklets, charts, or murals depicting favorite things at school, at home, or in the neighborhood will help children clarify their preferences. You can remind children to be honest and make decisions based on their likes rather than those of their parents, peers, or teacher.

Playing store is another way in which children make concepts of consumer and producer real to them. Taking on the role of clerk and purchaser, children gain insights into the roles of consumer and producer. Researchers have found that children's store play begins simply, gradually building in complexity and becoming closer to reality:

- *Stage 1.*   The very young child uses imitative play, often with a mother or a father, and uses imaginary goods. Usually the child has no concern about purchasing or exchanging money.
- *Stage 2.*   This is the beginning of creative play. Children improvise play materials, use buttons for money, and play at purchasing items.
- *Stage 3.*   Children appear to desire more representative goods; empty cartons, canned goods, and play money are useful at this stage.
- *Stage 4.*   Children construct the store and goods, build counters, cut money out of paper, make signs, and take parts in purchasing and in exchanging money.
- *Stage 5.*   A continuation of free play leads to more involved projects and teacher-contrived explorations of children's interests. Children use signs, prices, graphs, and scales and hold sales with reduced merchandise or actually sell small boxes of raisins, cookies baked by the class, or plants grown from seeds.

As with other play, children need time to develop complex responses and to become involved in store play. To obtain the full potential from shop play, children need the opportunity to progress from the imitative stage to the creative and complex stage. Thus, shop play should continue through the primary grades rather than stop at kindergarten or first grade.

The best way to learn to become a wise consumer, however, is to practice consuming. You need to provide as many opportunities as possible for children to make choices about purchases. In deciding on materials to purchase for the class or themselves, children need to consider: "How long will it last?" "How many ways can it be used?" "Is it something I really need or just want?" "If I spend my money for this, will I have any left for other things?"

As consumers who watch 3 to 5 hours of television daily, children should be aware of advertising's influence on their decision making. Children do not distinguish between programs and advertisements and cannot understand that a commercial's intent is to sell something. Even worse, the advertisements are aimed at breaking down the resistance of rational adults.

Based on strong psychological research and theory, advertisements do affect consumer behavior. Teachers can begin introducing children to the idea that advertisements are designed to influence the purchase of goods and services. Children can begin to analyze ads. The language arts activity of writing ads about real or pretend products helps children to see how words are selected to influence purchases and to realize that commercials are written by people. If children do not have writing skills, the commercials can be dictated or orally presented to the class by a committee.

Children can send for an advertised cereal-box toy and, on its receipt, compare the toy with its ad. Ask, "Does the toy do what the advertisement promised?" "What else could you have bought for the same amount of money?" "Would another purchase better fill your needs or wants?" "How does the toy received differ from the advertised one?"

Primary children can also analyze ads for other toys. Ask the children to watch a particular ad on television, arrange to have it shown to the class, or bring in an ad from a current paper or magazine. Read the ad and then compare the claims with the product. The children can, if it is convenient, take a trip to the toy store, or the product can be made available in class. Have the children determine if the ad distorted the product. Typical questions include "Did the doll really move the way it did on television or the way the ad said it would?" "Did the car really move as fast as

Let's play store!

it appeared to in the television ad?" "Did any parts of the ad make you think something different about this toy? Which parts?" "Were all parts of the ad true?"

At times, certain advertising slogans become popular and can serve as another vehicle for analysis of ads. Any slogan that is popular can be tested by kindergarten or primary children: "Will this candy mint make your mouth feel fresher than another?" "Does this soap really clean the clothes better than another?" "Does this towel absorb better than another?" "Which soap makes your hands softer?" "Let's try it for ourselves."

To be truly effective, consumer education must involve parents. Let the parents know about the activities the children are involved in at school. Tell parents that the activities will help children (1) weigh their purchases in terms of their goals, values, and resources; (2) make selections from the alternatives; and (3) accept the consequences and responsibilities that arise from their decisions. Inform parents about things they can do to reinforce children's abilities to analyze ads and make wise purchases. Parents can include children in their decisions about food purchases: "Would you like this box of cookies? It contains more cookies than this other box, but the cookies in this other box are made with real chocolate." Parents can also include children in discussions about larger purchases: "We need a new carpet and a new washing machine; how can we decide which to buy?" You can invite parents to school to tell the children about their experiences as consumers, how they make decisions for purchases, or about the time an advertisement lured them into making a foolish purchase and how they felt about it.

Consumers have rights and responsibilities. Their rights are to choose which goods and services they will buy, obtain accurate information about goods and services, shop in safe places, and be able to register complaints and seek redress of grievances. Consumers also need to respect the property and rights of others when shopping. You could take a shopping trip with the children to observe good and bad shopping manners. Children can make a list of all the things they think are improper shopping behaviors: running in the store, opening packages, or crowding at the checkout line. Ask them to add a list of proper shopping behaviors. Children might be able to role-play both good and bad behaviors.

Consuming Services

Children see the exchange of money when their parents purchase goods and materials, but they may never witness the exchange of money for services. The doctor and dentist are paid by check through the mail; the teacher, librarian, police officer, and postal employee are paid indirectly through taxes. You can focus children's attention on the services their families use by making charts titled "Goods Our Families Consume" and "Services Our Families Use."

Other children can investigate the services that are supported by their parents' taxes and the taxes of others. Ask, "Who pays for the school?" "Does the teacher get paid?" "Where does the money come from?" "What would happen if no one paid for the school building, the services of the janitor or teachers, or materials and supplies?"

Children learn we consume services as well as goods.

You might arrange trips into the community to observe other services paid for by taxes. Children can observe police officers, firefighters, street cleaners, health workers, and other people whose services are paid for by tax money. On another trip, children can identify public property used by everyone—streets, parks, hydrants, fireboxes, street signs, lights, and sidewalks. Ask children to speculate about what would happen if people had to build their own streets or parks or buy their own firetrucks. Bulletin boards, booklets, or murals labeled "Things Families Buy Together" and "Things Families Buy for Themselves" will reinforce and clarify the concept of using public services.

Production of Goods and Provision of Services

Although everyone is a consumer of goods and services, not all are producers. Interwoven with the concepts of scarcity, wants and needs, and consumers' responsible use of money is the concept of producer. Children can begin to develop the concept of producer by understanding the work they do at home and at school and the work their parents do (Figure 10.1).

```
┌──────────────────────────────────────────────┐
│   Work at School           Work at Home        │
│   ─────────────            ─────────────        │
│   Goods    Services        Goods    Services    │
│                                                 │
│            Our Parents Produce                  │
│            ───────────────────                  │
│            Goods    Services                    │
└──────────────────────────────────────────────┘
```

Figure 10.1   Children's chart of their work.

Goods that children can produce at school include gifts for parents, greeting cards, books, garden products, and cookies. Ask, "What things do you produce at home?" "What do your parents produce? Food? Clothing? Furniture?" "What services do you produce at school?" "What services do you produce at home?"

The concept of specialization—job diversification—arises from the identification of producers. Within the school building itself there are many specializations. There may be a building engineer, a nurse, or a lunchroom worker; there are teachers, a secretary, and a principal. Children can interview these different workers, finding out about their particular jobs—what they produce and how. Ask the children what would happen if each teacher was responsible for heating the school, cleaning the room, preparing the meals, repairing the windows, and answering the phone.

Children can experiment with diversity of jobs within the classroom. One day, instead of preparing materials for the children, let them prepare their own paints, salt dough, and so forth. Discuss what happened. Ask the children which way was easier and more efficient. On another day, ask each child to prepare a snack instead of the usual committee or teacher preparing for everyone. Children might time their preparation and cleanup and compare it to the time it takes when these jobs are divided and conducted by a few for the entire group.

The study of producers leads to a study of the resources used in the production of goods. Production depends on people but also on natural resources, tools, machinery, and money. In the classroom, children can see that different materials are needed to produce a painting or to construct a playhouse. Children can make a chart of all of the tools within the classroom; they can take a trip through the school to identify the tools used by producers in the building. You can initiate a discussion of the tools used at home or by parents at work or the tools, machines, and materials needed to keep the community functioning.

Preparing for Careers

Everyone needs a career—something that gives purpose and direction to life, something that is significant to the individual and useful to society at the same time. Without a career, whether it is to make a house into a home or be a doctor, a lawyer, or a construction worker, humans lack purpose or direction in life and are aimless, capricious, and in danger of becoming parasites (Dewey, 1944). Recognizing the critical need for each child to become a productive member of society, school systems, state departments of education, and the U.S. Office of Education have mandated that schools begin education for careers in the preschool and primary grades.

The idea of beginning career education in the preschool-primary classroom, of asking young children who are barely able to comprehend concepts of yesterday, today, or tomorrow to plan for a vague and distant future, might seem inappropriate. Intent on living each day fully and on developing skills, knowledge, and attitudes required for life in the present, young children have little real concern for future. Yet the preschool-primary class is the ideal place to begin education for a career; during these early years, children's attitudes, values, and essential skills are formed. These attitudes, values, and skills will remain with the children and serve to direct their entire lives. Career education seems much more a function of attitude, value, and skill development than an artificial addition to the curriculum.

Attitudes and Values

Toward Self. Children must grow with a strong sense of self that will give them the confidence to shape their own destinies. Whether fostering career education or fulfilling the general goal of all education, you will want to plan for children to achieve all the self-confidence they need to go on growing and developing into socially responsible and constructive members of society.

Self-confidence is acquired as children are given jobs to fulfill in the classroom. Real responsibilities for preparing materials, cleaning up, and caring for pets, plants, and equipment help children feel successful, competent, and sure of their abilities to contribute to the welfare of the group and, later, to become productive members of society.

Toward Work. Attitudes toward future work are developed through programs designed to increase children's awareness of career opportunities. Children need to be aware of the choices they have and the things they can do.

Children can interview the workers in the school building, neighborhood, or community to determine their attitudes toward work. Children can ask the following:

- What do you like about your job? Why?
- What do you dislike about it? Why?
- How did you decide to do it?
- What preparation did you need?
- Do you feel proud of your work? Why?
- Have you ever thought about changing jobs?

Help children think about the questions they will ask, perhaps listing them on a chart for reference. Children can compare the interview responses, exploring the different job choices available as well as discovering how people feel about their jobs.

Children can begin to speculate about the future. You might ask, "What kinds of jobs do you think you might have when you grow up?" Remind them that they might be able to do several things, such as being a student, a parent, an engineer, or an interior designer. By asking children to think about the future, you increase their awareness of career choices and opportunities.

Toward Sex Roles. The question "What do you want to be when you grow up?" continues to be answered on the basis of sex. Despite the ever-increasing numbers of women who have entered the work force, the occupational awareness, exploration, and decisions of boys and girls tend to remain stereotypical (Derman-Sparks & the ABC Task Force, 2003). Sex differences in attitudes toward careers and career aspirations begin during early childhood and persist into adolescence (Chrisman & Couchenour, 2003). Boys know what their fathers do more often than girls do and are able to identify twice as many career options as girls can.

The American Association of University Women (2000) suggests creating awareness of the role of women in the work force by taking trips into the community. The focal point of the trips is to observe people working. Younger children may take trips a few blocks from the school building. You will want to emphasize the nonstereotypic jobs and workers the children observe on the trip. Older children can extend trips over a larger area. They can explore their city, suburb, or rural area by bus, car, or train. Children of all ages can photograph their observations. You will need to guide the children skillfully: seek out the unusual; challenge the stereotypes that are present; and point out the options that exist in career choices for all people, both men and women.

Discussions follow each trip, or children can make a mural or booklet of jobs they have seen, jobs their parents hold, or jobs in one store. The emphasis should always be on people in the variety of roles in which they actually function rather than on the stereotypes found in books, the press, and other media.

Other experiences may be vicarious. Selecting books, photos, posters, and pictures showing women in a wide range of career options, both traditional and nontraditional, may be useful. Challenging children's stereotypical thinking is also recommended. When children announce, "You can't play here; only men can build houses," or "You're the girl; you have to make the dinner," teachers can challenge them: "Remember when we went to the construction site? There were three women builders," or "Men can make dinner as well as girls can. At the fast-food restaurant, we saw only men making waffles."

Essential Skills

To succeed in an unknown future, children will be required to have essential skills. These include the hard skills—basic mathematics, reading, the ability to make decisions and to use computers—as well as the soft skills—the ability to work in groups and make effective oral and written presentations.

The essential skills of reading, writing, communicating, and learning to learn are basic to career education. But if these skills are taught in isolation from the rest of children's lives, they will have no meaning (Helm & Beneke, 2003). An integrated approach to the curriculum is essential. As Dewey (1900) suggested, teachers can relate mathematics to career education as children observe carpenters using measuring devices. Then teachers can help children to construct their own playhouse using measurements. Following a trip to the gas station to see what attendants and mechanics do, children can read to find out where gasoline comes from, how it is produced and refined, how it gets to the gas station, and perhaps how world politics are involved.

The skills involved in solving problems and making wise decisions are equally essential. You can incorporate decision making into the curriculum by telling children, "Do it your way." "You decide." "It's entirely up to you."

Skills in relating to people are essential to career education. Children who cannot relate to others will have a difficult time developing a career. Schools afford children the opportunity to learn to work with others and to develop firm interpersonal relationships.

With attitudes of respect for self, work, and others, and the development of essential skills, children are prepared to find their places in a rapidly changing society where occupations appear and disappear. Children who have developed (1) respect for the dignity of people and the worth of occupations, (2) knowledge and understanding of the opportunities available, and (3) willingness to gain skills and an openness to learning throughout life are those who have been educated for careers.

SUMMARY

The major economics concepts that are appropriate for preschool-primary children are ideas about scarcity, decision making, and the function of production and consumption, as well as future career choices and roles. You introduce these concepts through children's experiences, both incidental and structured.

Every day, children experience the concept of scarcity. They must conserve materials and energy. They must consider their needs and wants in relation to available resources, and they need to make responsible decisions and learn to live with the consequences of their decisions.

As consumers, children develop an understanding of the producer concept. Some produce services, others goods. Money is required to pay for both services and goods. The diversity of producers' work leads children into a study of different kinds of jobs as well as the resources that producers use in their jobs.

Even though their working lives are far in the future, preschool and primary children are not too young to learn basic attitudes toward self and work that will prepare them to make wise decisions about future career choices. The skills of decision making, relating to others, and learning basic skills are part of career education.

Although research supports introducing young children to economic concepts, it is important to ground your teaching of concepts in children's concrete, everyday experiences through an integrated, whole curriculum. If children are to gain necessary awareness of and develop initial economic concepts, they must be involved in experiencing, doing, and acting for themselves.

Extend Your Knowledge

1. With a small group of children, visit a supermarket or a neighborhood store. What things are the children interested in that you could use to build economic concepts? List how you could extend these interests in the classroom.

2. Select one concept from economics. Interview a group of children to determine their understanding of that concept. What experiences could you plan that might build more accurate, complete understandings of the concept?

3. Interview a 5-, 6-, and 7-year-old child. Ask each child what he wants to be when he grows up, why, and what he thinks he'll have to learn or do to achieve his career choice.

4. Nearly every state in our nation mandates some form of economics education in elementary or secondary schools. Write, call, or search the Internet to locate information about your state's guidelines for economics teaching. Even though these plans and guidelines will probably be designed for older children, review them and identify concepts, activities, or plans that could be adapted for younger preschool and primary-grade children.

Resources

The Foundation for Teaching Economics is a nonprofit organization providing leadership in economic education for educators and young people selected for their leadership potential. The foundation welcomes inquiries, comments, and suggestions:

Foundation for Teaching Economics
160 Russell Boulevard, Suite B
Davis, CA 95616
Phone: (530) 757-4630
Fax: (530) 757-4636
Website: *http://www.fte.org/fte.index.html*

The National Council on Economic Education is the leading source for materials and information dealing with economic literacy in the K–12 environment. Their Website includes a large list of lesson plans for the instruction of economics for K–12 children, which can be ordered by fax, phone, or mail.

Website: *http://www.ncee.net*

The Center for Economic Education provides economic education programs to prepare students for life in a global society and offers instruction for classroom teachers.

Website: *http://www.udel.edu/raker/ccenters/cee.html*

The following books offer parents and teachers ideas for teaching economics to young children:

Bodnar, J. (1993). *Kiplinger's money-smart kids.* Washington, DC: Kiplinger Books.
Bodnar, J. (1996). *Mom, can I have that?* Washington, DC: Kiplinger Books.
Estess, P., & Barocas, I. (1994). *Kids, money, and values.* Newark, NJ: Gateway.
Modu, E. (1996). *The lemonade stand.* Newark, NJ: Gateway.

References

American Association of University Women. (2000). *A license for bias.* Washington, DC: Author.
Berti, A. E., & Bombi, A. S. (1988). *The child's construction of economics.* Cambridge: Cambridge University Press.

Brophy, J., & Alleman, J. (2002). Learning and teaching about cultural universals in primary-grade social studies. *Elementary School Journal, 103*(3), 93–98.

Chrisman, K., & Couchenour, D. (2003). Developing concepts of gender roles. In C. Copple (Ed.), *A world of difference* (pp. 116–117). Washington, DC: National Association for the Education of Young Children.

Derman-Sparks, L. & the ABC Task Force (2003). Expanding awareness of gender roles. In C. Copple (Ed.), *A world of difference* (pp. 118–119). Washington, DC: National Association for the Education of Young Children.

Dewey, J. (1900). *The child and society*. Chicago: University of Chicago Press.

Dewey, J. (1944). *Democracy and education*. New York: Free Press.

DiSalvo-Ryan, D. (1997). *Uncle Willie and the soup kitchen*. New York: Demco Media.

Freedman, R. (1995). *Buffalo hunt*. New York: Holiday House.

Helm, J. H., & Beneke, S. (2003). *The power of projects*. New York: Teachers College Press.

Holst, C. B. (1999). Buying more can give children less. *Young Children, 54*(3), 19–23.

Leedy, L. (2002). *Follow the money*. New York: Holiday House.

Maestro, B. C., & Maestro, G. (1995). *The story of money*. New York: Mulberry.

Meszaros, B., & Engstrom, L. (1988). The voluntary national content standards in economics. *Social Studies and the Young Learner, 11*(2), 7–12.

Mollet, T. M., & Lewis, E. B. (1999). *My rows and piles of coins*. New York: Clarion.

National Council for the Social Studies (NCSS). (1998). *Social studies for early childhood and elementary school children: Preparing for the 21st century*. Washington, DC: Author.

National Council on Economic Education (NCEE). (2002). *Economics America*. Bloomington, IN: Author.

Searls, M. J. (1997). *Allowance kit, junior!: A money system for little kids*. Washington, DC: Summit Financial.

Seefeldt, C., & Galper, A. (2002). *Active experiences for active children: Social studies*. Upper Saddle River, NJ: Merrill/Prentice Hall.

VanFossen, P. J. (2003). Best practice economic education for young children? It's elementary! *Social Education, 67*(2), 90–94.

Viorst, J. (1978). *Alexander, who used to be rich last Sunday*. New York: Atheneum.

Wells, R. (2001). *Bunny money*. New York: Dial.

Index